Summer

SUMMER
KARL OVE KNAUSGAARD

With illustrations by Anselm Kiefer
Translated from the Norwegian by Ingvild Burkey

Alfred A. Knopf Canada

PUBLISHED BY ALFRED A. KNOPF CANADA

Copyright © 2016 Karl Ove Knausgaard
English translation copyright © 2018 Ingvild Burkey
Artwork copyright © 2016 Anselm Kiefer

www.penguinrandomhouse.ca

Excerpt from Emanuel Swedenborg's *Journal of Dreams and Spiritual Experiences
in the Year 1744*, translated by C. Th. Odhner, 1918.
Excerpt from Gunnar Ekelöf's *En röst, Efterlamnade dikter och anteckningar,*
1973, translated here by Ingvild Burkey.

Library and Archives Canada Cataloguing in Publication

[Om sommeren. English]
                 Summer / Karl Ove Knausgaard ; Anselm Kiefer, illustrator ; Ingvild
Burkey, translator.

Translation of: Om sommeren.
Issued in print and electronic formats.

ISBN 978-0-345-81112-7
eBook ISBN 978-0-345-81114-1

    I. Kiefer, Anselm, 1945–, illustrator II. Burkey, Ingvild, 1967–,
translator III. Title. IV. Title: Om sommeren. English.

PT8951.21.N38O4513 2018   839.824'74   C2018-900737-0
                                                     C2018-900738-9

Set in Scala

Printed and bound in the United States of America

10 9 8 7 6 5 4 3 2 1

Penguin
Random House
KNOPF CANADA

JUNE

JULY

AUGUST

JUNE

Lawn Sprinklers

That I have my own lawn sprinkler has never quite dawned on me, it was just one of the many things I acquired when we bought this house, like the lawnmower, the garden shears, the rakes and all the other equipment that belongs in a garden. Though I have fastened the hose to the tap in the porch of the summer house countless times, have heard the water first hiss, then rush through the hose, and then seen the thin jets of water rise in the garden, maybe five metres into the air, often glittering in the sunlight, and, slowly wavering, fall to one side, before rising again and falling to the other side, in a movement that has always made me think of a waving hand, I have never connected it with myself or my life, as if what it represents doesn't represent me, or in other words that the life I lead here isn't really mine, but merely something I happen to be doing right now. To draw such a far-reaching conclusion from something as insignificant as a metal arm full of holes through which water flows may seem overblown, but of all the things I remember from the summers when I was growing up, the lawn sprinkler is the most emblematic, it is the single object around which the greatest number of moods and events cluster in my memory and which evokes the most associations. Every household in the development had a lawn sprinkler, and all of them were of the same type, so that these fine, glittering arcs of water could be seen everywhere on summer days when the sun was shining. Often the lawns they stood on were deserted, as if the sprinklers led their own independent existence, like some large friendly water-based creatures. When water landed on the lawn the sound was nearly inaudible, nothing more than a fine light sprinkle, which might be drowned out by the rushing noise from the hose or from the tap if the hose wasn't screwed on tightly, while the sound could rise to a rustle or even a patter if the sprinkler was positioned so the water struck the leaves of trees or shrubs. These sounds, which rose and fell seemingly methodically and patiently, as if from some painstaking labour, and which also contributed to the feeling that the arc of water was an independent being, could last all day and into the evening, unaffected by the other activities of the residents, sometimes even throughout the night, though that was rare, for some reason or other it wasn't thought proper to water the garden in the dark. At our house my father was in command of the sprinkler, I can't remember ever seeing my mother moving it or turning the water on or off, though I don't know why this was so. The tap was in the basement laundry room and the hose ran out into the garden through the narrow rectangular basement window, which on the inside was high up, right beneath the ceiling, while outside it was low down, just above the ground. That the window couldn't be properly shut while Dad was watering produced a faint ache in me, while on the other hand the window's different height above the ground inside and outside the house exerted a magical pull. The arc of water in all its aspects, visual and auditive as well as its usefulness in the garden, represented something unconditionally good. That I myself am now master of a sprinkler and both turn it on and move it around unaided, in my own garden, ought therefore to mean something to me, if not a lot, at least a little, since the life which back then I only observed – the life of grown men and women – has now become mine, something I no longer regard from the outside but fill from within. It doesn't, I take no particular joy in turning on the sprinkler, no more than I find pleasure in buttering a slice of bread or taking off my shoes as I enter the house. Now it is the world of the child that I observe from the outside, and what more fitting image for this asymmetry in life could there be than the basement window, which is at once high up beneath the ceiling and low down near the ground?

Chestnut Trees

We have a chestnut tree in the garden, it stands in the corner between the two houses and towers more than twenty metres into the air, maybe as many as twenty-five. The longest branches extend at least ten metres from the trunk, and one of the first things I did when we moved here was to saw off the bottom ones, since some of them partially blocked the path between the houses while others had grown across the roof and rested upon it. But even though this chestnut tree is so large – from a distance that is what one sees of the property, not the roofs – and though I have climbed it and sawed into it, I never really noticed it, never thought about it. It was as if it didn't exist. Now it seems inconceivable that I have lived side by side with such a huge creature for five years without really seeing it. What kind of a phenomenon is that, to see without seeing? Presumably it comes about because the thing one sees doesn't stick. But what do the things we really see stick *to*? We say that something gives meaning, as if meaning is something we receive as a gift, but actually I think it is the other way round, it is we who give meaning to what we see. And this chestnut tree, which I am looking at as I sit here writing, I didn't give any meaning to. It was there and I knew it was there, it wasn't like I bumped into it on my way between the houses, but it meant nothing to me and therefore had no real existence.

What happened is that this spring and summer I have been studying paintings by the artist Edvard Munch. I've looked at all his paintings, again and again, and I've become familiar with most of them. He painted several chestnut trees, and there was one painting in particular that struck me. It depicts a chestnut tree on a city street and is painted almost impressionistically, in the sense that all surfaces appear as colours rather than as solid objects, they are more for the eye than for the hand, more for the instant than to endure. The chestnut is blossoming and its white flowers are painted like little posts amid all the green, where they shine like lamps. When I look out at the chestnut tree beyond my window, nothing about its flowers resembles the flowers Munch painted – they don't look like vertical lines but like little puffs of white arranged in four or five tiers, and they are not pure white but tinged with beige and brown. And yet it was Munch's painting which, when our tree began to blossom at the end of May, made me understand for the first time that a chestnut tree was standing there. The same thing happened with the trees that grow along the pavement on the road into the centre of Ystad, the one that runs along the railway tracks in the harbour, where the big ferries to Poland and Bornholm rear up. But they're chestnut trees, I thought when they began to bloom. And it wasn't the name that made the difference, it wasn't that now I could say that they were chestnuts whereas before I hadn't known – for I had, I knew all the time what kind of trees they were – it was something else, the chestnut trees now occupied an intimate place in my mind. And I think it is this intimacy we mean when we talk about authenticity. For intimacy radically suspends distance, which is the central element of every theory of alienation advanced in the last century, and which remains an active force in our yearning for the tangible, which we feel to be closer to reality. The opposing poles are not modernism and anti-modernism, progress and retrogression, these are merely the consequences of the balance between intimacy and non-intimacy, a question of where we place the emphasis, and that in turn depends on what we have use for and what we want from our lives. Do we want to take the chestnut tree in, do we want to see it and let it occupy a place within us, do we want to feel its presence every time we pass it, its very own place within reality? What the chestnut tree articulates, what it expresses, is nothing other than itself. And perhaps the same is true of us, that what we articulate, what we express, is nothing other than ourselves? A particular presence in a particular place at a particular time? More and more that is how I think about it, that thoughts are just something coursing through me, feelings are just something coursing through me, and that I might just as easily have been someone else; the crucial thing isn't who I am but that I am, and the same holds for the chestnut tree, standing there outside the window right now, towering silently amid its whorl of green leaves and white flowers.

Short Trousers

I am wearing short trousers today, they are moss green and reach to just above my knees, and although they are more comfortable than long trousers in the heat, there is something faintly unpleasant about them, it is as if they make me smaller, as if I am too old for them. The very term, short trousers, is infantile in its simple descriptiveness, like a word a child might have come up with, akin to foot ball, tree house, sand box, see saw. If instead I write that I am wearing shorts today, it feels somewhat less childish, and if I add that they are army green it no longer sounds like I am dressed in the outfit of a ten-year-old, more like a young man in his early twenties heading for a music festival. In the mid-1990s I read a novel which made a big impression on me, and which gave form to certain inclinations and zones within me that had remained undefined until then. The novel was *The Child in Time* by the British author Ian McEwan. The main narrative is about the greatest fear of all parents, a child who goes missing, but what stayed in my mind was one of the novel's parallel stories, about regression and infantility – a man, who as far as I can remember was a member of parliament, regresses to his childhood, he dresses in short trousers and begins to climb trees, builds tree houses in them, plays the games he played as a boy. It seemed grotesque to me, for his fall was completely stripped of dignity to an extent and in a way quite different from a descent into alcoholism or drug addiction. At the same time it held a certain allure for me, for not only was I filled with a powerful nostalgia for everything to do with my childhood – the smell of melting snow and the sight of the white ice banks from which water trickled into the road beneath a foggy sky, for example, might produce a yearning to return to the time when I experienced the same thing as a child, so strong that it hurt – I also longed to be taken care of as I had been then. Not explicitly, the longing wasn't even articulated until I read *The Child in Time*, and all these vague, unacknowledged emotions flowed into the novel's mould so that I could see them from the outside as something objectively existing in the world. The grotesque side of it was also apparent to me. The adult who wants to be a child is even more grotesque than the old person who wants to be young, an insight I had used to write my first novel, in which the longing to be a child again is transformed into longing *for* a child – I remembered the intense feelings my very first infatuations produced in me when I was still in primary school, and I let my protagonist go there, into that zone, and fall in love with a child. Now all these yearnings and feelings seem peculiar, and when I put on short trousers this morning, since it looked like it would be another hot day, I felt a little jolt of distaste, for there is something life-denying about always looking backwards, and I had to tell myself, it's just a piece of clothing that lets you go about bare-legged. But although the nostalgia has passed, or has been weakened to the point where it is no longer recognisable, I know that there are other such unconscious inclinations and patterns within me – my whole adult life, for instance, I have entered into relationships that resemble those I was in while I was growing up, so that the person I loved came to hold the same position my father had had, as someone I wanted to placate, someone I wanted to satisfy, whom I also feared and could be spellbound by – and becoming an adult is perhaps primarily to liberate oneself from these patterns by becoming aware of them and acknowledging them, so that one can live in harmony with the person one is or wants to be, not the person one was or wanted to be in the past. The advantage of maintaining the old patterns is that they feel safe, regardless of how painful or destructive they may be. Freedom is unsafe, when one is free anything can happen, and one of the paradoxes of life, at least one of the paradoxes of my life, is that now, as I head into a free and open existence, I no longer have any use for freedom, it was during the first part of my life, until I reached my forties, while all possibilities still lay ahead of me, that I had use for it and could have enjoyed it. For what use is freedom to a middle-aged man in short trousers?

Cats

Yesterday afternoon the head of a hare lay on the lawn beneath the chestnut tree. Its eyes were gone and the face was mangled, so only the long ears allowed me to identify it as a hare. The cat had got it, it was the second hare it had killed in two days, with the same modus operandi, a torn-off head with eyes missing and bloodied fur left in the garden. As I write this the cat is sitting on the windowsill looking into the house and waiting for someone inside to get up, notice it and let it in. It is a Siberian forest cat with long grey-black fur and a bushy tail whom the woman we bought it from called Amaga, which is still her name. Amaga likes to sleep in enclosed spaces, the narrower the better, it seems – crates, boxes, suitcases, prams – but she will also snuggle up on windowsills, stairs, beds, sofas and chairs. More than anything, she lives like a tenant of the house, she comes and goes as she pleases, eats her own food in a special place, sleeps the days away, is out all night. Occasionally acquaintances of hers come to call, sometimes I see them sitting in the garden waiting for her to come out. In the literature the character of her breed is described as sensitive and resourceful, and while the description seems excessively anthropomorphic, it matches my impression of her fairly well. We had several cats while I was growing up and they each had distinct personalities, from the wary but mild-mannered Sofi, a grey long-haired Norwegian forest cat, to her daughter Mefisto, also long-haired, completely black and both more elegant and more devoted than her mother, to her son Lasse, who was impulsive, undisciplined and markedly more dull-witted than his progenitor. He would begin to purr if you so much as looked at him, was never properly house-trained and loved to be petted. Petting was clearly the high point of his existence, he tried to turn it into orgies of bodily contact, his nose would run, he pushed his paws in and out with their claws extended, he turned over on his back, splayed his legs, rubbed himself against everything within reach. Lasse had no dignity and no integrity, and when he tried to chase Mefisto away and take over the house, he was eventually taken to the vet, where he met his fate. Amaga is Lasse's complete opposite, she has total integrity, and if she is as wary as Sofi was, she is nowhere near as mild-mannered. There is something sharp in her character, noticeable even when she surrenders herself, for if she purrs and closes her eyes when she is petted, the watchfulness never entirely leaves her; at any moment she might twist around, jump to her feet and leap to the floor to walk off by herself. When we got a dog two years ago, the first thing she did was attack it, she scratched it near the eye so that blood ran down its snout, and from that moment the dog was terrified of her, she ruled it entirely. The baby girl we had had the year before she didn't pay any attention to at first, but when the girl began to walk and toddled after the cat, she would lower herself turtle-like towards the floor and run off, as she always does when she senses danger. 'The tack, the tack!' the girl would shout – that was her word for cat, which was felicitous, since *tack* means 'thanks' in Swedish, so that whenever I saw her I could point to her and say, 'There's gratitude for you!' – and try to grab her by the tail. She rarely succeeded, since Amaga was so much faster than her and just slunk away, except when she was sleeping, and if we didn't get over there quickly enough then, Amaga would hiss at her, and if that didn't deter the little girl, she would scratch her. It happened twice, and now she has respect for the tack, no longer throws things at it, doesn't grab its tail, but likes to pet it, which the cat lets her do although I don't think she gets much enjoyment out of it, for she lies there with watchful eyes, looking somewhat tense as the small hand strokes her soft and often tangled fur. The self-control Amaga displays then is admirable, considering the torn-off heads, the gorging on blood and gouging out of eyes that her instincts can lead her to at other times. In fact, through living with cats I have come to wonder what instincts really are. I used to think they were a form of automated actions, something preprogrammed and ineluctable in animals, separate from what little they had in the way of thoughts and emotions, and that taming animals meant implanting a different system in them, just as automatic, which caused their instincts to be held back or channelled into other directions. And that the instincts of large carnivores such as lions and tigers were more powerful and might therefore more easily break down the wall that their taming had erected, so that without warning they might attack those who had tamed them, who fed and sheltered them, and tear them to pieces. We can call it instinct, we can call it nature, we can call it the animals' essential being. But when I see a lion or a tiger in a zoo somewhere I never get the feeling that they are ruled by what we call instincts, that they are in thrall to their instincts and thus confined to a limited number of possible reactions. It is more as if they do as they please, that they never consider or judge any action, they just act. That the decisive difference between us and them isn't that we think while animals don't, but that we have morals and they don't. I am certain that Amaga has sized us up, that she knows who we are, the six members of the family that lives in her house. I am also certain that she sees us as some sort of large, stupid cats, slow and dim-witted, and if she doesn't think that she is superior to us, I am certain she feels it with her whole being.

Campsites

Campsites are delimited areas set off for overnight stays, usually outside cities or small towns, often in the vicinity of beaches or other recreation grounds, where in exchange for payment travellers can spend the night in their own tents or caravans. Other than the small pitch of a few square metres that the owners of the tent or caravan has at their disposal for as long as they have paid for, the campsite also offers visitors certain common facilities, such as toilets, showers, a kiosk where basic necessities are sold, often a playground for the children, and if it is well appointed, a swimming pool. The campsite is akin to the hotel, which is also a place where travellers spend the night, but while the hotel demands that one relinquishes one's own habitual existence and for a few hours lives one's life in an unfamiliar room, which over the years has been occupied by hundreds or thousands of people who have all subordinated themselves to its four walls and for a few hours allowed themselves to be framed by their unfamiliarity, the campsite accommodates travellers' desire for independence by allowing them to erect their own homes and thus to establish an intimate, homely zone amid the unfamiliar. One might think that this possibility of remaining independent would be considered superior to the lack of independence of the hotel, that in our so-called individualistic age we would value the freedom of the campsite more than the constraints of the hotel, but that's not how it is, the campsite has a low status, and it has been decreasing for several decades. The reason is a simple but hidden and perhaps even deliberately concealed fact: money and freedom are opposing entities. The diminishing status of the campsite has coincided with the rise of market liberalism and privatisation, and money establishes differences between things, it grades and demarcates in a system that restricts access to the world and in which whatever cannot be assigned monetary value is relegated to the outside, so that openness is directly linked with worthlessness. The freedom of the wanderer, the person who goes wherever he wants and sleeps where he happens to find himself, now exists only among the homeless, who occupy the lowest rung of society's ladder, while driving around from place to place carrying one's own dwelling and one's own food, which in one sense opens up the world and retains a remnant of the freedom of the wanderer, isn't considered enviable either. Just think of the Roma people and their status in society. Thus there is a scale, from the homeless person who sleeps on benches and in gateways, in parks and woods on the outskirts of cities, to the person who lives in an enormous apartment or house, secured with alarms and by guards at the entrance. It is therefore unthinkable that a man like the Norwegian billionaire businessman Kjell Inge Røkke, who comes from a working-class family but is now one of the richest men in the country, would spend his holidays in a caravan, even though he may have done so with his family when he was growing up and thus knows well the smell of dewy tent canvas in the evening and the safe but also exciting feeling of falling asleep to the sound of low voices from outside other tents, where women and men are sitting in their camping chairs, chatting in the gathering darkness of the summer night. The joy of being on the road, for the next day the tent will be dismantled, the luggage will be stowed away in the boot, you will head on to the next campsite, where you never know what you will find: will there be a pool? Will they sell soft ice cream? Will there be other children the same age as you? Will there be trampolines? Is it by the sea, with a sandy beach? Is it by a river, is it near the forest, in the mountains, next to a field where bellicose bulls are grazing? I still remember the excitement of family camping trips in my childhood, in the 1970s when camping was the most common form of holiday-making and one could see heavily loaded cars lined along the roads next to unfolded camping tables and cooler bags, in an age when it wasn't yet considered shameful to bring your own home-cooked food (which stands in the same relation to the restaurant as the tent does to the hotel) simply because people then had less money. Campsites still exist, but since people have more money now, the logical thing has happened: slowly the mobile tents and caravans became less and less mobile, gardens sprang up around them, they became filled with conveniences and knick-knacks, TVs and computers, refrigerators and dryers, and became more and more like ordinary homes, into which their transformation has now become complete, so that campsites are now places where people live half the year, fenced in and enclosed and immobile, and the only things which remind one of displacement and mobility are the wheels of the huge caravans, which no longer bring freedom but are merely symbols of freedom. These campsites embody a sort of congealed longing, not unlike the posture of the poet in his tower writing about the open and the free.

Summer Night

One night I sat on a hotel terrace with the woman I loved, we had just been downtown, where we had eaten at a restaurant. I had been uncommunicative and troubled, she had tried to get me to snap out of it but had finally given up, so that we had sat there as two silent people who spoke only once in a long while, to break the silence when it became too oppressive. We had been sitting outside in a yard, rose bushes grew along the fence, the roses were big and blood red. The sky above us had been blue, the roofs of the houses around us shone golden red in the sunlight. The mood at the other tables was good, many had finished their meals and sat relaxing with legs outstretched drinking coffee or wine while they chatted and let their hands toy with something on the table, a box of toothpicks, a glass of cognac, a coffee cup. We paid, the waiter ordered a taxi for us, it happened to be a minibus, and as it tore through the streets leading out of the little town it was as if we, what we were together, disappeared between all the seats. The hotel lay at the end of a long tree-lined avenue, on a low rise above the channel. Our room, which we had hardly been in since we arrived late that afternoon, was white, decorated in nautical style, with a view of the sea. She ran water into the bath, which was so big that there was room for two side by side. I turned off the lights, and we lay down in the warm water. The sun had gone down, but the sky outside was still light and hovered over the dark channel. A big tree stood black and silent on one side, and above it shone a single star. It must be a planet, I said. Yes, it must be, she said. Are we friends? I said. Of course we're friends, she said. We made love in the bedroom, got dressed and went downstairs to the restaurant, where the door to the terrace stood open. The restaurant was empty, the bartender was tidying up, jazz playing low over the sound system. We went out on the veranda and sat down at a table. The water in the channel lay perfectly still. On the light sky several stars had appeared, and behind the three old trees, which looked like a single tree from where we sat, the moon was rising. I couldn't see it, only a shining yellow column on the dark water between the leaves, but I knew it was full. A bat flittered through the air. Except for the low music in the bar, the hotel was silent. Everyone was asleep. Down by the water a duck quacked a few times. From the other side of the channel, where a forest grew all the way down to the water's edge, another bird emitted a long, hissing noise. Then everything became quiet again. I turned my head and looked towards the little town where we had just been. Its lights shone and glittered, surrounded by darkness beneath the light sky. It was a magical night. After a while we got up and walked down the path to the water, the last stretch of a long flight of steps. A wooden pier extended into the water, at the end of it stood a bench where we sat down. We didn't say anything, we didn't need to say anything, I thought, it would just spoil it, for the silence was like a vault above the landscape. From here we could see the moon suspended high above the forest, perfectly round. With no competition from mountains or cities it owned the sky. Though the water around us was still and smooth, it seemed to well up, I thought. Now and again a faint splash sounded, from fish feeding near the surface. Isn't it beautiful, I said. Yes, she said. It's very beautiful. And soon it will start to get light, I said. Yes, she said. Neither of us knew then that it would be the last night we spent together, but over the next two days everything that had lain unspoken between us came out, and we found no other way to handle it than to break up. It still hurts to think about it, that we were together that night, which is the most beautiful night I have experienced, and that we can't have shared any of it, as I thought we did. The 'we' I had felt so strongly held only me.

Summer Afternoon

Earlier that day, which would be our last together, we had visited another town, and after strolling through the provincial pedestrian precinct, past the Renaissance-style town hall and the large brick church, we entered a park and lay down on the grass in the middle of it. Except for some teenage girls sitting on a bench in the shade of a tree maybe thirty metres behind us, there wasn't a person in sight. Birdsong sounded all around us. Usually I don't notice it, now I heard nothing else. Isn't it strange that birds sing in ways that we too find pleasing? I said. It didn't have to be that way. No, it didn't, she said. In my parents' garden there are some birds that sound awful. Just hoarse, ugly croaking. And then gulls. They're the nastiest birds I know of. The really big ones are like dinosaurs. They *are* dinosaurs, I said. I know, she said. But not all birds bring up that association. The birds here in the park don't. No, I said and imagined dinosaurs chirping like little birds. That would have changed our impression of them entirely. But I didn't say anything about that, instead I lit a cigarette and lay back on the grass. A few chalk-white clouds drifted across the blue sky. The leaves on the trees rustled in the wind, which blew stronger now that it was past noon. In autumn and winter the day nears its end in the afternoon, coming up against a wall of darkness, in spring it seems to become diluted, while summer after-noons deepen it and make it richer. The light becomes fuller, the blue of the sky grows more intense, and in the landscape the heat of the sun is preserved throughout the day, in some places by accumulation, as in the sweltering tarmac or the air in little glades in the forest. The sea breeze coming in across the land makes the crowns of trees sway slowly, as if waking from a sleep, while their leaves rustle with a sound like a purling brook or a drawn-out sigh of pleasure. 'Look there,' she said, 'at the tree, do you see how it shimmers?' I sat up and glanced at the tree she was nodding towards. It grew on the other side of the narrow river that ran along the edge of the park. The course it followed lay too low for us to see the water. Instead the reflection of the light, fragile-seeming and transparent, that flickered over the thick trunk seemed to be coming from the tree itself. We sat there look-ing at it. The light moved like water, swaying and trickling. I wondered how it is possible to walk into a school and fire wildly at everything around one, to kill everyone in sight, children and adults, when the world is so calm and beau-tiful, so full of sunlight and birdsong, flowing rivers and unmoving trees. It must be because what is and what hap-pens follow two different courses: that the unchanging and constantly recurring, the immobility and eternal beauty of the world is something the other course, that of actions and emotional drives belonging primarily to humans, only brushes against in passing. If the channels are not kept clear, if they are not left open and free but instead get clogged up and darken, which happens to all of us to a greater or lesser extent, then they become predominant, then they become us. And that – to be merely a human being, not a human being in the world – is dangerous. It has always been dangerous and it always will be dangerous. That's what I was thinking as I watched the reflection of light from the water gliding back and forth over the tree trunk on that summer afternoon, and at the same time I knew I would always remember it, since I saw it with her.

Intelligence

Intelligence is the term we use for the ability to understand connections. All human beings have this ability, which is perhaps primarily characterised by its being limited: everyone understands something, no one understands everything. But the limits to understanding are drawn differently and are final in each one of us. That traumatic experiences or great sensitivity to external conditions can lower one's level of understanding and that great efforts of will can increase it doesn't mean that intelligence is a relative quality, only that it is potential, in the sense that it can be either fully exploited or not used to the full. The concept of intelligence is by its nature comparative, for if the ability to understand connections was equal for everyone, as the ability to scratch oneself is possessed equally by everyone without differentiation, then the concept of intelligence would be meaningless. One is only intelligent if one is more intelligent than others. And since intelligence is itself a connection that must be understood based on one's own mental ability, those more intelligent than oneself are often difficult, even impossible, to distinguish. The person who is more intelligent will perceive you clearly, all your cognitive limitations will be apparent to them, whereas you won't see the more intelligent person as being more intelligent than yourself, but only that part of the intelligent person which is visible within the limits to your thought, rather like how a dog sees everyone else as dogs. In egalitarian societies intelligence is one of the most ambivalent entities, since the difference which intelligence represents is insurmountable, and insurmountable differences are of course fundamentally non-egalitarian. In that respect intelligence resembles beauty, which is another problematic entity in egalitarian societies. The solution has been and still is to pretend it doesn't exist or that it isn't important, a game of pretence which begins at school, where both intelligence and beauty are communicated through mixed messages: on the one hand one is taught that looks are not important, that what counts is the inner person and that all people are equally valuable, while at the same time this fundamental ethical principle, which everyone agrees on and which pervades every level of knowledge, on the other hand is continually contradicted by the disproportionate attention and better treatment accorded to beautiful pupils over ugly ones by teachers, other adults and fellow pupils. Intelligence also breaches the doctrine of equality, but in a different way, for while beauty isn't a threat, perhaps because it is so ineluctable and in a certain sense so final, intelligence is threatening, for we all know how to think, we are all able to understand connections, and that some people think better, that some people understand more connections and with greater ease, can be hard to accept. While the threat is constant, it feels more acute during one's school years, since that is one of the few phases in life during which one's mental abilities and capacity to understand are not only continually tested but also graded, thus exposing the differences between people in this respect. All the intelligent people I went to school with at some point or other tried to hide their intelligence, to tone it down, since the consequence of appearing intelligent was that they were ostracised, they were unpopular and in a few cases were even bullied. That never happened to any of the beautiful people I went to school with, on the contrary, they were all greatly sought after. In the *gymnas* the most intelligent pupil was named Gjermund, and during one break we wrote with a black marker in large letters on the noticeboard that ran along one whole wall of the classroom, GJERMUND IS UGLY. We meant it ironically, for that is the kind of thing primary school students would do, while we were in the *gymnas* and we felt that by parodying primary school pupils we were changing the message and turning it into something else, something harmless. But it didn't seem that way to Gjermund, his face went white when he saw it, and there were tears in his eyes. He pretended not to notice, however, and so the moment passed, at least for us. But no one removed the letters, so for him it must have been different, since he had to see that sentence every day for the rest of the school year. How he has done later in life I have no idea, but I do know one thing, that society's view of intelligence changes in adulthood, for even an egalitarian society needs people who distinguish themselves through their superior intelligence, and the function of school is not primarily to convey knowledge but to differentiate, so that the intelligent students end up on the right shelf, while all the others are taught that there is no difference between people, so that later they will accept being governed by the intelligent.

Foam

Everything happens in accordance with the laws of nature. Air moves because a difference in atmospheric pressure has arisen somewhere and all the invisible particles rush into vast pockets to fill them. The force of this movement drives the surface waters of the sea ahead of it, and since no hollows open into which the water can flow, it piles up instead, forming waves. These waves, driven by the wind, continually fling themselves forward, and every time they strike the surface they pull air down with them. If air and water obeyed other laws, one might imagine that the air dragged down by the waves would gather and form vast underwater shafts, grotto-like systems of air, but of course this isn't the case, for air is light, water is heavy, so that water immediately fills all the air spaces just below the surface. But this movement is mechanical, the air doesn't unite with the water, it is just forced into smaller and smaller pockets, which are all of the same shape, namely tiny round bubbles enclosed within fairly thin walls of water. In a matter of seconds these bubbles form enormous structures, which the waves keep pushing up and forward and which we can see every time there is a gale at sea, when white heads of foam spring up and vanish again on the grey-black or grey-green surface.

Snorting, hissing, soughing, they surge forward like horses' heads, go under, then reappear. This foam is extremely short-lived; when the wave is flung forward and disintegrates, the foam may remain in the water for a few seconds as winding veils of white, only to dissolve and disappear in the next instant. What makes it seem lasting is that the same thing happens again and again, in that incomprehensible abundance of repetition which characterises the universe. How infinitely many tiny air bubbles are formed on the ocean's surface in the course of a single windy day? Nothing is stinted in this explosion of formations, structures, patterns and shapes. It is brief, the next day the sea may lie still as a mirror and every whorl of foam may be gone, but it is brief only to us, just as the universe's explosion of formations, structures, patterns and shapes seems nearly eternal to us. Rather than in fractions of seconds they disintegrate over the course of billions of years. But it isn't hard to imagine a being with a different perception of time, one for whom one second is an eternity, and for whom the ocean and its foam therefore appear immobile and crystalline. If one further imagines that not only time but also space is relative, then a whole universe could be contained in one of these air bubbles, which then, to this being, would be eternally immovable and governed by laws that could be observed and recorded but never understood. Perhaps this being would eventually notice that all the heavenly bodies in this infinite space were drifting outwards from the centre and draw the inevitable conclusion that the universe was entropic and inexorably heading towards its end? That the Big Bang was like the pop of a champagne cork and the universe like a mass of bubbles rising through the narrow, chilled bottleneck and down into waiting flute glasses, which sparkling with light were raised in a toast somewhere, in some apartment?

Birch

In the monochrome majesty of the forest, where almost everything is green or underpins green, like the grey of the spruces' bark, the birches with their white trunks stand out, and it is easy to imagine that they belong to a finer species, a sort of sylvan aristocracy, erect and stylish, beautiful and highly strung. But beauty and genealogy are both human notions and have little of essence to say about either animals or trees, so when we think of the spruce as sombre and brooding, the pine tree as proud and freedom-loving, the aspen as anxious, the oak as majestic and the birch as sensitive and perhaps in its nature more like a horse than a tree, we are transforming them into ourselves, we are transplanting our inner selves into the exterior world. But even knowing that this is so, that everything which grows in the forest is indifferent to us and our notions about it, including Darwin's theory of evolution and Linnaean taxonomy, the sight of a forest floor covered with wood anemones, for example, always wakens a thought in me that wood anemones are not merely beautiful but good, while the sight of a birch, like the one that grows in the garden here, right next to where I park the car, is for me always associated with fragility. This is of course precisely because the birch stands out among other trees, and because in the world of humans I have come to expect that those who stand out are also fragile. When I was growing up, I knew exactly where all the birches were, they seemed to define the places they grew in, as did the bus stop, the bridge buttress, the outcrop of rock, the marsh and the pond, each in their own way. I was familiar with the different appearances of birches, how in winter they lost their volume entirely, like dogs or cats with shaggy fur who seem to shrink when they get wet; how their thin twigs were covered with pale green buds in spring, which no matter how old the trees were – and some of them must have been my grandparents' age – made them look young and bashful; how their small sequin-shaped leaves hung in dense garlands in summer, so that their foliage resembled gowns; and how in the early-autumn storms they could look like ships with sails stretched taut by the wind, or swans beating their wings as they rose from the water. Birches were one of the few trees we didn't climb, the bark was slippery and difficult to get a grip on with one's shoe soles, and the trunk usually didn't divide into larger branches until some way up. Yet birches were not for the eyes alone – every spring we sought them out, selected one and cut off a branch, inserted the stub into a bottle, tied the bottle fast and let it hang there until the next day, when it would be full of a clear green liquid which we then drank, it was as sweet as fruit squash. I don't know where that knowledge had come from, but everyone had it, this was in the 1970s, so people still picked berries, not just for the sake of the outing but to supplement the household budget – they went fishing for the same reason – and children's lives were interwoven with this manual world, we made flutes of the bark of willow branches and the stems of dandelions, bows and arrows from young broadleaf trees, we drank birch sap and built huts from spruce twigs, but we also sat in our rooms listening to Status Quo, Mud, Slade and Gary Glitter. The unfathomable age of tree species wasn't something we related to, but then nor did we relate to the unfathomable age of our own species; for us everything was here and now, everything was contemporary, the birch, the car, the classroom, the forest grove, the blueberry bush, the music, the fish, the boat. And in a certain sense we were right, for with the exception of the mountains and the sea, almost nothing of all that surrounded us lasted longer than a human lifespan, including the birches, which in rare instances can grow to be three hundred years old but which usually live for about a hundred. But while the music we listened to changed from English glam to English punk and post-punk, and the clothes we wore went from the bell-bottoms and knitted sweaters of the 1970s to the black coats and Doc Martens of the 1980s, and we moved away while the children who came after us were no longer drawn to the forest, the birches stood as they had always stood, in poses first struck millions of years ago, in the Cretaceous, when the white and black trunks and tender green leaves of birches began to appear in the forests and their characteristic movements in the wind were for the first time performed on the world stage.

Slugs

All the names we have given the small, soft, slimy, dark animals that slither slowly around on the ground wherever it is moist – molluscs, lung snails, bladder snails, forest snails, nude snails – themselves have something moist and soft about them, it occurs to me, and every time I see a slug these days I am struck by how it inverts qualities that normally belong to the intimate human sphere and there express great beauty – nude is vulnerable, soft is arousing, lungs are the spirit of life, the forest is pure nature – for the slugs' nakedness, the slugs' softness, the slugs' lungs and the slugs' forest are instead repulsive, deeply undesirable and loathsome. That snails with their shells are less repulsive than slugs, as a turtle is less repulsive than a toad, would seem to indicate that it is the nakedness in itself that puts us off – and that sounds probable, for isn't the most repulsive thing about a rat its hairless tail? – and yet there are plenty of other animals that lack a clear distinction between their outer and inner body, for instance jellyfish or earthworms, which should therefore seem just as repulsive to us. Could it be because slugs resemble us more, are closer to us than jellyfish? Is it precisely that they have lungs, that they have a heart, that they have eyes which makes their nakedness seem so repulsive? To be sure, their eyes are of a very different and alien construction, placed as they are at the end of tentacles, one of two pairs, the upper pair being for the eyes, the lower pair for smells, like a kind of nose extension. What is it we see when they come slithering out after a rainy night, slowly and with heads raised? They resemble aged majesties, the rulers of the forest floor, emperors of rotted leaves and moist soil. But this striking dignity, which should make us venerate them, rather like the Egyptians venerated cats and Indians venerate cows, is entirely lost sight of due to the repulsiveness their nudity and slimy smoothness exude. Isn't there something almost provocative about them? Something counter to nature? They seem to belong to the interior, organs in a body, lungs, livers, hearts, which are all smooth and rounded and naked, without any distinction between inner and outer. Is that why they disgust us, because they look like little lungs creeping around by themselves, with antenna-like eyes, like little livers, like little hearts? Is this why they seem almost provocative, because they are counter to nature, and then they go creeping around like it was the most natural thing in the world, eating and reproducing, and everything has to happen so damned slowly, everything has to be so damned dignified – who the hell do slugs think they are? Millimetre after millimetre they slide along between the moist blades of grass, the wet ferns, across the soft moss, and live their lives in harmony with their abilities and limitations, as all living things do. When I was growing up all slugs were black, and they appeared after a downpour, as if from the bowels of the earth, suddenly they were everywhere, in the middle of the lawn, on the paths, even on the black asphalt roads of the housing development. It was said that it would start to rain if you stepped on a slug, so we took great care to avoid that. Still, sometimes it happened, sometimes inadvertently, other times deliberately: all children must have stepped on a slug at one time and seen its soft innards ooze out on the asphalt and the black blend with orange and white. Since then a new species of slug has invaded Scandinavia, so-called killer slugs, big brown slugs from Portugal or Spain which reproduce with amazing speed and cause great damage to gardens, since they gobble up everything they can find. One year the garden here was full of them, they were everywhere, as if they had rained from the sky. My mother-in-law used to gather the children around her and go slug-hunting. Armed with a bucket and sharp garden scissors they would walk across the grass, and when they found a slug they cut it into two and tossed the parts into the bucket. I couldn't watch, much less participate, it was too gruesome. But a raid like that, during which maybe twenty slugs were eliminated, was of no avail, a few days later there were just as many. At last, some time after my mother-in-law had gone home, I myself went out with a bucket and garden scissors. I knelt down in front of one of the brown slugs. It was as long as my long finger, thick as a sausage, with some sort of lengthwise grooves in its skin, and its broad foot, which reminded me of a belt, was beige. As I lifted it up it squirmed slowly in my grasp, and when I placed it between the blades of the sharp scissors its tentacles moved. I pushed the handles of the scissors together, and as the blades sliced into its body I heard it screaming, low and shrill.

Redcurrants

Redcurrants are small, round, smooth berries which hang in clusters from the branches of currant bushes, usually between five and fifteen on each stem. While the stem is thin and flexible, fairly soft, its substance more like the leaves than the branches, the berries fastened to it are remarkably hard. They resemble little marbles and bundle together in big bunches, for the clusters often grow close together so that in places up to a hundred berries might hang side by side, like pouches beneath the branches. Often these pockets are concealed by the dark green foliage, and that is one of the great joys of picking currants, to come across a rich ore of berries deep in the mountain of leaves. One picks redcurrants by pinching off the stem at the top, and what one then has in one's hand can sometimes resemble a caterpillar, where the thin green stem is the legs and the string of berries is the lumpy body. The commonest type of currant is red, but there are also yellow-green and pale yellow varieties. Redcurrants in their unripe state are first green, then they turn pale red, sometimes nearly orange, until late in June or early July they get their mature colour, a bright red which then, if the berries are not picked, turns dark red. The currants' bright red colour is intensified by their shiny translucent skin, which sparklingly reflects the sunlight and at times makes the berries look like glass pearls. When one bites into a redcurrant, there is first a little snap when the taut skin bursts, before the teeth penetrate to the flesh within, which is juicy – almost like melon flesh, one might imagine, except that redcurrants are so tiny and the quantity of flesh so small that a comparison with melon seems too asymmetrical, since precisely the abundance, the very quantity of flesh, so coarse and slobbery juicy, is typical of melon – but also tart, so that one's mouth automatically puckers as the currant's interior comes into contact with the tongue. Together with its petite size the tart taste gives the redcurrant an exclusive aura, it is not at all easily available and cannot be consumed in large quantities. This adds a contradictory element to its nature, or our relationship to it, since redcurrants are at once delicate and come in great, almost inexhaustible quantities. If we say that the redcurrant is the princess of berries, and transfer this to the human realm, it would be as if each country had thousands, even tens of thousands of princesses. The solution to the conflict between the redcurrants' exclusive air and their inexhaustible supply has been to mash them into a pulp, add sugar and make either juice or jam of them. Then the redcurrant loses its air of elegance and refinement, it no longer dangles like glittering little strands of red pearls amid the green leaves of the currant bush and no longer pricks sour needles into the freshness, but becomes either a sweet and sticky mass which is stored in sealed glass jars in the cellar and during the winter half of the year is spread on slices of bread – which has a similar story of origin, from the yellow grain in the field, saturated with sunlight and warmth, to the dry white flour and the soft, faintly moist bread with its hard crust – or a translucent red, concentrated, sweet and somewhat viscous liquid, stored in bottles throughout the autumn and winter, and mixed with water in a glass in summer and drunk standing in the kitchen, or to meals served outside in the shade of the apple trees, not far from the redcurrant bushes but no longer associated with them but rather with the bottle it has been kept in and with summer, when it is drunk. Everything we surround ourselves with undertakes similar journeys, which are not necessarily long in a purely geographical sense but which by traversing different spheres of life are like miniature-continental or micro-interstellar crossings, and once one understands that, then the richest of lives may be lived in a house within a garden, with a lawn, a few fruit trees and some berry bushes.

Summer Rain

While I was sitting here writing, it suddenly began to rain, in the middle of the day on the tenth of June 2016; without the slightest warning the air outside was streaked with raindrops plummeting through it. The drops were not big, they didn't rattle on the roof but fell gently against all surfaces with a soft whisper. The sky above the trees up by the churchyard was blue, the clouds that seemed to drift past behind the trees were white, some shone in the rays of the sun. This gave the rain an air of unreality. The light both in the sky and in the garden contradicted it, and perhaps that is the very definition of unreality, the simultaneous presence of two mutually exclusive entities. But there is nothing eerie about summer rain, it doesn't represent that form of unreality which for instance the sight of my daughter walking along the flagstone path would have if at the same time she was also visible in the kitchen – it is more that the unreality of summer rain sharpens the senses and allows it to appear in its true form, which is unique: this rain rained for the first time. For a few minutes it streamed down, so rapidly that it looked like a grating of silver threads hung in the air above the lawn, until it ceased just as abruptly, leaving the landscape exactly as before, only wetter. The flagstones were dark, the grass glistened, a few drops trickled down along the leaves of the willow and one by one fell to the ground below. Later that day, when everything had dried out, it rained again. This rain was different, it began quietly, just a few drops, as if feeling its way. I was sitting in the hall with my youngest daughter on my lap, putting on her sandals, and the door was open, so that I saw the big drops shattering against the flagstones outside. The raindrops slowly became more frequent, and as we headed over to the car, it poured down. But they fell at a conspicuous distance from each other, at the same time as the sun shone on the lawn, and as I walked behind the little girl, who was running as fast as she could and shouting it's raining! it's raining!, I thought that this too was an unusual rain. As I drove to the grocery shop, the drops pattered against the windscreen, and though they were immediately swept aside by the wipers, a film of water covered the glass. Outside the shop, where people were running to or from their cars, the mood was excited, there was laughter and smiles and cheerful comments, as sometimes happens when it suddenly rains after weeks of sunshine and everyone knows it will soon be over, unlike the autumn and winter rains, which produce a grimmer or more resigned mood in social settings. When we came out of the shop, it had stopped raining. Puddles of water stood on the tarmac, the bonnet of the car glistened, some of the passing cars still had their wipers on. The sun shone, but in the north-east, above the trees lining the avenue, the sky was almost completely black. I put the shopping bags on the floor in the back of the car, strapped the girl into the child seat, got into my own seat in the front, started the car, backed out and began driving uphill towards the grey-black sky, which made the dark green crowns of the trees along the road stand out brightly. A thunderclap sounded from far away.

Bats

So much about the bat is out of the ordinary that it is easy to think of it as a bizarre exception, a survivor from an age whose creatures were radically different from what we are now, but the fact is that there are so many kinds of bats – every fourth mammal species is a bat species – that it is rather at the centre of contemporary biology. That we are less familiar with bats than with other animals or birds, such as mice or crows, guinea pigs or pheasants, is not only because they are shy nocturnal animals that fly, for so are owls, but also has something to do with their innermost being, that they exist in the world in a way so idiosyncratic that they have made it their own, and it is this world that is incommensurable with our own. We share the same reality with owls, but not with bats. For such small animals, bats live remarkably long, up to forty years, and this makes their experience very different from that of mice, for example, who only live for a year or two. And since bats are mammals while all other flying creatures are either birds or insects, it is not impossible that they experience flying differently, that the bat's flight is a unique experience in the world, not found anywhere else. And while there are many creatures which are blind and slow and earth-bound, living in environments and following behavioural patterns that privilege the other senses, bats navigate by sonar at a breakneck speed and in spaces that alternate between open and closed, like those between buildings in cities or trees in forests. That too, life in a dark and sonar reality, is an experience unique to the bat. During the years we lived in Malmö, every spring a bat would fly back and forth between walls and roofs in the evenings, I saw it from the balcony on the seventh floor when I sat there smoking, once in a while it whizzed through the air only metres away from me, with that jerky motion characteristic of bats. It had maybe been doing this for five years, maybe for thirty, I would never know. Nor will I ever know what it was experiencing, what kind of images filled its mind while it flew. The sounds it emitted, at a frequency beyond my hearing range, were flung back from the wall, and the length of the sound told it whether the space in front of it was open or closed. What did it see? Not bricks or cement, not chimney or cornice, only something that must be steered clear of, an obstacle. But there is nothing crude about the bat's biosonar, on the contrary it is extremely finely tuned, for it enables it to locate even tiny insects in the air. Is it like a dense mesh, where the world appears in reverse depth, rather like one of those toys with screens full of little metal pins which one can stick one's face into and then see one's own features appearing as hollows? Bats can't glide the way birds do, a bat has to flap its wings to stay airborne, and this demands a lot of energy: its heart beats five hundred times a minute. In winter, when there are no insects to be found, it hibernates, a state where life processes are reduced to a minimum and it approaches the border with death, for then its heart beats only four times per minute. When it wakes in spring and its heart begins to beat faster, is it then immediately familiar with itself and the life that awaits it? Or does it feel as we sometimes do when we return to our house after a long holiday, that everything has a faint shimmer of strangeness? Most likely it has barely registered its absence from the world, it probably falls back into itself and its own existence within a fraction of a second. But that may be enough for satisfying or even pleasurable sensations to arise within it: once again it will fling itself into the mesh of sonar impressions and fly through the labyrinth of its own mind.

Clinker-built Double-ender

Every object whose form is dictated by necessity rapidly becomes fixed, the initial stage of experimentation is whittled down to a standard shape, that which has proved most functional. Today all spectacles are fixed to a thin bar which runs along the temples and whose ends are bent to fit around the ears. The monocle and the pince-nez are no longer in use. All bicycles now have two wheels of the same size; the velocipede, which had an enormous wheel at the front and a tiny one at the back, quickly proved impractical. The same rules apply to really old objects, those which humans have made use of for thousands of years, and whose shape must have been perfected early on and then have passed unchanged through the endless stream of time. The bowl for making and serving food, the jug for storing water, the knife for cutting meat, the plough for ploughing the soil, the boat for travelling on rivers, lakes and oceans. The basic shape of the boat, which narrows to a bow in front, to knife through the surface of the water and the waves as efficiently as possible, and narrows into a keel beneath, to stabilise it if it is of a certain size, has remained the same whether it has been paddled, rowed or sailed, whether the boat was big or small, whether it was used for transporting goods or people, for fishing or warfare. The engine was a revolution in many respects, but not for the boat, since its form was already perfect, and the engine was simply integrated into it. Not that I thought of this when we got our first boat, an open wooden launch which one spring day was carefully lowered onto some trestles on the lawn from a crane mounted on a lorry parked in the road beyond the hedge. My father had bought it. We lived on an island, and perhaps he had a notion that a boat belonged to the way of life here, or to his life, the way he imagined it then. The boat was a traditional clinker-built double-ender, made of wood and with a built-in engine, a Volvo Penta. It was relatively wide and moved slowly, the engine thumped soothingly at normal speed, sputtered wildly at full throttle. I came to know it well, for my brother and I were the ones who had to strip the paint and varnish off it that first spring with triangular scrapers, and then sand it with sandpaper, while our father varnished the hull on the outside and painted it on the inside. It was boring and monotonous work, and we could hear the voices and shouts of the other kids while we were at it, while the peculiar pleasure of engaging in an ancient craft, preparing wood for water, was of course completely lost on us: children live in the moment, and we just wanted to get away and play like the others. Yet when one day in June the same crane came and lifted the boat out of the garden and a while later lowered it onto the water a few hundred metres away, I did feel a faint sense of satisfaction which had to do with the work, for it felt good that the wood had been prepared and that water couldn't penetrate it, but it was quickly forgotten, the boat soon became a part of the everyday, with occasional openings into the fantastic, as when we glided slowly through a narrow sound and the greenish sea floor was visible through the cool, clear water, or when at the mouth of the fjord we saw the silvery fish come up from the deep after they had taken the bait, the frantic jerks on the line as they fought for their lives, how hard one had to squeeze their smooth tensed bodies to hold them still enough to get the hook out of their mouths, and how limp they suddenly went afterwards. My father smoked a pipe at that time, and I remember him sitting on the aft thwart with the pipe in his mouth and his hand on the tiller as the boat thumped its way slowly out of the sound. I also remember thinking there was something not right about it, that it was a mismatch, the boat was much too slow for him. Now I think of it as a child's way of understanding a fundamental thing about him. That the speed he had inside him was greater than the life he was living, and that it was only a matter of time before the force of this asymmetry would fling him out of the trajectory which included the wooden launch, the pipe, the house and the children, and into another one, faster and wilder.

Wolf

That reality changes radically faster than the language we use to describe it is shown by our relationship with animals, for when I was growing up in the 1970s the wolf was still conspicuously present in culture, even though it was no longer found in nature, at least not in Norway. I remember one evening when I was sitting in the kitchen and told my mother that I was as hungry as a wolf, she asked whether I knew that 'lupine', which comes from *lupus*, the Latin name for wolf, is a synonym for ravenous. I didn't, but I knew well what a wolf was. A lone wolf, that's what one called a man who went his own way, like the Western heroes Morgan Kane or Jonah Hex. To them, being alone was a good thing and the wolf was not an image of loneliness but of willpower. That was a comfort, something to aspire to. Other Norwegian folk names for the wolf were *gråbein* ('greylegs'), *gråtass* ('greypaws') and *varg* (from Old Norse *vargr*, 'robber' or 'outlaw'), my mother said. I knew that wolves hunted in packs and that they howled at the moon. I also knew that in fairy tales the wolf was the ruthless one, while the fox was clever and the bear was good-natured and a bit stupid. Later I learned that in Norse mythology it was the wolf that brought on the end of the world, in the shape of the terrible

Fenrir, or Fenris Wolf, while the werewolf, half-man, half-wolf, was a demonic figure who kept cropping up in comic books, films and books. Real wolves, on the other hand, were not something I ever related to, I have never lived anywhere that had wolves, so when one time a few years ago I saw an animal loping across the stubble fields as I was driving across the plain at Tågarp in Österlen, just past the old abandoned train station, my first thought was that it was a fox, for there are plenty of foxes around here, and yet it didn't look like any of the foxes I had seen, its running gait was different, and it was grey, long-legged and gaunt. Could it possibly be a wolf? Just around that time a story was circulating in the daily papers, there was a wolf on the loose in Skåne, it had presumably come down from Småland, and one could trace its route, for at regular intervals it killed sheep on farms in the area, which resulted in more or less identical news stories with photos of mangled animals and farmers whose faces expressed dejection, anger or despair. When I caught a quick glimpse of the loping animal way out in the fields, therefore, I gradually became convinced that it had been that very wolf. I had seen wolves before, but only in zoos. To see it running free across the fields was something entirely different, it was like coming into contact with another age, back when the forests were deep, people were few and animals were many. In the fields of Österlen beneath the pale blue sky so many years later, all this was difficult to connect with the mangy, thin, long-legged animal whose movements as it ran across the yellowish-white fields were so economical. If it really was a wolf I saw. The one that was traipsing around Skåne was probably young and inexperienced and had ended up here, where there hadn't been any wolves since the 1800s, when it left or was chased away from its pack. It must have begun to wander and then just gone on when the landscape opened up and the forests disappeared, not least because here there was plenty of prey, which it caught and killed in almost dreamlike sessions without meeting any resistance, where the warm blood flowing out of the throats it had ripped out excited it more and more, an aggression caused as much by there being no end to it, that death didn't put a stop to everything the way the wolf was used to, as by the excitement of the blood.

Some time after I saw this animal on the plain I received an early-morning phone call. One of our daughters had spent the night at a school friend's house, it was her mother calling, they ran the biggest farm in the area, and now they wanted me to come and pick up my daughter even though it was only eight o'clock, for the wolf had been there and taken their sheep. Her voice was full of stifled anger, I sensed that she was outraged, grief-stricken and distressed. On the way home my daughter said, sitting in the front seat next to me, that she hoped they weren't going to shoot the wolf, it couldn't help it. You didn't tell them, I hope? I said. No, are you crazy? she said. And that's how we, the culture worker and his daughter, who live as removed from the world of animals and nature as it is possible to get, became wolf lovers, while the farmers, who spend their lives tending animals and caring for the soil, became wolf haters, depicted in the newspaper the following day standing in front of the mangled carcasses, while the young wolf continued its loping journey across the open landscape, oblivious of what it represented, until a few weeks later it was shot.

Tears

The eyes, with their vitreous body and their membranes, are kept continually moist, a thin film of water always covers them so that they don't dry out, and so that dust and dirt don't stick to them. This water comes from a small sac-like cavity beneath the skin at the corner of the eyes and is led out towards the relatively large surface of the eye through a narrow channel, where it is evenly distributed by the eyelid, rather like a wet cloth across a windowpane. Or perhaps a better image would be like wipers across the windscreen of a car, for it all happens automatically without any thought or planning on our part. The amount of water is regulated by the hypothalamus, which controls the body's autonomous processes, those that have to do with body temperature, circadian rhythms, hunger, thought and digestion. Normally the amount of water on the surface of the eyes is so small that it doesn't even form drops, but disappears unseen down into tiny perforations below the eye. Drops are only formed when something out of the ordinary occurs, either when the eye is irritated – through direct contact with for example a twig or a large grain of dust, or through a more indirect contact, for example with the gas that an onion exudes when it is cut – or when one coughs, sneezes or throws up. Then

the eye suddenly overflows with water in a reflexive occurrence where the excess water gathers at the corner of the eye
and forms, from this perspective, some enormous drops,
which either run down along the root of the nose and on to
the cheek, or, if the head is bent forward, the water loosens
in little clusters and falls through the air, rather like raindrops. These drops, which differ from rain in that they are
salty, are what we call tears. Neither in the continual clean-
ing and maintenance work performed by this liquid or in the
reflexive emergence of tears do thoughts have any say; it all
occurs exclusively in those parts of the body that are self-
sustaining, and which our thoughts can only contemplate,
never penetrate or alter. When you are kneeling in front of
the toilet bowl and vomiting, your eyes fill with tears and
what you see becomes fluid and seems to tremble, whether
you like it or not. This extra-conscious distribution of moisture to the eye is something humans have in common with
all mammals. What is unique to humans is that tears can
also form as a result of powerful emotions, in other words,
independently of this mechanical maintenance system,
which is unheard of in any other animal. This, that our eyes
fill with salty water when we experience grief, despair or
powerlessness, and that our inner life is thereby given form
externally in a sort of language of liquid, is one of the most
beautiful natural phenomena I can think of. But precisely
because they are a kind of language, these tears are drawn
into culture by being regulated and subjected to a system of
values.

If for the sake of argument one imagines a purely natural
man – which I suppose is what one would call a contra-
diction in terms – he would cry every time he felt like it,

openly and without inhibition, and every fluctuation in his inner life, every emotional reaction, would be exposed, just like a small child, whose most distinctive feature is that nothing is hidden, it has no secrets. Since society and the social realm are constructed around the dynamics between the open and the closed, the secret and the accessible, where the unspoken is always more important than the spoken – similar to how what isn't used but is rather saved is always more important than that which is used at once – the openly crying person, the person who displayed everything, would also be the uncivilised person. In the north, where I grew up, not speaking about emotions and not displaying emotions has always been an ideal, and this has probably been so because nothing has been spontaneous, everything has always had to be planned, saved up, hardly anything has been available for one's immediate enjoyment, but has always had to be postponed, has always been stored for later. That I didn't stop crying uninhibitedly as a small child but just kept on crying for the least little thing was considered a failing, for in that way I showed myself incapable of saving, delaying, waiting, but squandered it all straight away at the same time as I also revealed secrets about myself and thereby my weakness. The tears produced by emotion are also mechanical and automatic, they too are released autonomously, so what one has to learn if one wants to prevent them from flowing is not to enter into those feelings which, when they reach a certain level of intensity, automatically release tears, but stay away from them, rather like in former times when one had to stay away from the seed corn even during lean years and in a famine. Only when the time was right and one's grief was obvious anyway, like at a funeral, could one let the tears flow freely and uninhibitedly, in a profusion of feelings not unlike the midwinter gorging one could indulge in and had scrimped and saved up for for so long at Christmas time, that lavish annual liberation from the restraints that life had imposed.

Electric Hand Mixers

Almost everything made by humans resembles, in one way or other, something in nature – a train resembles a caterpillar or a worm, a car resembles a beetle, a house resembles a den, a helicopter resembles those seeds from certain deciduous trees which in late summer swirl through the air by means of their organic rotor blades, a vacuum cleaner resembles an elephant's trunk, a toilet bowl resembles a giant's cauldron, and the water which flows down along its smooth sides is like a waterfall. What does the electric hand mixer resemble? Not a hummingbird, though both are full of rapid movement yet at the same time they stand still, nor a wader, who like the mixer has long thin legs – no, the mixer exists fully in its own right, a machine for stirring and mixing with two propeller-like beaters at the end of two shafts fastened to the underside of a compact, cube-shaped machine, each in their hole, which begin to rotate when the machine is switched on. The movement is transferred to the beaters, which are made of metal and shaped like little cages or globes. On the upper side of the cube there is a handle with which one controls the appliance. Though the mixer is small, no larger than a magpie, it dominates the kitchen entirely once it is switched on, sometimes even the adjacent rooms, due to its shrill, irascible whirring, which for a time forms an auditory centre in the house. To a small child the whirr can be terrifying, which isn't so strange, since it starts abruptly from an apparatus that in itself looks innocuous, and it is made louder by the material of the bowl which the beaters strike against – a high-pitched, almost piercing sound is sometimes produced if the beaters are pressed against the bottom of a plastic bowl – moreover if they want to say something or give an instruction adults often raise their voices in order to be heard above the din, but the child probably doesn't understand why. Suddenly the room is transformed into an inferno, so it's no wonder if the child starts to cry. But gradually its dread diminishes, not least because the child will come to associate the sight of the appliance with something good: the mixer is used for whipping cream for cakes or berries or to stir batter for pancakes or waffles, so even though the sound it makes is infernal, it almost always holds a promise of something good. Personally I hardly ever use the mixer any more; when I make waffles, pancakes or whip cream, I use an ordinary hand beater, it feels better: quieter and simpler. Since the result is the same – the waffles and pancakes become a batter that can be fried, the cream becomes fluffy – hand power and engine power are placed on an equal footing, and both become a matter of expending energy, the nature of which I have never quite understood. The mixer, or the electric beater as it is also called, this hummingbird of kitchen appliances, is connected to the electrical grid by a power cord, and the electric current which flows through it is what makes the beaters revolve. How much electricity it needs to whip cream can be measured. The electricity, which is what the movement of my hand must be compared with, is produced in hydroelectric turbines, in coal- or wind-powered power plants or nuclear reactors, in other words by the power of running water, blowing wind, burning coal or controlled nuclear reactions. But whereas electricity has to be produced or extracted before it can be used, the tiny effort I make doesn't feel like it is either produced by or extracted from anything, it happens almost imperceptibly, a movement among other movements, and I feel neither drained nor emptied of anything when it is over, merely a little stiff, perhaps, able to continue as before. That 'continuing', in other words doing something, always also involves expending energy, combusting fuel, can't have been obvious until after the invention of engines, which in a sense was also the invention of ourselves, in that our activities became separate from us, demanding a certain amount of energy, thereby becoming a separate entity or a function of ourselves. That we can now let water whip cream, let coal brush our teeth, let petrol transport us to places, let wind wash our clothes and the reactions within atomic nuclei vacuum-clean the dust in our house, enables us to hoard our own movements, but this stored power doesn't make us stronger, on the contrary we become weaker and fatter, so in order to compensate we leave the house in the evenings and start running along the roads in a perfectly aimless waste of energy, power simply drains out of us and produces nothing of any use to anyone, and about this one might say that humans have painted themselves into a corner, or alternatively that nothing is more human than that, and it represents the very pinnacle of human achievement, making man supreme among the animals: the creature who runs aimlessly.

Diary, June

Wednesday 1 June 2016

It is a few minutes past eight thirty in the evening. The sun is still shining upon the trees above the churchyard, whose tops I can see from the window here. A fairly strong wind from the east has been blowing all day. All the branches move constantly, and it is as if they follow different rhythms, some undulating slowly, others fitfully and jerkily, some circling, all while the leaves shimmer in the sunshine and the light from the sky behind them pierces their crowns at irregular intervals and in constantly shifting places. It is like a whole orchestra of movement, which even the trees here in the garden are a part of, the low, unkempt willow – its branches grow so densely and so droopily that there is something of the cocker spaniel about it; when I was pruning back one side of it some days ago, I wouldn't have been surprised if a pair of eyes had been concealed behind the foliage, which grew dense as fur – and the towering chestnut have also been tossing and pitching back and forth and up and down all day, like moored boats in a rough sea. When I was sitting out there earlier this afternoon I was in fact thinking of the ocean, for the rushing of the wind was so loud that it reminded me of the sound of waves striking land, and the trees, especially the birch, seemed to be stretched out by the wind and resembled large green sails. I liked that thought, and I liked the rushing noise, it felt as if I was surrounded by bustling activity, as if a great undertaking was going on around me. And I liked that birds were singing in the middle of all this, but as if withdrawn, from a greater depth than usual.

You are asleep now. I just went upstairs to pick up the book I began reading yesterday, Swedenborg's *Journal of Dreams*, and as I passed you, the book you enjoy most these days, *Sam's Potty* by Barbro Lindgren, was covering your face. I removed it and you opened your eyes and looked at me but without any sign of recognition appearing in them, and the next instant you were again lying with your eyes closed, breathing gently. I should have written today, my plan was to finish the piece about cynicism and then write another one, maybe about slugs, but then they called from the kindergarten and said you had a fever. They also said you had told them your tummy hurt. Your mother was on her way to Copenhagen to have a lunch meeting with her agent, so there was nothing for it: I got into the car, drove down there and picked you up. You love riding in the car, so getting you to come with me wasn't a problem, and you also like to express yourself, so when new things happen you think it's fun to pronounce the words for them. Anne sick, go home with Daddy, you said, and Anne tummy hurt, ride car, sit in Anne's seat.

Yesterday evening you stood watching me roll up your sisters' sleeping bags, they are at a school camp today, and said Daddy roll! Daddy roll! And yesterday morning, when a heavy rain fell and lightning struck nearby, while thunder roared above the house and the mood in the hall as we were about to drive to school was excited, you shouted The moon! The moon! and went to stand on the staircase, where you could look up at the sky through the little window there. You had realised that the flashes of light and the thunderclaps came from the sky, and since the sky for you was associated with the moon, you must have thought that the moon was making it all happen.

You weren't all that sick, it turned out, you had only a light fever and no other symptoms. I brought my computer out into the living room, turned on *Laban the Little Ghost* on Netflix for you and tried to read a manuscript by a friend of mine, but it wasn't easy, you wanted to sit on my lap, and I was really too sleepy to concentrate. I fell asleep with you on top of me for about half an hour, and then, when I put you to bed upstairs and lay down to read in the next room, I too fell asleep. We slept for two and a half hours. When I woke up, I had to wake you so we could be at school in time to pick up your brother. I removed your nappy, put panties and some new clothes on you – a little flowery skirt I had bought in Simrishamn some days ago and a white sweater – put you in the car and drove to Ystad. We took your brother to the hairdresser, she had a few minutes to spare between two customers and agreed to cut his hair at top speed. She cut it very short, using clippers at the sides, and she dyed his hair green with a dye that washes out after one wash, though he would have preferred a more permanent one. You played for a while in a playground, I bought a yellow cap for you, we ate at a hamburger restaurant before driving home, where your mother was waiting, and I came in here to answer emails that have piled up.

*

Swedenborg begins his journal in Ystad in the summer of 1743 with the following summary account:

1743. July 21. I started on my journey from Stockholm, and arrived at Ystad on the 27th, having passed through the cities of Tälje, Nyköping, Norrköping, Linköping, Gränna, Jönköping. At Ystad I met the Countess De la Gardie with her two young ladies and two counts; also Count Fersen, Major Lantingshausen and Magister Klingenberg. On July 31st General Stenflycht arrived with his son, and Captain Schächta.

The town of Ystad where Swedenborg stayed during these summer days, before he sailed on to Stralsund in present-day Germany, can't have been so very different from Ystad as it was when we walked around it earlier today. Several of the houses in the old town date to the fifteenth and sixteenth centuries, many are from the seventeenth and eighteenth centuries, and although tarmac, concrete, motor vehicles and motor boats have been added, the town structure is the same, with the harbour like a stage and the houses like the seats within an assembly hall around small pockets of squares and parks. What has changed is the speed. Swedenborg's journey from Stockholm to Ystad took six days, a distance I cover by car in six hours. The landscape he travelled through was different too; back then Skåne was covered with large deciduous forests, not cropland as it is now. His journal entries are brief, dutiful notes about what he does and whom he meets, and how many churches there are in the small towns he travels through on his journey southward across Europe. Then something happens. Six pages of the original manuscript have been torn out, and after that the external world vanishes completely and is replaced by an inner world, hitherto uncommented on, through a fevered and wild description of dreams he has had, the significance of which he ponders.

The shift from the outer to the inner world is so abrupt, and the inner world so chaotic and heavy with meaning that at first it is nearly impossible to orient oneself in.

What is happening within him?

When I was reading his journal earlier this evening it struck me that my inner being, the person I am to myself, has changed in recent years, and how often I get the feeling that I am no one, that I am merely a place which thoughts and feelings pass through. The last time I had that feeling was in Buffalo a few weeks ago, as I was walking down some long, high-ceilinged and deserted corridors in a large art deco hotel, on my way from my room down to the street to smoke. How can I explain it? That the thoughts and feelings weren't mine, that I had hardly any sense of a self that could lay claim to them? It is an eerie feeling, also because it is so different from the feeling I had earlier in my life, when everything that had happened to me and everything I had experienced, especially in my childhood and early youth, was so important to me, and all the relationships I had were so significant – my father, his role in my life, my mother, my brother, my grandparents, my friends and acquaintances. That what they had done and said to me, and what I had done and said to them, was somehow bound to me, and that I understood myself on the basis of that.

Now it is as if that whole rigging has come undone and the life-determining parts are merely parts that exist within me, the way a dwarf birch stands by the side of a path or a stone from a terminal moraine lies next to it, surrounded by heather, but the heather, the stone and the dwarf birch say nothing about the path, nor do the path, the stone or the dwarf birch say anything about the heather, they are just there, side by side, and the identity of the place they thereby constitute is as distinct and unique as it is accidental.

Your elder sister has called twice from the school camp while I have been sitting here writing this, she wanted me to come and get her. The first time she said that the mood there was icy, the second time she said she was scared. She knew I couldn't simply come and get her, she just needed someone from outside to tell this to, someone connected with the home she was missing. She is twelve years old, and everything she experiences feels intense and important, charged with meaning. She has begun to think about who she is, she has begun to see herself as herself, and that hurts and also feels good, it is terrifying and exhilarating, she is so full of life and her newfound self, and is now, I think, at the point where human beings are at their most vulnerable.

It feels strange to observe it, for I remember what it was like to be there, yet at the same time I have never been further away from it. Perhaps it is meant to be that way? That whatever it is that holds the life-determining parts of the parents' lives together begins to decay and finally comes undone at about the same time that the children's selves begin to acquire greater weight and, as it were, draw the life-determining parts towards them? That meaning diminishes in the one at the same time that it grows in the other?

The day after tomorrow I am seeing a doctor. I have been to the doctor only twice in my adult life, both times it was your mother who made me go, and so it is now: when she read the last book I wrote, *Spring*, three weeks ago, the first thing she wanted to talk about was a scene I described in it, where there was blood in the toilet bowl. 'You have to get it checked,' she said. My mother said the same thing after she had read the book. 'That blood,' she said. 'What was it? Have you been to see a doctor?' I hadn't, but I made up my mind to do so when I was in Buffalo, for during that whole book tour, which began in Buffalo, continued on to New York, Santa Fe and Chicago, there was blood whenever I went to the bathroom, and though it is probably the most trivial of trivial matters, namely haemorrhoids, all that blood did something to my mood, in the hotel corridors, in the cars going to the theatres, on the stage, in the restaurants, at the airports, it took me even further away from myself and my surroundings.

Now it is ten minutes past eleven, and outside it is completely dark. For some reason unknown to me, your brother is sleeping on a mattress on the floor next to the bed, it was your mother who put him to bed tonight. She is asleep too, in the innermost bedroom, where I will soon go to lie down.

Your two sisters are lying each in their dormitory together with their classmates many tens of kilometres from here, in a forest by a lake.

The trees above the churchyard are barely visible as a deeper darkness against the black sky, which at its lower end merges with the roof of the house, the wall and the lawn and is indistinguishable from them. The faint light from the two windows in the kitchen, where the fluorescent tube beneath the fan above the stove is lit, shines in the middle of this black mountain, and as always I see them as eyes, peering out into the darkness as mournfully and silently as the kitchen windows in the house I grew up in once did, for that is something I have preserved from my childhood, the animation of things. Even now everything I see has a face, everything I look at has a certain aura that I think of as its soul. The cup on the table in front of me, so mild and friendly, the palette leaning on its edge against the bookcase, speckled with paint, with the hole for the thumb like an eye, the notch below it like a slightly gaping mouth, the profile vaguely fish-like.

Thursday 2 June 2016

It is seven minutes past nine, and I am looking out at exactly the same landscape as I did yesterday evening. The colour of the sky, pale blue, almost white near the horizon, grey-blue higher up, is the same, the colours of the trees, the bushes and the grass are the same, from the dark green of the trees in the churchyard to the light, dull green of the willow, and the light of the setting sun, grey along the ground, golden in the treetops, is the same. The only difference is that the wind from the east is meeker and the movements of the trees gentler. I love repetition. Repetitions turn time into a place, turn the days into a house, where the repetitions form the walls, floor and ceiling. Inside this building, this latticework of routines, it is as if time doesn't pass, since every act and movement repeats the preceding ones and in this way holds them fast. The strange thing is that outside time passes all the more quickly. Just now it was autumn, it was winter, it was spring. I was just thirty-four years old, forty-two, forty-five. While I was having dinner with your sisters after driving them to and from their musical rehearsal in Simrishamn I noticed a photograph sticking out from a pile of papers on the sideboard by the wall, I took it out, it was a group photograph from the kindergarten, your elder sister, who is smiling her biggest smile, must have been four years old, the youngest, who is sitting in the row above, two, nearly three. I showed them the photo, they grabbed it and examined it eagerly, almost greedily. I looked at them, to me there was hardly any difference between who they were then and who they are now, the clothes they were wearing were familiar to me, it was as if they had worn them yesterday. To them it was a photograph of two strangers whom they only recognised from other photos. But routines help to make this avalanche of days and years manageable, for if one does the same things and holds fast this place in time, walks around in this house of routine, then one is nearly untouched by it, it is like living on a hillside above a river, as if it is only outside that time flows. And in a way this represents a true experience of time, or at least one that is valid, for the soul doesn't age, it stays unchanged throughout life, while the body grows, changes, weakens, wrinkles, is bowed, is bent. Time tears into the flesh, that is what the avalanche of days changes, while the soul is only a witness to it, like something seen from a window, a swelling river that slowly overflows its banks and, when it recedes, leaves behind a very different landscape.

Before Swedenborg had these violent dreams, which seem almost like an assault by alien powers, he was interested in the relation between the flesh and the soul, matter and spirit, like many contemporary philosophers, such as

Descartes. Swedenborg came to this problem not from philosophy, but from biology. When he travelled from Stockholm to Ystad and onward to Stralsund and Groeningen, his intention was to gather material for a major treatise he was working on, called *Regnum animale*, or *The Animal Kingdom*, in which his plan was to examine the soul from an anatomical point of view. The dreams overwhelmed him, but he continued work on his treatise on the materiality of the soul until one day in the spring of 1745 when he was dining alone in a private room in a restaurant in London and suddenly saw a man sitting in the corner of the room. The man said, Do not eat too much, and Swedenborg took fright and hurried out. That same night the man appeared in a dream, it was God, he wanted Swedenborg to reveal the spiritual meaning of the Bible, and of course his life changed for ever.

To me, the truly fascinating thing is not the world of spirits and angels that Swedenborg gained access to in London, the parallel reality which opened before him and into which he gazed from his everyday existence, but rather what he was working on before that, the materiality of the soul, the physical origin of dreams, their foothold in the flesh. The science of the Baroque, I can't imagine a wilder place to visit in thought. Descartes, who imagined he saw fixed images in the bulls' eyes he dissected. Rembrandt, who was staying in the same city at the same time as Descartes, Amsterdam, and his anatomical paintings, especially the one where the top of the skull has been removed and is held like a bowl in the hand of an assistant. That arms can be lopped off like branches and continue to feel. That everything we see and feel passes through bundles of wires, that blood flows through tubes, that images flicker through us as we sleep.

Last summer I observed three brain operations. I saw how the top of the skull was sawn off, and I saw the assistant holding it like a cup in his hand. I saw the membranes covering the brain, as if doused with blood on the underside, like rags, and I saw the shiny surface of the brain, how it pulsated faintly. I saw the doctor, the British neurosurgeon Henry Marsh, stick an instrument resembling a knitting needle into the brain, and when the current was switched on, I saw the patient's arm flail up into the air. I saw how they fastened the lid to the cranium again with metal clips, and I saw how one whole side of the patient's face and body was partially paralysed the next day, after they had removed certain parts of his brain.

The brain was like a small animal, weighing well over a kilo, which had grown into folds inside the narrow skull. We know more about it now than Swedenborg and his contemporaries did, yet we don't, really, for the link, which Swedenborg compared to the relation between the finite and the infinite – that is between spirit and matter – we cannot say anything about. The spirit is the angel in the room, life is the mystery. It is the vast oak forests that Swedenborg travelled through on his journey from Stockholm to Ystad and the fortifications and the harbour he saw in Stralsund, the churches he counted in the German towns he travelled through and the noble men and women he met on his journey, they are the miracle. The grass and the stars, the trees and the people, the branches and the hands, the stones and the heads, the bulls and the birds, the fences and the teeth.

You saw all this today, you know. While I drove your brother to school and your mother to the train station, you were with the babysitter, you walked to the playground down here, you sat in the pram and looked at the sky, blue and summery, the sun and the trees, the horses and the houses while I sat in here finishing a piece about cynicism. When I was done, I put you in your seat in the car, picked up your sisters at school, and we drove to the minigolf course, ate at the fast-food stand there, before we went to the beach, where you sat down with your youngest sister and ate ice cream. The sand, dry and golden, the sea, dark blue, a mild breeze sweeping by. The sea, you said when you saw all that blue water.

Your sisters were tired after the school camp and a little sullen as we drove home, but they said they had had a good time, and I think they had, although darkness and loneliness had overcome the older of them and had made her call home.

The feeling that I no longer belong with my memories and thoughts, that they are just passing through me as if I were a sort of station, doesn't have anything to do with my age, nor does it have to have anything to do with any kind of existential dimension, I thought today as I sat at an outdoor café drinking coffee while your sisters were dancing and singing at a nearby school. I felt a little chilly in the shade, for even though it was twenty-five degrees today, it is as if summer hasn't quite settled in yet, the air gets cold as soon as the sun goes down, and it is still cool in the shadows. It seems more likely that it is connected with what I do: that I have written down my thoughts and memories, and that others have read them, and that in all the events I take part in I sit talking about my thoughts and memories in front of an audience. The feeling that they don't belong to me is reasonable, I have given them away, and I continue to give them away. Is there a freedom in that, in the feeling that I no longer belong to myself or don't have any ownership over my inner self, which has rather become a place that thoughts and memories pass through while I look on, as it were? Yes, there is. There is a great freedom in it. It resembles the freedom I seek in writing, which has to do with being in a self-less state, where what is put on paper doesn't concern me personally, is not a part of my own identity, merely a product of it. But all freedom also has an element of destructiveness. If one is free in a community – that is unbound by others – then one can be reckless with them. And if one is free within oneself – that is unbound by inner restraints – then one can be reckless with oneself. I like recklessness, to me it is a sign precisely of freedom but also of abundance.

Why was Swedenborg tormented?

For tormented he was.

He was at the mercy of his inner visions, they overpowered him with great force, and of course he was unable to ignore them, their significance was obvious. Not what they meant, but that they were meaningful.

For a long time he defines them as dreams, images within him, created by his soul or spirit or, as we would say now, his subconscious. Then it changes, for the images are somehow torn loose from him and become something that comes to him from outside, a tendency which gains in strength until he himself can visit at will the place they come from: a whole world, a whole universe that exists in parallel with this one where everything corresponds to everything else.

It isn't difficult to explain, it was a way he had of handling the tremendous pressure, of channelling it away from himself and out into the external world. I have seen people in a state of psychosis, and that's what they do, they project their own conflicts and inner images outwards into a world which they then communicate with and in some cases also receive orders from. But what if it really was God who appeared to him in that restaurant in London? What if a parallel dimension really exists which only a few chosen ones can see into?

There is nothing to indicate that this is the case. But nor does anything disprove it.

At least I can't think of anything.

It is completely dark out now. It is twenty-three minutes to midnight and you have already slept for four hours. What you will dream of tonight, no one will ever know. Even if you were to remember it when you wake up, you wouldn't have a language in which to communicate it to us, nor do I think that you quite understand what dreams are, I think that is still undefined for you, your thoughts haven't grasped the concept yet, and it therefore lies within that strange zone where it neither exists nor doesn't exist.

Friday 3 June 2016

It is eleven minutes to eleven in the evening. When a few minutes ago I was sitting in the living room next to your brother, who was watching a cartoon version of *Star Wars* while I read a book about Swedenborg's view of science and his theories, which I've had on my bookshelf for several years but never opened before, it seemed dark outside. But when I opened the door to walk over here, as your brother disappeared into the bathroom to brush his teeth, I discovered that the light was still alive, for the sky above me was blue, though darkened, and the first stars had emerged. In the garden around me there was a strange atmosphere, for it was neither light nor dark, or rather it was both light and dark at the same time. The crowns of the trees were dark, but the air between them was light, and the flowers in their canopies shone white. The grass was dark, the hedge was dark. And everything stood perfectly still, there was no movement anywhere. I have never seen such a light before. That must mean that I have never been outside in the garden between ten thirty and eleven at night in June before, after a sunny day with clear skies, for I would have remembered this atmosphere.

Something coursed through me then. Not exactly happiness, but a current of something good. It was as if I was being tuned up one step.

Now it is dark out there, the only light that remains is in the sky, at its blue rim, which is modulated into darkness with infinite delicacy as one moves upward. The rows of trees above the roof, up by the churchyard, which have been dancing in the wind the past two evenings, now stand motionless. I can see seven of the trees. They stand as if on duty, jet black against the faintly lighter sky behind, which here and there pierces the foliage.

What kind of life is it that they live? Why do they live at all?

You are sleeping. You have been running around in your panties all day in a good mood, no fever, just a runny nose and a slight cough. You have repeated almost every word you hadn't heard before, it is as if the words become yours when you say them, as if they then become a part of you. As if you capture them. And that catch will last your whole life, for once words have entered you, they don't go away. Then I notice them too, all the different words that move in the air between us.

When someone laughs, you laugh too.

This morning, while we were standing in the hall getting ready to go out, your sister asked how warm it would be today. Recently they have started asking about that, to decide whether to wear shorts or not, whether they'll need a jacket or not. I got out my phone, navigated to the Norwegian weather site yr.no, found the weather forecast for Glemminge and looked at her. 'Twenty-five degrees,' I said. 'Oh,' she said. 'Just oh?' I said. 'It was twenty-six yesterday,' she said.

Your siblings climbed into the car, two in the back and one in the front, I connected the phone to the stereo and clicked on the playlist of fifty hits which we have been listening to this week after three months straight of *Hits for Kids*, started the engine and drove out into the road. The sky was perfectly blue, the flat wide landscape yellow and green with the sea a darker band in the east. The fantastic cloud formations that usually hang on the horizon in summer, enormous mountainous shapes, still haven't begun to form. But there were plenty of other things to look at. The wall of lilacs, which are blossoming now. The gentle hills to the north, which in the last few weeks have been lit up by white apple and cherry trees. The wind turbines, white and slender and visible from a distance of several kilometres. The islands of separate farmyards, the little river which I didn't discover until we had lived here for two years, and the herd of cows grazing in the area where the landscape opens up towards the sea, there are maybe sixty of them, yellow-beige like camels.

Your elder sister told me about an episode during music class when they were listening to music by artists who had taken drugs. She said something about her teacher, he didn't like Justin Bieber, but this one song he thought was good. Or was it her who thought so?

What was she really saying?

I looked at her. But at times she became irritated if she was asked to repeat something, so I let it go.

Had the teacher played music by people who took drugs, making a point of it?

Surely that couldn't be true, could it?

'It is a good song,' I said. 'I think so too.'

We were playing 'Love Yourself', the simple guitar theme was incredibly catchy.

We drove into the narrow forest that continues all the way into Ystad.

'I accepted the offer to go to Los Angeles in October,' I told her. 'Are you sure you want to come?'

'Yes,' she said.

'Nothing is definite yet,' I said. 'But I'll try to arrange it.'

There was a silence.

'Maybe you'll have to do something for us if you kids want to come along,' I said, since I am a little worried that I am spoiling them.

'Like what?' she said.

'There's always something you can help out with,' I said.

Two days earlier she had said that everyone sooner or later has to get drunk, to find out what it's like.

Suddenly she is at the age where they talk about things like that. Suddenly she has become interested in clothes, in make-up, in pop music.

I said that I would come to bring her home from every party she went to when she was older.

During the last part of the trip we talked about Trump and about the US election, which she had also taken an interest in, while the other two sat silently in the back seat staring straight ahead.

After I had dropped them off at the car park in front of the school, I changed the music and drove on into Ystad, up to the hospital, which lay a few hundred metres from the town centre, parked, opened the windows and lit a cigarette while I waited for it to be nine o'clock, when I had my appointment.

I had hardly sat down in the waiting room when my name was called and I was able to go in and meet the doctor, who was waiting in the corridor, a small man maybe ten years older than me with an Eastern European accent.

'We can go in here,' he said, gesturing towards a half-open door.

'Sit there,' he said as we entered, and gestured again, this time towards a chair.

I sat down, he asked how long I had been bleeding. I said a year and a half. But that a long time passed between each episode. The last time it had lasted for five days. 'How long ago was that?' he said. 'A month ago,' I said. He sighed. 'You should have come then,' he said. 'Oh well. You still smoke?' 'Yes,' I said. 'How much?' 'Twenty,' I lied, the truth is closer to forty, but he didn't really need to know that.

I undressed to the waist and lay down on the bench with my white rolls of fat bulging over my waistband. He took my blood pressure, which was first rate. He listened to my lungs with the stethoscope, asked me to breathe in and out, hold my breath. Everything was first rate.

'Now you can take your trousers off,' he said.

I did as he said.

'My underwear too?' I asked.

He nodded without meeting my gaze.

'Now lie on your back with your knees bent towards your stomach.'

I did as he said. The rolls of fat, my pants around my knees, it didn't feel so great.

My dick looked puny now that I was seeing it with his eyes.

Is it really that small? I thought as he began to knead and press his hands against my belly.

I would have felt so much better if I had had a large, impressive dick.

How much better everything would have been then.

'Does it hurt?' he said.

'No,' I said.

And nice teeth.

My ugly teeth bother me so much that I can hardly speak to people, I keep thinking of my teeth.

'OK,' he said. 'Now lie on your side. With your knees up.'

'Like this?' I said and turned over on my side.

'Yes,' he said. 'This won't hurt. But it won't be pleasant either. Neither for you nor for me.'

He laughed a little.

I laughed a little too.

'So, now you are going to feel something,' he said. He smeared something moist on my anus. Then he stuck a finger into it.

'It isn't pleasant,' he said.

'No,' I said. 'It isn't.'

'Does this hurt?'

He moved his finger back and forth a little inside my rectum.

'No,' I said.

'OK,' he said, pulled his finger out quickly, handed me a tissue.

'You can wipe yourself now,' he said.

I did, threw the tissue into a waste bin, pulled up my trousers.

'Are we done? Can I get dressed now?'

'Yes, you can get dressed. You just need to take another blood test, in another room.'

I put on my shirt, my suit jacket.

'You're fine,' he said. 'No haemorrhoids, no fissures and no tumour. As far as I can tell. But we'll still do a proctoscopy. Since your mother has had colon cancer. It isn't hereditary, but you've eaten the same food and lived in the same environment. So we'll check.'

'But it's nothing?' I said. 'So why was I bleeding?'

'It's just bleeding,' he said. 'It can happen. Could be hard stool, for instance. But you should have come at once. Then I could have seen.'

'But everything is fine?'

'Everything is fine.'

Outside I put on my sunglasses, buttoned the top button of my jacket and walked to the car park. It was already over twenty degrees. I drove downtown and picked up a picture I had had framed, a sketch Anna Bjerger had sent me in the mail after I interviewed her at the Louisiana Museum of Modern Art outside Copenhagen, it was one of the paintings reproduced in *Spring*, the one with the girl wearing an orange sweater. I had been very happy when I received it and I felt happy again now, looking at it. Then I had a coffee at Espresso House, sat on the terrace and looked out towards the quiet square flooded with sunlight, the shadows of the buildings stretching across it. I called Geir to talk about his book, which I have read for the third time. He read to me from the new book he was working on, an episode at the airport in Turkey, on the way to Afghanistan. When I got back into the car, I received a text message from your mother asking how it had gone, I replied that it had gone fine, there was nothing wrong with me. On the way out of town I called my mother, your grandmother, I knew she was anxious and told her that everything was all right.

Back home you were standing in the doorway as I arrived, I gave you a hug and told your mother a little more about my visit to the doctor, you went down to the playground, and I sat down in here to write a piece about slugs. When I had written half of it, I answered emails, then I went to sleep a little, but as I was lying down Eirik called. Our publishing house, Pelikanen, was short twenty-seven thousand kroner for customs dues, if the amount wasn't paid by Sunday the printed copies of three books would be stuck at the border. I came in here again and paid the bill. Then I succumbed to the temptation of reading the first few lines of the reviews of *Spring* which had come out today. One reviewer wrote that the first two books, *Autumn* and *Winter*, were uninteresting as a whole, and the other wrote that *Spring* was like a poetic mummy blog.

I sat in front of the text on slugs for a while longer, but I was unable to concentrate, so when I got an email from Kari at the Munch Museum with an updated list of works for the exhibition, I spent the next hour looking at the paintings and going through the exhibition rooms thinking about possible changes. Then I slept for half an hour before driving back into Ystad and picking up your younger sister and brother. Your elder sister was going to sleep over at a friend's house. The plan was to buy your brother a new bicycle, the old one was far too small for him, but he got a little cross when I told him he wasn't allowed to take his computer to his friend's house, and when he realised that we weren't going to the little bicycle shop where we had bought the previous one but to a much larger, warehouse-like shop, he became rather uncooperative, and I became cross, I had thought it would be a big thing for him, but instead he just shuffled sullenly between all the rows of bicycles. In the end we went home empty-handed. I dropped him off at his friend's place while your sister and her friend played on the lawn in the warm windless garden, and then I wrote the final part of the text about slugs. You were here in the office for a while, the insane mess is exciting to you, since you can hardly take a single step without knocking something over, a stack of books or papers. And all the rubbish on the floor! Bottles, cartons, boxes, cigarette packs, newspapers, periodicals, plastic bags, magazines. I fetched your brother and his friend, while your sister and her friend were picked up by her father so that we were only five for dinner. We ate outside, on the patio behind the summer house, which is nearly completely overgrown even though I cleared it last year. I told your brother that none of my friends had ever been to my house while I was growing up. That none of them had been inside my house until I turned twelve. He wondered why. I told him that my father hadn't allowed it. He wondered why.

I said I thought my father hadn't wanted other people close to him. Then I told him that he had been a teacher, and that he was used to children. The rule only applied at our house. Your brother said that my father should have been a writer, then he could have been alone all the time.

'Yes,' I said, smiling.

'So why wasn't he a writer?' he asked. 'Didn't he want to be one?'

'I think maybe he wanted to but that he wasn't able to,' I said. 'Being a writer is pretty difficult.'

That made him laugh. 'Being a teacher is much harder!' he said.

'No, I don't think it is,' I said.

'Being a writer is easy,' he said.

'Not that easy,' I said. 'It's just that all the grown-ups you know are writers. But actually not that many people are. But he was a very good teacher. I know someone who says he was the best teacher he ever had.'

'Wasn't he strict?'

'Yes,' I said. 'He was. I know one person who thought he was terrible. Once my father hung him on a coat peg in the corridor.'

Your brother stared at me in disbelief.

'It's true,' I said. 'It was in the 1970s. It's a pretty long time ago.'

'That's not allowed any more,' he said.

'No,' I said. 'In many ways you are living in the best of all times ever for children.'

When we had taken his friend home and you had gone to bed, your brother and I stayed up watching TV in the living room while your mother watched a movie on her computer at the other end of the house. That is, he watched TV, I lay on the sofa leafing through the book about Swedenborg's scientific enquiries. He put his feet over mine, that made me happy, I still felt guilty about our failed trip to buy him a bicycle, that I had overruled him. And then the book was interesting. Swedenborg had published writings in nearly every discipline that existed. Mathematics, geometry, physics, chemistry, anatomy, biology. He had theories about everything, and he made several sketches for mechanical inventions, including a flying machine. He had developed a new, octal numerical system, based on the number eight rather than ten, and presented it to King Charles XII of Sweden. But his main theory concerned tremblings or what he called 'tremulations', waves that travelled through man like rings in water or sound through air: all bodily movements, all movements of the spirit came about through the action of such waves, from the nervous system out into the limbs, from the world into the nervous system, a kind of fluid-mechanical system where the physical and the spiritual merged. When he had his dream crisis and everything w upended, he was working on a treatise on the material fo of the soul, where it was located and what it consisted of strange thing is that all this, which for so many years been his entire life, what he lived and breathed for, in the course of a few months lost all meaning, all relevance, and that for the rest of his life he concerned himself with matters that, at least as seen from the outside, had to do with the exact opposite.

I found another book by Swedenborg here, *The Spiritual Diary*, and when I opened it at random, I saw the following chapter heading: 'Those who have for an end magnificence

and honors in the world, and also in heaven; those who have
for an end wealth and gain in the world, and those who have
for an end the fame of erudition, all such neither see and nor
find anything of genuine truth in the word.'

Here he writes about figures he has encountered in the
spiritual world who believed they would shine as stars in the
heavens since they had kept the Word of God, but after their
souls had been examined it appeared that they had done so
out of self-love and ambition. It isn't hard to see that he is
writing about himself here, and that this is what his life
crisis was about. And that the two paths, the path of external
truth and the path of internal truth, the active and the contemplative life, are still the two alternatives facing us.

Saturday 4 June 2016

When I woke up this morning unusually late, past ten, it was
to a strong feeling of shame at what I wrote last night. I have
never felt ashamed of anything I have thought, and never of
my inner self, but only of what I have said, done or written, in
other words when something in me has been made visible to
others. It is odd, a kind of double standard, that everything is
fine as long as it is hidden and not seen. Writing is a way of
getting under this fence, since it involves expressing the
inner, as it is in itself, which is only possible if one forgets
that one is writing, forgets that writing consists of tech-
niques, rhetorical moves, manipulations and modulations of
tone, since all this belongs to communication, that which is
directed towards the other, and thereby implicitly opens up
the internal world to one who sees, and consequently

introduces shame, or the possibility of shame. Only by forgetting that one is writing can one write and give an external expression to the internal thought without it being marked or prevented by shame, as all other external expressions are.

I find it interesting that one can think all kinds of forbidden thoughts without any consequences for one's self-image. Perhaps everything we think is a part of who we are, rather as a community is made up of all the individuals in it, and its elite may well despise the stupid, dislike the trivial, hate the vulgar, at the same time knowing that they have as much right to be there as themselves, since the community is defined through all its members, not just some of them, and the presence of the basest neither diminishes nor changes the whole, which is the community itself. That an idiot lives in Norway doesn't make Norway an idiotic country.

And then, an absolute familiarity reigns among the elements of the inner self, nothing is alien, everything is regarded with sympathy; a stupid thought is like a little brother, an evil notion is like an uncle who in good company says what he really thinks about immigrants. If the inner self belongs to a person hostile to immigration, the role of the uncle may be played by the notion that we should help people in need. Within, everyone is one of us, whom we support, and even if we don't back up absolutely everyone, we understand them. Yes, at times the inner self resembles a sheltered workshop producing things which no one needs, but it doesn't matter, what matters is the process of production and the community it offers.

What was it I felt so ashamed about when I woke up this morning?

It was what I wrote about having a small dick.

Did I really write that? was my first thought.

Why, oh why?

Not only did I write it – then I could simply have deleted it and forgotten all about it – but I also sent it to my editor, as I do with all the texts I write.

What must he think?

Why did I write it?

It's not *that* small, is it?

Isn't it actually pretty average?

Maybe even a little bigger than average?

Just thinking it to myself doesn't do any harm. But writing it down gives it weight. Not only is it a private matter and therefore inappropriate, it is also banal and unworthy of a literary text, moreover infantile. By writing it I reveal that not only do I think about it, I attach importance to it. That it is a part of my identity. This makes me a small human being. I have a hard time imagining Heidegger writing about the size of his penis and reasoning about how this had contributed to his own image of himself, or that he thought about it constantly even as he was writing infinitely slowly, calmly and comprehensively about Presocratic philosophy. That he was unable to enter a public bath without straight away looking at the other men's penises, at how long they were, and when he saw someone whose penis was longer than his own, being filled with envy.

That's what I do.

I was just now in the main house putting your brother to bed – I read from Harry Potter until he fell asleep and I had to put the book down a little disappointed, for I myself wondered how things would turn out for Harry – and then I sat on the sofa with your youngest sister, she was watching

Friends and about to fall asleep too, I saw how her eyelids slid down, like two little garage doors, and how they sprang back up when the thought that she was falling asleep reached them, since she didn't want to go to bed yet – and when I went out into the dark, the thought of what I was writing struck me again with full force – what was I doing, why did I go on torturing myself by writing about my penis when it was so terribly silly, so frightfully childish, so appallingly undignified?

It is fourteen past eleven and you are lying on your back sleeping in the darkness up on the first floor, after a long and eventful day, at least by your standards, you who still don't distinguish between big and small, boring and interesting, important and unimportant. A few days ago you stopped and bent down as we were walking across an asphalted square, you had noticed some ants and they absorbed your attention entirely, you quite forgot that we were on our way to pick up your siblings.

It was even hotter today than yesterday, and I spent nearly the entire first part of the day in the car. First your brother, your mother, you and I went to a bicycle shop, then I drove you to a café in town and went up to the house where your elder sister had spent the night, then back to town, where I picked up your brother so we could collect the bicycle we had bought and which was going to be fitted with a light and a lock, back to town to pick you up, drive you to the beach, then drive your brother to a friend's place in Glemminge, then back to the beach, where your sister discovered that the bikini she had bought was too large, so I took her back to town, she changed it, and when we got back to the beach your youngest sister called, she was at another beach with the family she had spent the night with and wanted to be picked up, which I did, and then I had to drive the friend of your elder sister to her home, since she was spending the night at our house and had to pick up some things, but she didn't have a key, so we had to drive by the hotel where her father was waiting with his cargo bike, with her little sister in it, and then up to the house, back to the beach to pick up you and your mother, and when we got home, I at once went out to Borrby with your youngest sister to get some pizza and shop for groceries. When that was done, she and I bicycled down to pick up your brother, who in this way got to try out his new bicycle on the way home, along the fields, beneath the sky, which was still blue, while the sun was sinking in the west. The first part of the day was sweltering, and I was irritable and frustrated, in good part because of the shame I felt about the text I had written the evening before. Long lines of cars everywhere, impossible to find parking places, the pram in and out of the car, the bicycle in the back seat, piles of kids, and the whole time I had to keep track of where you all were – you were there, your brother was there, your sisters were there and there – for the fear of leaving one of you behind somewhere is constantly present within me, not least after your first summer, when I forgot you in the car one afternoon, we were on our way to a restaurant, and if a friend hadn't asked about you, I might have forgotten about you for a long time – in a car in a car park in the sun . . .

The second part of the day it was raining, with distant thunder. In the evening the weather lightened again, but the temperature was ten degrees lower than it had been just a few hours earlier. It's June: indeterminate and changing, warm and cold, wet and dry jumbled together.

But a stressful and unsatisfactory day like today can be made up for by a simple little event, an insignificant moment of increased density, as when after dinner I walked along the corridor towards your elder sister's room, where she was sitting with her sister and a friend. Dad is coming, I heard her say, then they laughed. I stopped in front of them, they were in such a good mood, I realised they were talking about boys. Your youngest sister has a boyfriend, they've been together for two weeks now, and your elder sister is in love with a boy, and not without hope that he might be in love with her too. They were so happy!

I didn't read anything today, I didn't write anything, and I didn't think of anything beyond the practical tasks I was involved in. But at least I saw something. When I was waiting in line to get out onto the main road, my gaze drifted over to a plaque on a memorial stone at the edge of the forest, where it was written that Sandskogen forest, which extends all the way from Nybrostrand into Ystad, was planted at the behest of Carl von Linné, which I knew already, but not the date. It was in 1749, only six years after Swedenborg had been here.

Sunday 5 June 2016

It is six minutes past ten in the evening. Even though the sun has just gone down, it is still light outside. From the trampoline outside the little house where I am sitting comes the sound of shouting and screaming, singing and laughing, your sisters are there rehearsing for the musical they are taking part in, which will be premiering a month from now.

I drove them to their rehearsal in Simrishamn this morning, as I have done every summer for three years now, and picked them up three hours later. The rest of the day I have mainly been sitting on the stone path between the houses clearing weeds, except for an hour in the middle of the day when I wrote a piece about bicycles, and an hour in the afternoon when I slept, and some driving in between – your brother was transported to his friend's house, where he is spending the night, and your elder sister visited a friend, with me driving her there and back. On the way there I saw a pheasant, a hare and a small roe deer fawn, it was running around confusedly in a field when I drove past, first towards me, then it spun round and ran the other way, leaving a cloud of dust in the air behind it. The landscape, so mild and fertile, stretched calmly out in every direction, lit by the low orange sun. It was peaceful and beautiful, and I thought of something Anna Bjerger said when I interviewed her a few weeks ago, about beauty. It is such an obvious property of her paintings, that they are beautiful. It has to do with the colours, for she is what one used to call a colourist, that is a painter who can make a painting come alive simply through the combination of colours, which at one and the same time is bold and confident: the two companions of intuition. I asked whether beauty was important to her. She said she had been trained to be suspicious of beauty, to be on guard against it. So am I, it is a tenet of our culture that beauty, at least the obviously beautiful, the eye-catchingly beautiful, the pastoral and the idyllic, but also the dramatically beautiful, represents poor taste in art, that it is inferior and banal. The only adequate reaction to it has been irony. Irony is distance, the opposite of empathy and presence. One of the most striking features of Bjerger's pictures is that they are all painted from photographs, most of which she hasn't taken herself but found in old periodicals and manuals and magazines. So the actual point of view belongs to someone else, an anonymous entity, and usually it is through point of view that the relationship to the person who has made the image is revealed, whether this person is a painter or a photographer. This makes Bjerger's pictures impersonal, in a way, there is something foreign about them, something non-personal and general, almost as if we were seeing something through the eyes of a culture or an epoch. The personal, the artist's own presence, lies in the colours, and these often show such clear signs of her presence, through pronounced brushstrokes or running paint, that it ought to dispel the realism, but this doesn't happen, perhaps because the tension and the quality of her paintings arises from this very doubleness: on one hand photographic realism, which is impersonal, on the other painterly realism, which attests to a personal presence. So if she had painted a sunset in a pastoral landscape, she would have done so based on an existing photograph, and we would have seen both the sunset and our own gaze at the sunset, we would have experienced both beauty and mistrust of beauty.

But why be mistrustful of beauty, isn't beauty good? I think that what is meant by beauty is the simple, the unresisting, the superficial, in other words the reproduced, what we recognise without really seeing it, because the gaze upon beauty was there before us. And the task of art is to see something as it really is, as if for the first time. And if we are serious about seeing, then the person who sees is also a part of it, for there is no such thing as a neutral gaze, a neutral landscape, it is always charged with an underlying meaning. To paint that charge, that is what Edvard Munch set out to do. By breaking free from representation, or by shifting the focus of representation, he placed a higher value on the sketch and the unfinished work, at the same time that the painting as an object in its own right, its paintedness, was given greater weight. In that way he distanced himself from the reality he was representing – he never let go of the idea of representation, it was too deeply rooted in him, which isn't so strange, after all he was born in the 1860s – some of the landscapes he painted hardly resemble landscapes, they are merely a few brushstrokes of colour on a canvas, while through this he also approached a different reality, which one might call, somewhat grandly, the soul's reality in the world. More than seventy years have passed since Munch died and a great deal has happened in art since then, but not so much within people, so there are still no more than three paths available to art: towards the external, towards the internal, towards autonomy. The exclusion of beauty as a criterion doesn't really mean anything, for if a major artist emerges, he or she will do as they like, and if that is to represent beauty in all its fullness and depth, it will happen in a self-evident, manifest, sovereign manner. At the end of the day art is merely a question of force, as all artists know. Which leaves us with three discredited, dubious, superannuated categories for the judging of art: force, soul, beauty. Why have they been disqualified? Because art is about getting close to something. About piercing through all our systems and notions, attitudes and prejudices, habits and routines. The soul, with its nineteenth-century ring of exaltation and nobility and the cult of genius, created such a distance, beauty and its conventional apparatus created such a distance, and the notion of force made contempt for weakness acceptable, which creates a distance to truth, for the truth is that the human being is weak and frail, like a frozen reed. And beautiful too, if one is able to get close to it, by dismissing everything that pretends differently, which is almost everything, and which it therefore takes force to pierce through.

But the landscape I drove through around nine in the evening, on my way to pick up your elder sister, was beautiful in a deeply unmodern way: the sun was setting as it has set over the earth for hundreds of thousands of years, it imbued the air with rich colour and here and there gilded the long furrows of dry, light-brown soil, while the trees, clustered around the houses and ranged along the brooks, stood perfectly still. Oh, the fall of evening, oh, the dusk, oh, the inexorable end of life! Oh, the sheep, oh, the cows! Oh, the low cars driving along the narrow road! Oh, the water tower on the hill! Oh, the white wings of the wind turbines! Oh, the row of oaks with their gnarled trunks and their knobbly bark!

I remember the first time I wrote down an exclamation like that, how much I liked it. For through its archaic form the eulogy opened up for irony, at the same time it was also sincere, an impulsive exclamation of joy, somehow unguarded, so that its meaning flew back and forth like an echo in a valley. Not that it really meant anything to me other than the pleasure I took in the archaic. Why the archaic gave me pleasure was something I never reflected upon. But I liked to look at Baroque paintings of motifs from antiquity, Lorraine's paintings, for example, or later those of Turner. I liked to read texts from antiquity too, but didn't find the same seemingly eternal peace there, except in Virgil's *Georgics*, where it is perhaps implied more than it is thematised. And I loved Lucretius's *On the Nature of Things*, but what I loved was probably the idea of it more than what it actually said. I read Aristotle's *On the Soul*, and Cicero's speeches, Thucydides' history and Ovid's *Metamorphoses*. We learned nothing about antiquity at school, and my first encounter with it was at university, in literary studies, where we listened to lectures about the Greek society from which the great tragedies had sprung, the enormous influence they had had and the contemporary conflicts they enacted. Another series of lectures covered the epic, from Homer to Dante. I never read anything thoroughly, just bits and pieces, it was more the feeling of antiquity I was after than antiquity itself. Nothing in Werner Heisenberg's autobiography impressed me more than the passage where he describes a walk in the woods – this was in Germany in 1920 – together with a group of friends of the same age, they are gymnasium students and can read Greek, and they discuss Plato, the Greeks' theory of the atom. That arc, from ancient Greek philosophy to European nuclear physics in the interwar period, what could be more exciting? The nature of things, atomic particles. Heidegger's reading of the Presocratics also belongs here, for while nuclear physics was in a febrile state in the 1920s, so that even mediocre scientists could make momentous discoveries – as happens in a culture when it reaches its zenith – philosophical thought during this era was almost infinitely slow and intricate.

'Have you ever heard Heidegger reading Greek?' Anselm Kiefer asked me for some reason or other when I visited him

Ecstases feminines

Mechthilde de Hackeborn
Marie des vallées

Thomas... ...thi

Marri...

at his studio outside Paris about a month ago to select paintings for this book.

'No,' I replied. 'How does it sound?'

'It is very beautiful,' he said. And then he produced some peculiar foreign sounds before laughing at himself.

Rarely have I wished so strongly as I did then that I could articulate some of my impressions, that I could say something about Heidegger and antiquity, something about Lucretius and nuclear physics, something about the materiality of things and luminous beauty, and about the infinite depths of time. But I couldn't, not a word came from my lips, instead I looked down with a slight smile, a little embarrassed by the sounds he had imitated not entirely successfully.

For that was what I experienced in Kiefer's paintings, the different velocities of time in the material and in the human world, and a continual search for depth in surfaces, which is the curse of every painter but with Kiefer seems to be an obsession. The only abyss we know is that of time, but not from personal experience, for we are contemporaneous with everything that surrounds us. Time is like death, we are shut out of it, and we can only be allowed in by becoming it. So when the gate opens, we are already a part of it and therefore cannot experience it. Perhaps that is why Kiefer was so interested in the artistic expressions of the very oldest cultures, both their texts and their buildings, for that is the only thing in the depths of time that we are able to identify with, the only thing issuing from it about which we can say with any justification 'we' or 'us'. In Kiefer's art I also perceived an interest in things, in objects, in matter as such, and in the principle of transformation, that something is what it is as the result of a determination and that with a flick of the wrist it can become something else.

But there I was, sitting on a sofa next to Kiefer, in a studio at the innermost end of an enormous several-hundred-metre-long hangar-like building, full of works of art in all sizes and shapes, with nothing to say. The studio was like a building within the building, it was located on the first floor, and the walls in the three large high-ceilinged rooms were covered with paintings he was working on or had just been working on. There was a strong smell of paint. The paintings were lighter and more colourful than anything I had seen by him previously, they represented rivers and trees, tangled vegetation and open stretches of water, some with light trickling through them.

He had come cycling through the hall dressed in a blue boiler suit as I was being shown around, and when he saw me he said, 'Ah, we have a visit from a Viking!' We exchanged a few words, and then he cycled away while I continued looking around. One painting hung in another building next to this one, it was at least twenty metres tall, with two full-sized fighter planes on the floor beside it, full of dried flowers. That one man could have produced all these thousands of works was difficult to understand, the incredible thing being not their number but rather everything they represented, the universe they made up in their totality. I would have felt exhausted just to wake up in the morning to the certainty that I would be working on one of the new, light paintings, which were maybe six metres wide and four metres tall. The kind of force required to do something like that every day throughout one's life, just climb up and get down to it, as it were, had to be a very special one, obstinate and blind to everything else, for there couldn't be room for much else in his life.

Munch had something of the same, he did nothing except paint every day from the age of sixteen until he died. And though he worked in monumental formats only exceptionally, in a similar way he created a whole universe, distinctive and peculiar and powerful. And Anna Bjerger, the same thing, every day at the studio, every day new pictures, which had to be created out of nothing.

Kiefer is probably the wealthiest artist in the world, or at least the one who is best paid for his works. It seemed as if all the money went into creating a sheltered world around his work. He slept in the studio, had cooks hired to make his meals, a dozen assistants helping him in his work, and a secretary and an adviser who made almost all decisions for him, as far as I understood.

'Do you fly helicopters?' he asked while we were eating.

I shook my head.

'You have to try it, you know. It's fantastic! You have to come for a ride some time!'

That's what he did when he was travelling somewhere, to London or Provence or Portugal, he flew there in his own helicopter. He loved flowers, grew them in all the places he owned, and threw none away, dried each one. He had a large library and had bought horses for his children so they would have something to do when they came to visit him. But all this magnificence, these grand gestures, which might lead one to think of him as a sort of prince among artists, were not the main thing about him, they weren't even important, at least that is the impression I got in the few hours I was there. Everything was about his work, his paintings, his artworks. And where did they come from, what had given rise to this possession, this obstinate blindness to everything else? It couldn't be anything other than a way of coping, he must at some point have discovered a way to open himself up to his inner greed, that which could never be filled or satisfied, only temporarily stilled. He told me that he hadn't known any other children when he was growing up, only his grandmother, they lived in Schwarzwald in the years after the war, and when I cast a final glance at the insane number of artworks before leaving, I suddenly saw trees and forest in everything he had made. Trees and forest, time and death, and his own biography running through it all like a thin, almost invisible thread.

When I parked in front of the house where your elder sister's friend lives, after crossing the sunlit plain and reaching the low hills that rise just before the sea, I looked straight at two large roosters with magnificent feathers and erect necks, staring at me. Some brown and considerably smaller hens were walking around them. I opened the gate, and in the same instant the door to the house opened and an enormous dog with a square head and muscular torso came rushing out, followed by a small, shaggy, furiously barking dog. I knew they weren't dangerous, but my heart still began to beat faster when I saw the teeth in the giant dog's wet jaws. I dutifully stroked its head, though I dislike dogs intensely, just as your sister came out, neck bent as if she was trying to make herself a little smaller at the moment of parting, to make it pass more quickly or to make it as small as possible was my guess; at least that's how I always felt.

We drove home the same way I had come, through the silent evening agrarian landscape that was now our home and which to her was also the place she was from. Sunlight shone against her cheek. If I had known how, I would have painted it.

Monday 6 June 2016

A few minutes ago your younger sister came out on the lawn, placed the phone on the table beneath the kitchen window, leaning it against a cup that stood there, and began to dance in front of it. She is rehearsing for the musical. This is the third one she is taking part in, but unlike the previous two, for which I sometimes sat inside the event venue waiting for the rehearsal to finish, I still haven't seen any of this one. Her head moved back and forth, her hands sketched patterns in the air as she sang to herself or counted. Then she grabbed the phone, sat down on the grass and watched the recording. When it was done, she glanced over at the window I am sitting behind, and when I lifted my hand in greeting, she greeted me in return before slipping into the house as abruptly as she had appeared.

It is six minutes past ten in the evening. The children have been home from school today; it is Sweden's National Day. All day I have had a Sunday feeling in my body and have been surprised to receive so many emails, usually my in-box is practically empty at weekends.

Your voice woke me up around eight this morning, it sounded unusually close, since, as I discovered upon opening my eyes, you were lying in our bed. I faintly remembered your mother lifting you up since you were crying inconsolably over in your cot.

You smiled at me and began talking. You said we had to pick up your brother in the car. I nodded and said we did, but perhaps not right away. No, not right away, you said. Shall we go downstairs and change your nappy? I said. Yes, you said. Anne need panty. Yes, exactly, I said and carried you downstairs but forgot about changing you, for when I set you down on the floor, you ran straight into the living room, and when I came in there, you had already turned on the television and were scrambling up on the sofa. I made coffee and had a smoke in the office before I ate breakfast with you, we sat facing each other at the table with each our bowl of Special K cereal with milk and raisins, and when your mother got up, I came in here to write a new piece. I started three different ones before I gave up. I usually never do that, but since I started writing this diary in the evenings and at night, I no longer get up at four or five in the morning, as I have done the last couple of years, and without those hours all alone, in the dark, at dawn or in the early-morning light, I have difficulty entering into a text. It is as if I start from zero when I get up, from a nothing that slowly becomes something if I concentrate, for concentration is really just a mental resetting, and the more impressions and feelings and thoughts the mind contains, the more has to be removed from consciousness before it can focus on the work.

I went out, dragged the lawnmower from the porch of the summer house, rolled it over to the lawn, started it and began pushing it across the lawn, around the edge of the garden in a slowly diminishing circle. Your mother went down to the kindergarten, it was our turn to clean it this weekend, and she had taken on the task. Around noon your younger sister had a visit from a friend, they jumped on the trampoline or sat on it, talking, they went for a bicycle ride around the neighbourhood, they sat up in her room each with her mobile phone, they turned cartwheels in the garden. They have known each other for five years and for a while attended the same school, and even though we moved your siblings to a school in Ystad, they continue to have contact. Your elder sister slept until I woke her up at half past one. Normally I wouldn't have let her sleep that long, but I promised her yesterday that she could sleep as long as she wanted to this morning. She had spent the entire weekend with friends and had been to a musical rehearsal, and being with other people for a long period of time takes it out of her, she gets irritable or tired and longs to be by herself or relaxing together with us.

It's incredible how different they are, and how much I like them for who they are.

I weeded the flower beds and between the berry bushes, but I don't always know which ones are weeds and which are decorative plants, so I only removed those I was absolutely certain didn't belong there, dandelions and an incredibly tenacious and persistent climber which coils itself around all the other plants and is difficult to remove without simultaneously damaging the plant it is growing on. Everything is growing and in bloom here now, up along all the walls and over the roof, everything is densely green, and the ground elder, which I damned well dug up a part of the lawn and resowed to get rid of, after having torn up what I thought was its whole network of white tangled roots, has exploded again and stands as dense as a small forest wherever the lawnmower can't reach.

At regular intervals I went inside to check on you, who were either playing with your sister and her friend, or playing by yourself, or sitting in front of the television watching *Laban the Little Ghost*. The latter made me feel guilty, not least because you could speak the lines before they were uttered, and you're only two and a half, but playing with you for more than ten minutes at a time is a test of patience for me, I feel I have to do something, preferably write, but if I can't do that, then work in the garden or tidy the house. I wasn't like that before, then I could sleep all day, watch TV all evening, be out all night, walk around aimlessly for weeks without being troubled by a bad conscience. Now it feels as if I am wasting time if I watch TV for half an hour; even reading, which after all is a part of my job, has become faintly dubious, something I can't do without feeling burdened with guilt, unless it is directly relevant to what I am writing or a book we are publishing.

That this is how it has become isn't really a mystery, it is a method I use to cope, and it works, so I see no reason to stop using it. All problems arise from relations with other people, and if one minimises one's relations with other people, one also minimises the problems. But since humans are fundamentally social beings and go under without contact with other people, relationships can't simply be done away with, they have to be substituted with something else, and few things are a more satisfying substitute for the presence of other people than writing, which at the same time provides an excuse for one's antisocial behaviour, for everyone knows that someone who writes has a great need for solitude.

Previously summer was always the worst time, it was accompanied by an expectation of pleasure and joy and groups of friends swimming or boating or on holiday, and there I sat, in Kristiansand or Bergen, at my mother's house or in the bedsit I rented, while the sun was shining outside and I didn't know where to go or what to do. One doesn't go swimming alone, one doesn't go boating alone, one doesn't lie alone in a park, one hardly sits reading in an outdoor café either, at least not when one is a young man of twenty-two. It bothered me terribly, and it marked me, not just who I was in the eyes of others, but also who I was to myself, which for a long time was practically the same thing. I ought of course to have been strong, not been bothered by it, and perhaps taught myself Greek there in my bedsit, or Hebrew or Latin or something else that might be of use to me. But I wasn't strong, it broke me down not to have anywhere to be in the summer, or anyone to be with. That problem vanished the very instant I began writing my first novel. I didn't need other people for that, and I didn't need other places, I could sit in a bedsit and work all on my own. And as long as I did that, there were no problems other than the ones that had to do with the novel itself. Since then I have continued in this way. When the children arrived, the problem of loneliness vanished definitively, since not much time was left beyond what their presence demanded, but by then the writing had become so entrenched within me, as a method and a solution to all problems, that not only did I continue but after the initial chaotic years of infancy also intensified it, until I got to the point where I am now, where I feel I have to do something all the time.

What happens when one carries on like this is that one becomes rigid, stiffening not just in an external posture, but also in an inner one, which must be why so many elderly people are unable to relate to change, they have developed their own method, mule-like they have bent their necks, and they have done it for such a long time that they are no longer able to lift their heads again.

One of my great-uncles was like that, stiff-necked, but then he became senile and the rigidity lost its grip on him entirely, not just in his thoughts but in his whole body, he became like a child again, his face permanently uncertain and faintly smiling.

Everyone must have a form particular to them, what we call identity. If the inner form is weak, if one's character is sensitive and indistinct, one needs an outer form. Bringing up children is really nothing other than helping them with this, offering them some fixed structures which make the world and themselves seem like fathomable entities. A child's greatest fear, the ultimate nightmare, is to have to decide everything for itself. This pattern is also found at the macro level in society, where the level of chaos determines how prevalent the yearning for a firm hand is, an unequivocal leader, a strong man.

The curious thing about strong men is that they so often also radiate weakness, something a little helpless, something self-contradictory. When I visited the US this spring I watched several of Donald Trump's speeches as the Republican presidential candidate on TV. He radiated an unmanly vanity, something faintly feminine which one might think that his voters, those who sympathise with his simple solutions and believe that prejudices are truths, wouldn't want, you would think they would prefer something hard and consistent and unambiguous through and through, not merely hardness as an easily seen-through posture, but that's clearly not the case, no one seems to be bothered by the ambiguousness of Trump's body language and appearance. The same was true of Hitler, though I don't wish to make invidious comparisons, his appearance was ambiguous too, there was something vain and unmanly about him also, an ambiguity which should have undermined his message but which didn't, quite the opposite.

Obama's personality is well integrated, he is sure of himself, composed.

On my visit to the US I met an editor of the *New York Times*, who had previously proposed that I cover the election campaign. I had declined, I couldn't stand the idea of being the European seeing it all from the outside, but after spending a week there, watching all the televised speeches and the studio debates and talking to people who not only supported Trump but grew agitated talking about him, angry about the immigrants, the Muslims, the government, I told him I would think about it.

'Would you like to meet Trump?' he said.

I went cold with fright.

'No,' I said.

'OK,' he said.

Why did I feel cold with fright at the mere thought of meeting him?

The power, the fame, the contempt for people?

Yes, that too, but primarily the authoritiarian side of him. With my fear of authority I can hardly imagine a more awful encounter. For would I try to ingratiate myself with him or wouldn't I? Renounce everything I believe in, in the hope of making him like me?

Unfortunately, that's what would have happened.

It is twenty-two minutes past midnight, and I am about to go to bed. Half an hour ago your elder sister came in here to get me, she had fallen asleep on the mattress that had been on the floor next to the bed on the ground floor since the last overnight visit, and then she had woken up, and now she wanted me to carry the mattress up to the bed on the first floor for her. I did, carried the mattress edgewise past your brother, who was asleep on his back with his arms close to his sides as if jumping off a diving board, with the duvet next to him, and you, little one, who were lying on your side with the duvet between your little legs and little arms. In about six hours you will wake up, cheerful and contented, ready for a new day in which nothing of what awaits will surprise you.

Tuesday 7 June 2016

Today I slept until seven thirty and just had time for coffee and a cigarette in here before I drove your siblings to school, across the fields through yet another sunlit, still morning, while your mother pushed you in the pram down to the kindergarten before she went in to Ystad by bus and on to Malmö by train. When I came back, I wrote a piece about playgrounds and sent it to my editor. He called just a few minutes later. We talked a little about the latest texts and a bit about the book as a whole; he tossed in a few suggestions which I liked but didn't note down, I thought my subconscious would take care of whatever was relevant. Then he asked me how things were going in my life. Although everything I write these days is autobiographical and in one sense deals with my life, life itself is still something entirely different. It plays out elsewhere, in a very different place, behind the writing somehow, a dark mountain which the text only glimpses in brief and limited flashes as if in the light of an electric torch. Something we have talked a lot about lately is how one can tell a story about something one has experienced personally without giving one's one version of it, as happens when it isn't the 'I' that is the main thing but the experience, which may sound like hair-splitting but isn't, the difference is great, and the first time my editor spoke to me about it, it was as if a whole new realm of possibilities opened up around what I wanted to narrate. These are the possibilities of narration, faced with which concepts like fiction and non-fiction fall short, they are too crude or not to the point. That is not where the real battle lies. It is commonly said that fiction can be truer than reality, truth being considered in an exalted sense as something crystallised and universal. Poetic truth, it used to be called. That the truth of reality, in other words the events as they occurred, is locked to the 'I' narrating them, with all the limitations this entails. And this is something I believe in, that's how it is, poetic truth is if not greater then at least more important than the truth of reality. But you don't need to write much about your personal experiences before you discover that the same principle of poetic truth is valid there. Not because one adds or invents things, but with regard to how the story is formed, which version of it you give precedence to. It is almost like an equation: as universal truth increases, personal truth diminishes. More than anything it is a question of how the narrative space is constructed, how much becomes visible around the 'I', and the extent to which the narrator identifies with the 'I'. If the identification is total, the narrative will be true in a personal sense, but then it is the only thing being expressed, and this is what lay in the old rule of thumb that literature should be personal but not private. Something is private when it is of relevance only to the person writing. This brings us to the paradox that the writer has to compromise his or her personal truth, that is to create an 'I' with which he or she doesn't fully identify, in order to express something that may be true for others. A colleague with whom I occasionally discuss such matters considers that this renders the concept of truth meaningless, since what is said has to be 'sweetened', as he puts it, in other words lied about. He also says that I write primarily to be liked. The question is not merely a literary one but also social, for in the social realm everyone has an external persona which is not identical to our inner self – or to put it more simply, we don't always say what we mean. Why don't we? We don't want to hurt others, that is perhaps more important than speaking the truth, or we think that it's more important to have a good time, or we think that the truth won't change anything anyway, for people are unchangeable. Or we think that others won't like us if we unburden ourselves and say what we really mean. So we pretend. But isn't literature precisely a sanctuary where the rules of the social game don't apply? Isn't literature the only place where it is possible to be absolutely truthful, since writing is one of the few social acts which takes place beyond the social realm? Isn't literature ruthless, and isn't the ruthlessness of literature its very core and justification? Yes, and that is one of the reasons why, for the greater part of literary history, fiction has been the preferred method, since it removes the personal truth of the 'I' from the equation and displays it as something other, in a social setting. Ibsen's plays were ruthless in the sense that they showed people as they really were behind their roles, and society as it really was behind the stage on which it was enacted. Peer Gynt is a crystallisation, Brand is a crystallisation, both are Ibsen himself, but not as he was to himself, they are as he was to himself at the same time that he was seeing himself from the outside, through the eyes of others. In this way he could write more truly about himself than if he had written a play in which the identification was total. This is so because the self is not an isolated entity – I am not thinking of loneliness or human isolation here, but about how the self is constituted – but is directed towards others, a turning towards others, as language is a turning towards others, and as is literature. To write about one's own self is in a certain sense the opposite of empathy, since empathy moves from the outer towards the inner, while writing about one-self means moving from the inner towards the outer. And yet both processes aim at the same thing, intimate know-ledge and, through that, understanding. When the person writing about him- or herself has moved out of the self, thus incorporating an external gaze, a strange kind of objectivity arises, something which at one and the same time belongs to the inner and the outer, and this objectivity makes it pos-sible to move around in one's own self as if it belonged to another, and then we have come full circle, for that move-ment requires empathy. The person one is when one is by oneself obviously doesn't require any empathy, since there is no distance involved, no 'inside' to penetrate to, for here the self is what it is. But as soon as one is no longer in that situation there is a distance, something objectifying which turns the self into something else while at the same time it is the same. These small differences grow with time and can represent so many different and conflicting things that the self is unable to contain them without becoming dysfunctional – for the self is also our frame of action – which makes it necessary to suppress and to forget, but also to remember. Memories constitute our story about ourselves, and that story is perhaps the most important part of our identity. The string of memories holds it together, unifies it, and by suppressing and forgetting we keep the string of memories pure, non-contradictory and manageable. There are people in whom narratives have been constructed that diverge so drastically from reality that eventually they become unable to maintain their identities, which collapse, and they become psychotic, depressed or bedridden and diagnosed with burnout. Psychoanalysis is really only about arriving at a truer narrative, that is why it so often tries to uncover old, perhaps suppressed memories, and focuses so much on emotions linked to relationships, since emotions speak a different language to thoughts and are less able to metamorphose or appear as something other than they are. Although they do that too, depression, for example, is nothing other than a congealed and immobile rage, a wave that strikes the shore just as the temperature plummets and halts its forward path, frozen solid. If one uncovers a truer narrative, a more relevant string of memories, the pressure on the self from the external world will diminish, and even if peace and joy may still elude one, at least a more manageable everyday life may be within reach. So directed towards others the self is structured as an address, similar to how the basic figure of language is the address, while to itself the self is structured as a story, made up of a string of memories. The latter is not unlike the mechanisms which hold couples together, they too have a story they tell each other, constituting their identity as a couple, and if the story is too far removed from reality, it too will sooner or later disintegrate. A couple's story has to be continually reaffirmed, the story of a self must be continually reaffirmed, for actually both the couple and the self contain so much, and often so much that is contradictory, that they have to be simplified in a few simple sequences, a few simple maxims: that's who we are, that's what I'm like. So if the self is a story, it is only one of many possible ones. My editor's latest novel is about the dissolution of a couple, and in the novel the rupture, the crack, the fracturing of the alloy between the two occurs when one of them, the man, begins to fantasise about the introduction of another man into their relationship and to make up stories about it, which she listens to and enjoys, it is one of the ways they have of being together, him loving her through an imaginary stand-in. Then it happens in real life, she meets someone else, sleeps with someone else, and that story is open to her but not to him, she turns her back on him and shuts him out as she begins a new story. The novel is the man's attempt to understand, by putting himself in her place, imagining from within her thoughts, feelings and choices. And in a strange way this openness towards her is related to the openness towards the other man; the lack of boundaries between people which the novel examines is both creative and destructive. This personality trait, which a psychologist might call ego weakness but which might also be considered a desire to understand others from within, or viewed as a radical openness to all the possibilities of the self, and which can be found in several of his books, in which some of the characters move between identities as one moves between the rooms of a house, is something that interests me, because that trait lies at the root of every novel, short story and drama ever written. I suppose the best example is Shakespeare, how open he was to everything human, all of which must have been contained within himself. The same is true of all major writers. But it is an inner openness, with no consequences in the external world except the books – it is something else entirely to allow this openness, this desire to understand others from within, this ignoring of the boundaries of identity, to play itself out in a life, in a character, in a person. It's interesting because the territory which emerges – reading a good novel is like seeing a landscape emerge when water subsides – lies somewhere between freedom and emptiness. A person who is everyone is no one, is empty. A person who is someone can always become someone else. I think the reason I think about this so much is that it is so relevant to where I am now. I mean where I am in life. I am nearly fifty years old, only four years younger than my father was when he died, but also the father of a two-year-old, an eight-year-old, a ten-year-old and a twelve-year-old, and when I look at them I see people whose lives lie ahead of them the way it once was for me, and it is hard not to ask myself why things turned out as they did, since through living with the children and watching them grow I also observe the mixture of innate characteristics, heredity and social environment that forms them, besides who they are as unique personalities, the light that burns within them and which in former times would have been called their soul. In theory I understand that a person's inner being is so rich that it can change and live out other aspects of the self, move in wholly new directions, but in practice my experience is that I am the same person and do the same things, think the same and feel the same as I always have. During a therapy session I had with your mother I said that I had found a method, one that worked for me, and that I didn't want to or didn't dare to change it. The therapist said with a smile that in fact the method didn't work, since I was a deeply lonely person. 'But what if it feels good to be lonely?' I said. 'It is never good to be lonely,' she said. I think she is wrong, but maybe I think so because that would threaten my story, who I am to myself, which I stick to in all weathers and every season, even if it means waking up dejected every morning, and even if I am constantly harassed by feelings of guilt and shame, for despite everything it works, the way the shell works for the crab as it crawls sideways in the darkness at the bottom of the ocean, or the way subservience works for the dog, that too is a form, something fixed, to which it can therefore entrust itself. The story that is my identity, this crab-like carapace, this set of notions which I don't challenge, is the very opposite of literature, for while I am not interested in freedom on my own behalf, in my own life, and haven't been since I was a teenager, freedom means everything in literature, that is its essence, and that is why I wrote that ruthlessness was the core and justification of literature, since freedom and ruthlessness are two sides of the same coin. In literature the simple story of the self encounters the complexity of reality, and this encounter is one of the basic structures of the novel, as in the meeting between the romantic self-images of Don Quixote and

Emma Bovary – both of which are founded on literature – and the reality they were a part of.

This evening I asked your brother if he wanted to come for a bicycle ride. He did. I suggested that we cycle out to the castle which lies just over three kilometres from here, and he agreed to that too. His bike is a little bit too big, I thought it wouldn't make sense to buy him a small children's bike that he will have outgrown by autumn or next spring, so it gave him some trouble, it was as if all his movements were just a little too small for it, but it went fine, we cycled up the hill by the church, turned left, crossed the main road and took the road to the castle, which ran straight west, towards the sun which hung low in the sky above the horizon at the end of the wide and deep plain which stretched out in front of us, green and lush, with water sprinklers here and there, a few patiently chugging tractors, houses surrounded by clusters of trees, planted at one time to provide shelter against the wind, which blew across the plain from the sea with great force in autumn and winter. I told him that one of the world's best-known astronomers had lived at the castle in the summertime five hundred years ago. What was his name? he asked into the air, since bicycling demanded all his attention. I was suddenly unable to remember and didn't reply. 'What was his name, Dad?' your brother said. 'Tycho Brahe,' I said. 'He was Danish. Skåne belonged to Denmark then, you know.' We stopped, he had to take off his jacket. I asked him to tie it around his waist, he did. He wobbled out into the road as we began to pedal again. After a few metres he stopped, it didn't work with the jacket around his waist. I took it and tied it to my handlebars. We continued for a few hundred metres, he stopped again, thought maybe his tyre was punctured. I squeezed both tyres, they were both rock hard. We went on. We rolled down a little hill, cycled across a bridge, and when we began climbing the hill on the other side, he pedalled more and more slowly and finally, when he was standing almost still, fell to one side and into the ditch. Fortunately tall thick grass was growing there – it must have come up to his thighs, so he didn't hurt himself, on the contrary, he looked quite comfortable lying there. On both sides of the road, beneath some trees, in fact as far as I could see, some plants resembling rhubarb were growing, plain and rather thick stalks with broad flat leaves. There were so many of them – they formed a dense cover that stretched away, dark and juicy green – that it was beautiful even though the plants themselves were not beautiful. We pushed our bikes up the hill, and at the top he said he was tired. I asked if he wanted to go back, but he shook his head, I want to see the castle, he said. I think you've been there before, I said. I know, he said. But I want to see it now too. So we continued, along meadows with tall grass up to the edge of the forest two or three hundred metres away, where the trees shone as if gilded in the sun. There were wild boar in there, I knew, but I didn't say anything about them to your brother, it might frighten him, since there were stories about wild boar attacking cyclists in the area. He repeated that he was tired, but since we were almost there, he could keep going. Down a hill, past three brick houses that were or had been connected with the castle, up again, past a small churchyard which belonged to the castle, and up a steep slope, alongside a wall, where lay first the church, also belonging to the castle, then the castle itself, small and unimpressive-looking for a castle, with thick, crooked, yellow-painted walls from the fourteenth century, behind a moat. 'There's the castle,' I said. 'Is that the castle?' he said. 'But I thought we were going to Glimmingehus?' 'No,' I said. 'We were going to Tosterup. Glimmingehus is twelve miles from here.'

To my consternation he began to cry. Tears ran down his cheeks.

'Are you that disappointed?' I said.

He nodded.

'Let's sit down here,' I said. 'We were supposed to go to Tosterup, not to Glimmingehus.'

'But you said so!' he sobbed.

'No,' I said.

'Yes,' he said. 'I asked you and you said yes.'

Then I understood. He had said something which I didn't hear properly while we were bicycling along the road outside the house, and I had simply nodded, maybe even said yes or sure.

'Now I'm too tired to bicycle back,' he said.

'Don't you want to see the castle after all?'

He shook his head.

'We have to bicycle home,' I said. 'There's no other way to get home.'

I stroked his back. Tears were still running down his cheeks. I was a little annoyed both at his tears and that he was too tired to cycle back, but I did my best to hide my annoyance.

'Let's just sit here and rest for a while,' I said. 'Then I'm sure it'll be fine.'

'OK,' he said.

It was perhaps the finest evening so far that summer, nice and warm, the air perfectly still, the sun a bright yellow against the dark blue sky. The trees in the forest immobile and beautiful.

'OK?' I said after a while. 'Are you ready?'

He nodded and stood up, pushed up the kickstand with his foot.

'You first,' I said. 'I'll follow you.'

He climbed up on the slightly oversized bike and began rolling down the steep hill, but somehow he couldn't get into the swing of it and lost control, heading straight for the ditch alongside the road.

'Use your brakes!' I shouted after him.

But he panicked and didn't use his front brake, instead he lowered one foot to the ground, without his speed diminishing, on the contrary it increased. He screamed and steered the bike down along the ditch, dust whirling around him, I shouted, 'Use your brakes! Use your brakes!' but he was in a panic, and a few seconds later he fell over with the bike on top of him.

I cycled down to where he lay.

'How did it go?' I said, lifting up his bike.

He was crying, loud sobs.

'Let me have a look at you,' I said, lifting him up.

He had torn a hole in his trousers at the knee and was bleeding from a cut there. Other than that he seemed to be OK. I held him close, and he wrapped his arms and legs around me, hanging like a panda from a tree.

After a while I set him down on a stone.

'The bike is all right,' I said. 'That's good, right?'

He nodded through his tears, his body was trembling.

'And you did all right too,' I said. 'You could have broken something, you know.'

'Yes,' he said.

'But what do we do now? You can't bicycle home, can you?'

He shook his head, and a new wave of tears broke from him.

'Can you sit here and wait? Then I can cycle home and get the car?'

'No,' he said.

That I could understand, we were a long way from home in his conception of the world, and there wasn't a person in sight.

'There's no other way,' I said. 'I'll bicycle as fast as I can.'

Finally he agreed.

'But you mustn't go anywhere, OK? You'll sit right here until I'm back?'

He nodded, and I started cycling home. I was too out of shape to be able to really exert myself, but it wasn't very far so there was no real danger, I thought as I pedalled along. Out of breath, I parked the bike next to the car, got in and drove back fast the same way I had come with my helmet on my head. Fortunately he was still sitting on the same stone, and I lifted him into the front seat, put the bike in the back, and then we drove home. Then his cut had to be cleaned and bandaged before I got him some ice cream from the freezer.

Now he's asleep, three metres from where you are sleeping, and tomorrow when he wakes up our bicycle ride will be a story he can tell his friends at school.

And perhaps, it strikes me now, this will become one of his strongest and clearest childhood memories, the failed bike ride with Dad. That my irritation, which he undoubtedly noticed, will be what he remembers of me from this evening. And that I drove him into panic and disaster.

When I asked him why he hadn't used his brakes, he said he had heard that you would be flung over the handlebars if you used the front brake, and that therefore you should never use it.

Wednesday 8 June 2016

Now it's your elder sister who is outside the house in the evening, filming herself. She is sitting at the table outside the kitchen, holding her phone up in front of her with both hands and singing. Either she is rehearsing for the musical or she is using one of those apps in which they make videos by miming to songs or spoken lines. Some of the videos they've made in this way are incredibly funny. They are aswim in pictures, these children and their friends, they are already experts at manipulating images and juxtaposing them in the wildest ways, and when they're not doing that, they are watching others' streams of images. When they talk to their friends, they do it on FaceTime or on Skype, so they can see them as they speak. Sometimes they sit on the sofa watching TV while they Skype, and at times they film us so that their friend can see the setting they are in, or they film the programme we are watching. Several minutes may pass without them saying a word. It is as if their friend is there in the room with them, and as if your sisters are in their friend's room. When they do something, for instance turn cartwheels on the lawn or on the trampoline, they sometimes film the exercise and watch themselves afterwards. They use their mobile phones as mirrors and take endless series of selfies, but also photos or videos of everything that surrounds them. Three or four years ago they made some videos about a character they called Old Maja, I remember; your younger sister played the part of the old woman, and the elder one filmed her and told her what to say. What all this will do to them I have no idea, but since it is such a big part of their lives, unlike when I was growing up, when moving images were something we could only see on TV and once in a rare while at the cinema, and were never something that represented us and our reality – I don't think there are any film recordings of me before I made my debut as a writer at the age of twenty-nine and was on TV for the first time, and the photographs from my 1970s childhood number no more than fifty at the most – it must shape them and their understanding of reality. Instinctively I dislike it, for it is as if the visual world, everything that happens on our screens, takes us away from the physical, material reality, and so much in the world of screens is about being taken away from reality and being immediately gratified and continually entertained. I just wish they would run around and play, climb trees and swim in lakes, be outdoors from early morning to late in the evening in the summer, play football, tennis, cycle, have sword fights, wrestle, build huts, collect bottles for the deposits. The reason I wish this for them is of course that my own childhood was like that. But that was on the surface, it was also filled with valleys of loneliness, despair and hopelessness, which I fled from by reading. And although letters demand a greater effort than images, the effect was the same, something in me was gratified and entertained by an imaginary reality which had practically nothing to do with the actual reality that surrounded me. And what am I doing while your siblings are swimming in a sea of pictures? I am sitting here writing about the world and all the things, animals and plants it contains, without taking part in it.

Your sister out there is wearing a pink sweater and a pair of white shorts, even though it is fairly cool, overcast and windy. Her little sister joined her while I was writing this, leaned forward and looked at the video being played on the phone. That those two girls, light-haired and quick to laugh, should have anything to do with me I find hard to comprehend. But I am glad they do, glad that I get to be with them while they are growing up. Actually the younger one has been in a sullen mood today, she has been for some time, much more quiet than usual, and more often alone in her room. No matter how I phrase the question, the answer I get is that it's nothing. That too is something they have to learn, keeping things to themselves, concealing part of their inner life. And I on my side have to learn to leave them in peace.

You, my little child, are unable to hide anything, you express everything you feel instantly, and there is never any doubt about whether you are happy or sad, whether you are in pain or enjoying something. What you like least of all is when I take the iPad away from you or switch off the television while you are watching. You lack the prerequisites for understanding why I do it, to you I am then just someone brutally inconsiderate who comes and takes from you something you like.

So it's no wonder you get angry and start throwing things about.

This morning on the way to school I saw a peculiar craft on the sea. It was large and square, like an enormous metal box, but it was so far away that I couldn't make out any details, merely this darkly luminous wall on the blue water. The road runs along the shore for just a few hundred metres before it disappears into the forest, so I didn't get to cast more than a few glances at it before it was out of sight. When I had taken the children to school and was on my way back, I saw it again, already further out. There was something menacing about it. I considered stopping the car and getting out to have a closer look, but that seemed over the top, after all it was just a vessel, probably a barge whose load concealed its tugboat, I thought and instead continued on my way home, along the green undulating fields which in some places were touched with yellow; the grain had already begun to ripen.

Back home the cleaner's car was parked in the little cul-de-sac across the road from the house, it is there every Thursday when I return from taking the children to school, and every Thursday it comes as a surprise. I always turn off there so I can back into the driveway next to the house, and I do it automatically, so every Thursday I have to hit the brakes so as not to run into the blue Volvo, which is hidden by a hedge as tall as a man.

'Hello!' I called out as I went into the house. 'Hello!' she shouted from the bathroom, which is always the first room she cleans.

'Everything good?' I said as she came out into the hall.

'Everything's fine,' she said.

'Have you had some coffee?'

'Yes, I helped myself to some.'

'I'll brew some fresh coffee. What's left in the pot is pretty stale.'

'Great.'

She came into the kitchen. She is maybe ten years younger than me, she has three children, all of whom live with her, but what she wants to talk about are always the various TV commercials and short films she has taken part in since her last visit, either as an extra or in a supporting part, and once in a rare while, usually in student productions, in a leading part. Sometimes she shows me video clips on her phone. She is the most positive and optimistic person I have met in the past few years, for her job is wearying, and I suppose that taking care of three children on your own is demanding, but she is energetic and enterprising and keeps getting new acting assignments, which she talks enthusiastically about every Thursday.

When the coffee was ready, I came over here and wrote a piece about redcurrants. From time to time I leaned back and looked out the window to my right, where the redcurrant bushes I planted some years ago stand. The currants were still green and small; the bushes are in the shadow of some big trees nearly all day, something I didn't consider when I planted them, like the amateur I was. I also thought of my maternal grandparents' smallholding while I wrote, for there were lots of redcurrant bushes there, and every summer my brother and I helped them pick the berries. We were given money for every bucket – as far as I remember it was ten kroner per bucket of redcurrants, twenty per bucket of blackcurrants. I guess they sold the redcurrants to a local jam and squash producer. Since I saw everything there through the eyes of a child, and since work on the farm ceased when Grandmother and Grandfather got old and I have hardly been back there since they died, my knowledge about what happened is limited and approximate. When I was there during the summer, I didn't question anything, didn't try to find out how things really were or ask myself what lay behind objects and events, but saw everything just as it appeared before me. The currants were one thing. Walk along carrying the empty bucket to a row of bushes, lift a branch, pinch off a stem clustered with berries, drop the cluster into the bucket, do this with cluster after cluster, until the bottom of the bucket was covered, and see the bottom rise slowly until the bucket was full, which could take all morning. Carry the bucket over to the house, walk down the little slope to the cellar at the lower side of the house, the cool, low-ceilinged, dim room with cement walls and floor, full of tools, a freezer, yarn, vats. Pour the currants into a vat, in which there might already be thousands of red berries. The feeling of abundance it gave me, of nature's endless repetititons and profligacy. A full bucket hardly made any difference when the contents were poured into the vat. I loved that room, especially on warm summer days, when it was like entering another world from the sunshine outside, but I also feared it, there was something in there I was afraid of – not dead people or ghosts – but the very activities that were carried out there, for to me there was something brutal and dismissive about all practical work, something hard and insensitive. Grandfather gutted fish in there and cleaned his nets in the yard, and the fish were a part of the same thing as the berries, an abundance, and they too came from the outside, only even further away, from the hidden and mysterious world beneath the surface of the fjord. Every morning and evening he milked the cows in the cowshed and trundled the milk churns down to the road in a cart, placed them on a wooden platform from where the dairy van collected them. The grass was mown and hung up on hay-drying racks or put in the silo, the hay was placed in the barn, and the only mechanised part of this work was carried out by a small two-stroke tractor. They didn't own a car, they hardly ever travelled anywhere, and when they needed something from the grocery shop, which lay three kilometres away, Grandfather drove there in the two-stroke, it was so slow that you could trot alongside it.

That's how things were at their smallholding in the late 1970s and early 80s. Except for the television and the supermarket, the washing machine and the dishwasher, life wasn't so very different there from what it must have been during the Second World War. The great change, what makes my childhood seem so different from my children's when I tell them about it – or told them, for now whenever I start to say something about how things were when I grew up, they interrupt me as fast as they can – came towards the end of the 1980s, and from then on the changes accelerated. The question is whether those changes are substantial, if they make an essential difference? Or whether Grandmother and Grandfather also felt this way when they were approaching fifty, that life while they were growing up was radically different from the existence their children knew?

My mother's father was born the year after Knut Hamsun published *Under the Autumn Star*, and the year before *Benoni* came out. He was seventeen when *Growth of the Soil* came out, twenty-seven when *Wayfarers* came out and forty-two when *On Overgrown Paths* came out. So to him Hamsun was a contemporary writer. I know that he read Hamsun and liked him. Hamsun often wrote about the world as it was when he was a child, in the 1870s, and I assume that world was recognisable to Grandmother and Grandfather; it was the world their grandparents had known. When I read those books, the customs and some of the thoughts seem foreign to me, but not as foreign as what I experienced in Japan when I was there this spring. And perhaps that is how we ought to consider our old people, as immigrants from foreign countries, surrounded by things and notions they have grown used to after many years here, and which they understand but lack the feeling of familiarity for that one has for things and notions in one's own country. When I look at my children and the things they do, at least that is how I feel.

Grandfather always told stories from his own life, about people he had met and what they had done. One of those stories made a greater impression on me than the others, and I have always, ever since I heard it for the first time, thought that I would write it down some time. Last autumn I took a personality test for the Norwegian sociologist, comedian and TV personality Harald Eia, who then went through the results on stage before a studio audience, and for me there were no great surprises, according to the test I was vastly more depressed than average, more than normally introverted, and while my imagination was average, my emotions were well above. In other words: I am bad at writing imaginatively, good at feeling. If I am to draw the consequences of this in my writing, I should set the story in places I know, let the action unfold between people I know, in ways I myself have seen. That's why I used some of the stories in the Bible as a theme when I wrote my second novel *A Time to Every Purpose Under Heaven*, combined with scenes from my own life, and it was not least for that reason that I set those Bible stories on the west coast of Norway, my grandparents' landscape, which I knew from my childhood. So if I am to write the story that Grandfather used to tell, it has to take place in a house I know, with characters whose traits are taken from people I know, or from myself. The story unfolded during the final months of the Second World War, it was about a woman who lived in one of the villages further out along the fjord, and an Austrian soldier who was stationed there. Grandfather knew them both, the soldier better than the woman. The soldier had visited Norway before, during the summers while he was growing up, and he spoke Norwegian. Grandfather had first gone to Voss and been mobilised when the Germans invaded the country in April 1940, but they didn't have any weapons there and people were drunk, so he went back home and eventually became friends with the Austrian soldier, who also visited him at home. Grandmother didn't like it, didn't like him, but Grandfather, who was as sociable as he was jovial, appreciated his company. However, the interesting character in the story was the woman, and it was the part she played that really caught my attention. The incident is well known, a book was written about it in the 1980s; it stood in grandfather's bookcase, and later I bought it myself. It is a work of non-fiction and the writer spoke to people who had been involved, but there are still gaps in it, in the sense that no one really knows what happened, they have to resort to guesswork. The only people who knew were the woman from

Outer Sogn and the soldier from Austria. After the war they lived together in Malmö, a city I too have lived in and which I know rather well. So what I intend to do now is to change the content of 'I' completely. While so far in this text 'I' has represented a forty-seven-year-old Norwegian man residing in Sweden with a wife and four children, 'I' will soon, as soon as this sentence ends, represent a seventy-three-year-old woman who is sitting at a writing desk in an apartment in Malmö on a summer evening. I am not used to sitting here, the last time I wrote a letter was many years ago, and I have never kept a diary. What it is that I am writing now, I don't quite know. I think it is a sort of letter, to you, Alexander, to you my friend. For the past came to haunt me today. It has haunted me every day for more than forty years, but only in my feelings and in my dreams, not in my thoughts, and not in reality. I am still shaken. When I hold my hand up in front of me, it trembles. And it is *not* because I am old.

Here things look exactly as they did the last time you were here. Not one new piece of furniture, not even a new tablecloth.

I wish you were here now. Most of all, I think – and don't get upset now – because I am used to you. We didn't actually share all that much – except for *that*. And although we never talked about it, it was always there, between us.

It is as if you are here when I write to you. That you emerge from among all my other thoughts. And perhaps that is where you have always been most alive for me?

I remember your back, and your neck, when you sat on the bed with your feet on the floor after the alarm clock had rung. How you used to bow your head and run your hands over your face a few times, and then you would sit like that for a moment, with your face in your hands. I am thinking now of mornings in autumn or winter, the darkness beyond the window.

You sighed, that was your ritual. Then you stood up and got dressed while I went into the kitchen and warmed up some rolls, put out cheese and jam, made coffee.

We knew we weren't like other people.

For we weren't, were we?

We ate breakfast, you put on your outer clothes in the hall and went to work, I opened the window a crack and lit a cigarette, and it is still autumn or winter in my thoughts, so the sky was dark and the street below lit by the street lights and by the headlamps of the cars that were queued up down there. Bicyclists, pedestrians, on their way to work or school.

Then I went to work myself.

You of course know how it was, you know how we lived, and I don't think that anything I might write about you or us would have surprised you. Not that you thought about it, but if a letter like this had arrived, from me to you, it wouldn't have seemed strange to you.

I am writing about this because I don't want to write about the place we came from.

But I have to. The past came to haunt me today, like I said. In fact it rang the doorbell. I was sitting on the balcony with the radio on, and then I had to go to the toilet, and when I came into the living room, the doorbell rang. It doesn't happen very often, so I became anxious, but then it struck me that I had nothing to be anxious about, what might that be, you were already dead, so it could hardly be a messenger of death.

I opened the door. A young man was standing there.

'Are you Mrs Jacobsen?' he said.

I hadn't heard anyone use that name for forty years, yet I nodded, for that was my real name – one might imagine 'I', which is now taken up by me again, writing as she sat later that same afternoon in front of the writing desk in her living room in Malmö, perhaps in an apartment in the part of town surrounding the high-rise known as Kronprinsen, not far from the big park, only a couple of blocks. The children don't remember much from those years, they were so young that only brief glimpses of all we did and all the places we went exist for them. That your sisters sat in a double pram and that your mother and I were loaded down with cool bags and bags with towels and swimming gear, even with a parasol, which we always dragged around with us through the warm summer streets, they can't remember at all. Nor do they remember anything from the city beach at Ribersborg and its throngs of people, or from the bathing place that lies at the end of a long wooden pier, where there is also a restaurant we often sat at.

But I think they will remember today. I took maybe thirty photos of them this afternoon, so it has been well documented – your siblings were standing in the garden in their best clothes while I took their photographs: it was the last day of school, and there was an end-of-year ceremony in the church in Ystad. You too were in the very last photos I took, a tiny tot beside the others. I picked them up early from school, we were going to buy a shirt for your brother, a denim jacket for your younger sister and a pair of shoes for the elder one. The babysitter who helps out when I am away arrived two hours before we were leaving, to do the girls' hair, and when we went into town, the girls in pink and white dresses, your brother in a blue suit jacket, it felt like we were going to a wedding or something. In front of the church we met up with your mother, who was returning from Malmö, and while your siblings sat with their respective classes near the front of the nave, we were given seats towards the back. Each class sang a song, then the principal gave a speech, then there was more singing, and then the summer holiday began. Afterwards we ate at the sushi restaurant before we drove home and I sat down to write this. You fell asleep a long time ago and your brother has gone to bed, but the other two girls are still up enjoying their freedom. I have the feeling it's going to be an exciting summer for them – a name was mentioned in the car, and your sister's face lit up, she was smiling from ear to ear and I could see that she was trying not to, but she couldn't stop. Her smile was inward-looking, heartfelt: she sat in the seat next to me, beaming. Your other sister is up to something too, there's a certain name she keeps mentioning, and I think it's the same person that she is texting and talking to on the phone in the evening. But I don't know anything, I'm just guessing, in these matters I'm always the last person to find out.

Friday 10 June 2016

Wrote a text about summer rain and watched the opening game of the UEFA European Championship. Dad died the summer France last hosted the championship, and since then I have always felt ambivalent about the World Cup and the European Championship, for I'm certain he watched the games alone, sitting in Grandmother's living room. It's not that his death makes the football matches seem meaningless, it's the other way round, the football matches make death seem meaningless, they turn it into something insignificant. At the same time I still get drawn into the game, the excitement of the matches grips me and quickly gets a hold over my emotions, including the feeling of nostalgia, the roar that filled the living room in summer when I was growing up. Football is pointless, to be sure, but on the other hand, what isn't?

Saturday 11 June 2016

Jacobsen, I think my father's mother's maiden name was. It must have risen to the surface from my subconscious when I needed a name for the old woman in Malmö. My father's father was surnamed Pedersen in his youth, his family changed their name to the one I have now when he and his brothers became students. My maternal grandfather's surname was Hatløy, a name still borne by my mother and her brother. Once I considered taking it; in that case I would have been called Karl Hatløy, the same as my great-grandfather. It is a beautiful name, but I seem to remember that I found it a little weak, somehow. I felt I needed a harder name because I myself was weak, and there is something a little hard about 'Knausgård', since *knaus* means 'crag' in Norwegian, giving it a stony ring. A name is like a bag with one's entire identity inside, or like a carrying case. When we die, only the case is left, gathering together all the feelings and thoughts associated with our person.

What the maiden name of my maternal grandfather's

mother was, I don't know. She died when he was small, and I have never heard anything about her except that her absence made grandfather learn how to cook while he was young, which was unusual for men of that time and which he took up again towards the end of his life when my grandmother was too ill to do anything practical. Her maiden name was Årdal, after the place in Jølster municipality where she was from. Parts of that family are also called Myklebust, which is a hamlet on the other side of Jølstervannet lake.

To get away from my name and all the associations it has come to evoke since I became a public figure, for a while I considered publishing my next book under a pseudonym. I thought again of Karl Hatløy, but my uncle is an author, his name is Kjartan Hatløy, it would have been an intrusion on his territory. Since the book was to have a religious theme and be a sort of thriller, I came up with the name Kristian Hadeland. It isn't a good name, I see now – but 'Kristian' means 'the Christian', and with 'Hade' I was thinking of Hades, the underworld.

Odd how you can always tell if a name is invented or not. If the writer has made a special effort to find a common name to use in a novel, for example Eva Vik, the reader senses it at once. Jacob Hansen? Even Ødegård? They positively reek of fictionality.

Karl Hatløy?

'Hatl' means 'hazel', so Hatløy is an island with hazel trees. There are few things I like better and find more beautiful or mysterious than trees. But both my father and my mother changed their names when I was growing up and I didn't like it, it created a sense of instability and uncertainty, as if something once firm was sliding away.

Grandfather's name was Johannes. Your elder sister's name is a diminutive of Ivan, which is the Russian version of Johannes, while your brother's name is a short form of Johannes. I found both these things out long after the children were baptised.

Time is a precipitous drop; in childhood visibility doesn't extend very far. To me, my grandparents' childhood was beyond reach, a thing I knew nothing about – and to my children it is my parents' childhood that is beyond reach! They have no idea about the lives of their great-grandparents in western Norway, with whom I spent every summer as a child. It doesn't help that I tell them about this, they have nothing to fasten it to, the stories I tell them involve people who are dead and have been dead all their lives. The cellar with the cement walls and the often wet floor with the hole where the water drained down, the white tubs with mounds of shiny redcurrants in them, the milk churns, the little tractor and all the other things that shine in my memory, these mean nothing to them, for it is from within that the world is lit up, it is from within that objects and places derive their significance. The thought that what surrounds us here and now will one day come to be just as significant to you and your siblings I find frightening because it passes me by, and for that reason I am probably careless about it. The bicycle ride with your brother some days ago is a good example, to me it was just another evening, albeit one in which something dramatic happened that will make me remember it, but it was still no more than something I observed, not something I was in the depths of, as was perhaps the case – or will later become the case – for him.

Yesterday, by the way, he called for me from the living

room, I was standing in the kitchen, he wanted to show me something. I went in to him. It was a video on YouTube, it showed a computer game that a young man was playing; in the top right corner of the screen there was an image of the player himself. Your brother looked at me expectantly. 'Now comes the fun part,' he said. 'Now!' He laughed and looked up at me to see if I was laughing too.

The reason he did this was simple. I've never liked it when he just watches others play, I find it so passive, he doesn't *do* anything, he's just staring at something others are doing. When he is playing himself, I am in a more forgiving mood, but that too I find problematic, that too seems passive, oughtn't he rather be outside playing instead?

He knows, of course, that this is my attitude. He senses that I don't like it, it is there as a constant if not always a conscious pressure on him, my thinking that what he likes best of all is bad for him. I don't need to say it, he knows.

A couple of days ago he was sitting on the sofa next to me, watching a game on YouTube. I looked at it for a little while and it was incredibly comical so I started to laugh. It involved a man on a bicycle carrying a small child in a seat on the bike, and he had to overcome various obstacles while riding, with his helmet, the child and everything else. If he made a mistake, the consequences were disastrous and bloody, he lost arms, legs, sometimes his head was chopped off. The contrast between the two levels made me smile, and then he crashed into something so that the small child was flung forward, hit a wall and ended up as a bloody mess on the ground, which made me laugh out loud. Your brother laughed too, he could hardly stop. We sat there watching the game for maybe ten minutes more before I went back to my own thing.

That's what he remembered, that's why he was calling me, he wanted to show me more.

That was the first time I realised the effect my disapproval of computer games had on him. I saw how happy he was when I liked a game and we watched it together.

After that we went for a bike ride together, just around the neighbourhood, and nothing happened, yet it still made me glad, for he was the one who had suggested it, so the terrifying ride down into the ditch couldn't have frightened him very much.

He is my son. I tend to think that I see my children, who they are, and that I am an OK father to them. This little incident made me understand how shut up within myself I really am. That I have never put myself in his place and thought: How is he experiencing this? Instead I have looked on from the outside, and the question has always been: Is this good for him? Or no, not 'for him', but 'for a child'. Is this good for a child? As if the situation had been an objective one. But that's precisely what it wasn't, since it was I, his father, who said it wasn't good for him, and that part, which has to do with him and me, is surely more important and should be obvious. Not least because I myself have had a father and still remember how much his approval meant to me.

Everything was different when my father came with us to visit my grandparents in western Norway. The best thing about being there was that we could do as we liked and that no one got angry at us if we did something wrong. It was a free haven. But when he was there, it no longer felt like one.

I know that he beat my brother there once. Something had been said around the dinner table, and Father hadn't said anything, had pretended not to mind, laughed along with the others. But as soon as our grandparents had lain down for an after-dinner nap, he had thrown him about, slamming him into the wall. I don't remember it and didn't hear about it until fairly recently.

The episode that I remember best from when he was there is different. We were walking in the meadow that belonged to the farm, the others were having a nap after dinner, I trotted alongside him, he was wearing tall gumboots, which were entirely wrong, I remember thinking, in relation to the fine shirt and pair of trousers that he also had on. I don't remember where we were going, but he must have asked me to come along, otherwise I would never have walked beside him. We didn't speak, but my chest still felt like it was exploding with joy simply at being together, just the two of us. There was pain too mixed with the joy, not much, but perhaps he was dissatisfied with something as we walked, perhaps he felt I wasn't talking enough, perhaps he didn't like the situation.

The ridge across from the farm was covered with spruce, dark green against the grey sky. A small lake lay at the foot of it, it was black as night.

'Could you imagine living here?' he said.

'Yes!' I said.

'Maybe some day we could take over this place. Grandmother and Grandfather are getting old, you know.'

'I would like that an awful lot,' I said.

He looked at me.

'Yes, it's a nice place.'

Had I shown too much enthusiasm? Did he realise that I would say anything at all just to please him?

My memory of this doesn't go any further. But while we

were walking, and Grandmother and Grandfather were taking a nap, Grandfather perhaps on the sofa, Grandmother perhaps in their bedroom on the first floor, and Mum was maybe doing the dishes in the kitchen and Yngve was maybe listening to music on the Walkman and reading, the woman whom I wrote about two days ago, the one who came from a village further out along the fjord, and who was one day visited at her apartment by a man, must have been somewhere in the world, for she did really exist, Grandfather had known who she was both before and after the war. Very likely she was in Malmö, since that's where she lived or had ended up. Other than that, I know nothing about who she was, what she looked like, what kind of thoughts she may have had. When I now, in the next sentence, let her take over the 'I' of this text, it isn't her I am seeking to represent but her story, which began in front of the desk in her apartment and then went back in time a few hours, where it ended, for the time being, as someone rang the bell and she opened the door and the man who was standing outside addressed her by her former name, Mrs Jacobsen. Perhaps he expected me to back away in alarm or slam the door shut. Or perhaps he thought I would hide my face in my hands and break down the way they do in the movies.

I wasn't brave, Alexander, you mustn't think that. Nor was I unaffected by it, even though all the years that have passed have built a wall between me and what happened back then.

Within me everything was collapsing. But at the same time it was as if I saw it from without, as if I were standing outside myself. And that part, that part was unaffected.

'Yes?' I said.

He introduced himself and held out his hand. I shook it. He said he was a journalist from Norway. I said I had thought as much.

'I would very much like to interview you,' he said.

'I'm afraid I don't have time for that,' I said.

'But you do understand what it is I want to talk to you about?' he said.

'I have nothing to say,' I said. 'You had better leave.'

I shut the door. I half expected him to put his foot out to prevent me from closing it.

'I'll be in town for some time,' he said outside the door.

My legs could no longer carry me and I supported myself against the wall. I no longer saw anything from the outside, you understand, and there was no longer anything inside me telling me what to do.

What would have happened if you had been here?

That would have been even more terrible. We were co-conspirators, and what had happened, which we never spoke about, we might not have spoken about even now. But it would have been there between us.

Now it was just me.

I lay down on the bed, and I must in fact have fallen asleep, for I opened my eyes and it was evening.

You know how beautiful sunsets can be here. Those were perhaps the best times we had in Malmö, when we sat out on the balcony in summer and the sun was going down.

As I went into the living room the sun was hanging low in the sky above Denmark, and it was as hot as in a sauna in there since it had shone straight into the room all evening.

I felt that what I needed to do was to write to you.

So now I am sitting here.

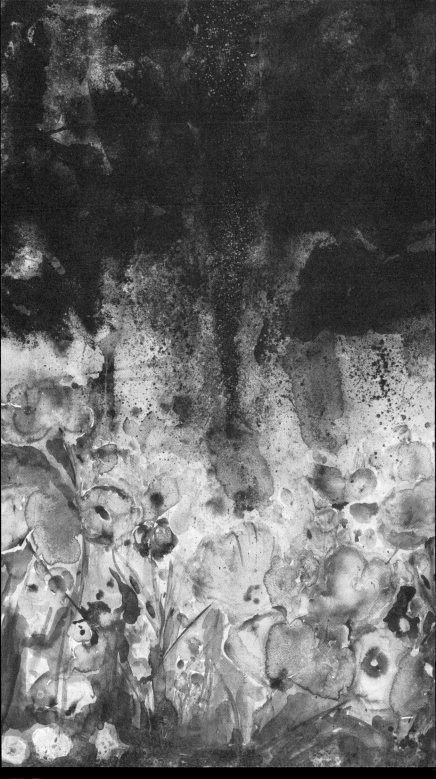

It did me good. Imagine, you are still able to help me!

Once I fell down in the street. You weren't here any more, I was alone. My chest hurt terribly, the pain was indescribable, and I thought my time too had come. No, I knew it. Now I will die, I thought. And the strange thing was that it felt so good. I was filled with pleasurable thoughts. I remembered my childhood, it shone within me, clear and green like the mountains back home. What I remembered were the days in summer. The fjord, smooth as glass. You know what it's like when everything is still and the days seem to have depth. I thought, I've had a good life. The thought filled me with gratitude.

As I lay there in unbearable pain thinking I was going to die, only childhood existed, I knew of nothing else, all the rest was gone.

Such grace, Alexander.

Then the ambulance came, and they saved me. I had had back pain for a long time but I had thought it would cure itself, so I hadn't been to see the doctor about it.

When I woke up from the anaesthetic, the strange experience I had had was also no more than a memory.

Why was that, do you think?

Does the brain release certain substances to make death easier?

Do we all die happy?

Sunday 12 June 2016

The wheelbarrow is standing on the flagstone path between the houses, half filled with weeds which have long since wilted and dried. On the ground various tools are strewn about next to a blue plastic tub – you were the one who brought them out, I shouldn't wonder – and in some places between the flagstones new weeds have sprung up, remarkably green and fresh next to the grey stone and the rusty wheelbarrow. I weeded maybe ten square metres before I called it a day, on an evening nearly two weeks ago, and I was so certain I would be continuing the next afternoon that I just left everything there. Every time I see it I am reminded of the unfinished job, which is annoying of course, but there is also something pleasing about it, for what has been abandoned possesses a peculiar beauty. Construction sites one passes in the evening, where the excavator rests its bucket on the ground and the workmen's sheds are deserted, where stacked pipes lie next to a freshly dug ditch and a spade is maybe planted in the clayish soil. A football field on a summer evening after a training session, the water sprinkler rhythmically slinging water across the grass, the small goals ranged down the long sides of the field, the forgotten track jacket that someone has hung over the crossbar. Or a campsite in winter, the kiosk boarded up, the cabins empty and dark, signposts indicating activities that are no longer on offer.

I'm not very observant when it comes to activities, I don't notice them; not until the activity has ceased and only its forms remain do I catch sight of it. Not the woman trimming the hedge but the garden shears lying by the hedge after she has called it a day. Not the family eating in the picnic area at the lookout point above the fjord, but the wooden table with benches when it is raining and there isn't a soul in sight.

Some days ago I wrote to a Swedish science journalist to ask if she knew any paleontologists in Africa whom I could contact, I am planning to go there, to Kenya or Ethiopia, to follow an archeological dig and write about the first hominids, who originated on those plains several million years ago, and who weren't apes but nor were they humans.

She sent me three names and wished me luck.

The excavation of these fossils concerns ultimate questions, but they lie buried in the soil and are nothing but bones, there was nothing great about them then and there is nothing great about them now, a living ape in a zoo is just as much of a mystery as the existence of the early hominids was back then, and that's where I want to go, into the small and the local and the concrete. They weren't many, these proto-humans, and they must have kept to a relatively restricted area. What is impossible to fathom is the time that separates us from them, the infinity of days and nights which millions of years entail.

I am going to try to get down there at the end of August.

Yesterday the father of your elder sister's friend came by to fetch her, she had spent the night here. We sat at the table in the innermost part of the garden, drinking coffee and eating ice cream. They moved here a year ago, bought a house in one of the developments in the town, it dates to the 1950s and sits in the middle of a small garden, so we talked a bit about that, the world of apples and plums, weeding and weeds, lawn mowing and vegetable gardening which had abruptly appeared in our lives. He had pruned their apple tree this spring, I had done the same thing with one of our trees two years ago, but unlike me he had researched it on the Internet and knew what he was doing. I just climbed into the tree and chopped away.

While we were sitting there your younger sister came walking from the bus stop. She had dressed up that morning and gone into town with your mother, who had sat in a café while your sister met up with a boy from school by herself.

I could tell that she was happy as she arrived.

I showed him the chestnut tree as they were leaving, and told him about the neighbour who had come by and said that the tree was dying. The trunk divides into four boughs a couple of metres from the ground, and one bough is already lifeless, with no leaves. It makes me so sad, not least because the tree adds character to the whole garden, it stands in the middle of the yard, towering above the houses.

Later that evening I took at taxi into Ystad and met up with another father, this time of your younger sister's friend, we were going to watch the England v. Russia match at a pub. It was a good game, but it seemed that what he really wanted was to talk, at any rate he kept bringing up one topic after the other, while I looked alternately at him and at the screen on the wall in front of us. Every football match has its own dramaturgy, and to me it only becomes interesting if I follow the entire game from beginning to end and become personally engaged in it. Then even a 0–0 draw becomes exciting. But even I understand that this kind of absorption is incompatible with watching a game with a mate in a pub. So I gave up on the match, following it intermittently while we talked and drank beer. He is German and had been close to his grandfather who took part in the war in Russia and had experienced the most horrific things there. He also told me about his father, who had played in the ruins in the post-war years, that they often found weapons and it wasn't unusual for them to come across dead people too. He is a home care worker now, but he used to be a policeman, and before that he studied history, especially the history of the Soviet Union, at a German university. He didn't like academics, he said, that's why he abandoned that career path. His face was entirely open, his eyes seemed younger than his face. He is fifty years old. He told me how difficult it had been to move here from Germany, how different the culture was; where he came from everyone was social, in that way it was open and magnificent, as he presented it, while here people kept to their own circles, it was almost impossible for outsiders to become a part of Swedish life. His best friend here was from Croatia. He said he had read Keith Richards' autobiography and it had made him want to learn how to play the guitar so badly that he bought one and set to it.

He walked me down to the taxi rank around half past midnight and then bicycled home. There were no taxis there, and when I called, they said the earliest I could get one would be in an hour. It was Saturday and gymnasium students were celebrating their approaching graduation, so the few taxis around were presumably ferrying the revellers to and from their homes.

A black car pulled up next to me, and the window was rolled down.

'Taxi?' said the young dark-haired driver.

Why not? I thought.

'How much will you charge me to go to Glemmingebro?'

'How much do you want to give me?'

'I don't know. How much do you want?'

'How much do you want to pay?'

'Three hundred?'

'Get in!'

'But I don't have any cash. Only my card.'

'We'll sort it out. Get in!'

We drove through the streets, everything was quiet, nightlife in Ystad isn't exactly lively, he pulled up in front of an ATM, I withdrew the money and gave it to him. We didn't speak and he turned up the music, which sounded Turkish.

'Where's the music from?' I said.

'Turkey,' he said. 'I'm from Palestine.'

'How long have you lived in Sweden?'

'Three years.'

'How do you like it?'

'They have been the best years of my life.'

He talked for the remainder of the ride. He spoke about his life in Palestine, that he had worked as a plumber with his brother, and that his entire family were still there. He was married with one child, they lived in one of the villages outside Ystad; I looked at the photograph of his wife and child hanging on the dashboard, there was a leather sofa in the background. I gathered that life was hard here too, he told me about all his expenses, and that all his jobs were on the black market. He had friends who lived in other villages, from Iran and Syria and Palestine. He said that many of those who came here as refugees didn't arrive straight from Syria, but via other countries, where they had lived well. I posed a few questions now and then, looked past him up into the pale black night sky, the grey clouds drifting slowly above the silent landscape, the dashboard glowing in the half-light, the headlights that seemed to rend the black tarmac ahead. He drove fast, and in ten minutes we were there. I told him to pull up at the fire station and walked the remaining hundred metres. It had been so long since I'd been out meeting people that it felt like I was returning home from a trip abroad.

Today I drove all of you to the outdoor pools at Nybrostrand and watched Croatia v. Turkey on my phone while you and your siblings were bathing. I hadn't even known that this was possible! You bathed in the small pool for children, which you had refused to go into the last time we were here, but now it wasn't a problem, you splashed and played and laughed. When we were getting ready to leave, you refused to come, and I lifted you up and carried you all the way to the car while you thrashed about and shouted. Your sister was sitting on the ground by the car and waiting with her head bent over her phone, she hadn't really wanted to come and was a little cross, but you stopped shouting and squirming when you saw her, and I strapped you into your seat and drove home. In the evening I took you along to the supermarket in Borrby, since you love driving in the car and you enjoy sitting in the trolley and being pushed through the aisles, so you had a great time. On the way home you fell asleep with the lollipop you had pestered me into buying stuck to your hand, and I carried you up to the first floor, put a nappy on you and laid you in bed before bringing in the groceries from the car and placing them in the kitchen cupboards.

Now you are asleep, while I am sitting here listening to Pink Floyd, of all things. I am playing *Meddle*, was reminded of that record when I heard a live recording of Midlake, who included a song from the album in their set. Mum and Dad used to play Pink Floyd when I was growing up, especially Dad, and for a while that impressed the other kids, since no one else had parents who listened to that kind of music. In the *gymnas* I listened to Pink Floyd with Hilde and Eirik and Thomas, usually in Hilde's basement recreation room, where we would sit into the night drinking tea or wine and playing records, watching videos, many of them with Monty Python, or we just talked. 'Wish You Were Here', 'Shine On You Crazy Diamond'. We weren't being cool, Pink Floyd was actually the opposite of cool, so I kept my mouth shut about it when I was with Espen and his friends, there we listened to Violent Femmes, R.E.M., Imperiet, Waterboys, occasionally U2, Wall of Voodoo, Stan Ridgeway, Prince, Green on Red, basically everything that came our way via the music magazines.

I haven't thought about those years in a long while now.

Once at a literary event I got talking to an elderly woman. She said, 'You might think that life is short, but you're just in your forties. I am over ninety and I assure you, life is long. Life is very long.'

The proto-humans who dwelled on the African savannah several million years ago, on the other side of that vast gulf of days, hardly lived to be ninety, I suppose, but some of them may have reached the age of fifty, sixty, as certain apes do, and although their faculties for remembering were probably not equal to ours, they too must have had a perception of time and the various stages of life, in one way or another they must have sensed that fullness of being?

I hope it's true what she said, the old woman.

Monday 27 June 2016

I am sitting on a balcony in Rio de Janeiro looking out over the beach across the road from the hotel. The waves of the Atlantic Ocean are striking land, light against the dark sand now that it is night, and their soughing fills the air all the way up here on the nineteenth floor, an even rushing melancholy murmur. Your brother is sitting on the bed beyond the glass door playing games on the new iPad he got when we were at Copenhagen Airport in Kastrup this morning. I had promised him an iPad because I will be working here, and he didn't want a babysitter but to be with me all the time, so he will need something to keep him occupied. He woke me up at half past five at our house, worried that the alarm wouldn't ring. I had set it to six, so everything was under control, but I got up anyway, showered, took the laundry out of the dryer and packed it in the suitcase. He took a bath, I washed his hair, then we ate breakfast, got in the car, and I turned the ignition key using pliers. The key broke five months ago, but for a long time it was still usable; the metal part stuck out of the lock, so you just had to fit the black plastic part over it and twist. Two days before we left for Brazil my mother called – she had come to help out at home while I was away – from the car park in Ystad to say that she couldn't start the car. It was no longer possible to turn the key with the black plastic handle, the opening that fitted over the metal part had widened with use so that it just spun around when you tried to twist the key. Now they were sitting on the bus on their way home. I fetched a pair of pliers from the kitchen drawer, called a taxi, stood in the road outside the house in the heat and smoked while I waited for it to arrive. I had thought it would be easy, that it was just a matter of turning the key using the pliers, but it wasn't, for when I did, the engine wouldn't start. 'Key not detected,' it said on the dashboard. It took me half an hour to figure out a method that worked. I stuck the plastic handle to the metal with tape, this allowed the key to turn halfway in the lock so that the electricity came on, but not all the way, the resistance was too great. But if I then, as fast as I could, removed the handle and used the pliers, the car was fooled and started up with no problems. This wasn't a sure-fire method, however, it didn't always work. So when I had driven the car home, we decided to rent one which Mum and the babysitter could use while I was gone. This morning my car started at the first attempt, and on the display it fortunately didn't say 'Key not detected,' just the regular warning that the car needs servicing, which has lit up every time I start the car for the last six months. It was a fantastic morning, perfectly still, sunlit fields, blue sky, no cars on the roads, the landscape green and golden. I thought of the summer mornings when I was eleven and twelve years old and bicycled to the strawberry fields, it must have been around seven o'clock, how the air and the light held a promise of warmth to come, the veil of mist across the sky, the glittering dew on the grass, and yet there were still corridors of cool air along the road. The pride I felt at being on my way to a job, the pride that I would be earning my own money, how the simple thought of what I would spend it on, a pair of slalom skis, was enough to motivate me to work as fast as I could for the five hours I spent with my back bent over the strawberry bushes, a situation I actually found unbearable. The unbearable part wasn't the boredom, it was that I was bound, that I couldn't do something else even if I wanted to. It wasn't something I thought about as we drove along the road this morning, merely something I felt: this whole spectrum of memories appeared in the form of a particular sensation, a summer-morning feeling, which lasted no more than a few seconds. Memories follow a logic similar to that of dreams, they fill us with a sense of duration that is disconnected from actual time: the second that elapses between a sound one hears while dreaming and the instant one is woken by it can be filled with a sequence of events that in the dream lasts several hours.

We flew from Kastrup to Paris, and from there we flew on to Rio. When the bus stopped in front of the enormous jet on the runway in Paris, I thought that it was like a ship. That it was made ready like a ship and that the passengers embarked as on a ship which would carry them to another continent. Slowly and ponderously the plane rolled along the runway, and although its speed must have been very high, since it eventually lifted from the ground and glided up through the air, it seemed low and the whole enterprise counter to nature. Your brother sat looking out the window, at a landscape – we were just outside Paris – resembling the one he is growing up in, only vaster. Fields upon fields, acres upon acres, green and yellow. I like to fly long distances, for there, aboard the plane, no demands are placed on you, nothing needs to be done, I can sit perfectly still for hours on end, sleep a little, watch a movie, read a little, doze off again. When we are about to land, I always wish we could have flown on. We flew over Spain and over Portugal, where we left the coast and glided out over the ocean. We passed the Canary Islands, and just as on the ancient ships they were our last glimpse of land until the American continent appeared on the other side. I saw dark green forests and here and there glinting water beneath the carpet of cloud. The sun went down, the western sky turned red, the landscape beneath us grew blacker and blacker, and then there was darkness. Your brother had woken up as the final rays of sun struck the clouds, I told him we were above the jungle, and as he looked out his gaze was greedy. But there's nothing but clouds, he said and lay back to sleep some more, curled up in a way I have always been affected by, with one knee pulled up to his belly, his head resting against his arm. When he woke up again, when the flight attendants switched on the lights – they were about to serve the final meal of the flight – his face was white. He was trembling a little. 'I feel sick,' he said. He reached for the airsickness bag and laid it on his lap at the ready. 'It'll be fine,' I said. 'You often feel nauseous, but you hardly ever vomit.' I thought of all the times he has had a bucket standing ready by his bed without ever using it. But this time I was wrong. Just as the meal trolley stopped next to us, he grabbed the bag, opened it and pressed it to his mouth, which he had opened wide. At first nothing came, only hawking noises and a sort of low moaning. Then vomit spurted into the bag. The air hostess gave us a resigned look and poured water into a glass, which she handed to me. I gave it to him. 'You can take the bag to the toilet,' the hostess told me. The whole trip I had felt that she had a grudge against us, for she had been annoyed with your brother when he didn't take the tray she handed him with the first meal, even though she obviously couldn't reach all the way to his table. 'Take the tray!' she had said then, a little too loudly, a little too tensely. Take it easy, he's eight years old, I had thought, but I didn't say it. Now I stood up with the full, warm airsickness bag in my hand and walked to the toilet with it. When I came back, he had been given a flannel with which he dried his face. 'Better now?' I said. 'Yes,' he said. 'Few things feel better than when you've just thrown up,' I said. 'No,' he said. 'Yuck,' I said. 'Are you hungry?' 'No,' he said and gave me a look as if I were crazy. He was leaning towards the window and looking out as we flew in over Rio de Janeiro, whose lights glittered in the darkness. It was my first visit to South America, but the continent's mythology has always been important to me, has run like an undercurrent of longing through my life, obviously because of everything I have read about it: it isn't the reality I long for or am fascinated by, it is what that reality is coloured with. And the colours were different here, it seemed to me, juicier and richer, more sizzling.

After a half-hour car ride through the city, we arrived at the hotel, where I am sitting now. It's midnight, the temperature is as on a Scandinavian summer evening. The waves are large, the lights along the beach promenade are many and darkly yellow. Behind the hotel, a few blocks down, a steep tree-clad hillside rears up. It looks peculiar standing there amid the blocks of flats, like a reminiscence of a time before the buildings, when this was merely a strip of shore, forested all the way down to the beach, which lay deserted receiving the waves from the ocean, unseen by eyes other than those of birds, animals, giant lizards.

Tuesday 28 June 2016

When the sun rose this morning and the darkness slowly lifted – that was the feeling, that the darkness was being hollowed out from within, and that its surfaces were raised up – I saw that the untouched hills and mountains, some forested, others with naked mountainsides, are a part of the city's rhythm, for steep hillsides rise at regular intervals as far as the eye can see, and interspersed among them are buildings, hundreds of thousands of white boxes and cubes, stretching part-way up the mountainsides.

All morning huge tropical birds circled in the air right above the hotel. Their wingspan was wide, the wings fairly narrow. There were perhaps twenty of them, floating on the thermals. I saw several others in the air above the city, little specks in the far distance or black shadows gliding over the green mountainsides. It was difficult to reconcile their primeval look with the life that unfolded beneath them, the people walking along the streets on what to the birds must appear like the valley floor of a mountainous landscape full of narrow gulches and deep incisions far below, the open bars and restaurants where people sat talking or watching TVs hung on walls, or the tremendous traffic of cars on the road along the beach, to the birds it must all be meaningless, or it meant something very different to them than to us.

I did some phone interviews in the room while your brother played computer games, and then we went to the beach. There weren't many people there and red warning flags had been hoisted all along the shore, the public was advised against swimming due to the powerful undertow.

We went into the water anyway, and the big frothy waves swept over us, your brother laughed, and I held his hand so he wouldn't disappear with the waves when they pulled back. The water was warm and so salty that it stung our lips. Afterwards we ate lunch at the hotel and took a swim in the roof-top pool. The view was spectacular. The city stretched out white beneath the green mountains, the waves struck dumbly and mechanically against the kilometre-long beach in cascading white patterns, and beneath the blue sky birds hovered and helicopters sputtered. Everything seemed open, and not only did the green forested hillsides in the middle of town bring the past into the present, the white, foaming waves striking the beach, glittering in the sun, in a similar way seemed to open on to the future, for their motion was eternal – at the same time that all of this was happening now, while your brother waded shivering in the pool with his hands up, for the water here was considerably colder than the ocean, and I stood holding my phone up taking photos of him. And perhaps all the labyrinths of the mind, all the difficult relationships and all interpersonal problems are also a way we have of holding on to our own time, a way of diminishing reality so that it becomes manageable.

In the evening we went out, I wanted to go to a restaurant on the promontory that had been recommended to us, three kilometres away, at the end of the beach promenade, and although your brother said he could easily walk there and back, we first hunted for an ATM to withdraw cash for a taxi home. Your brother said the streets here reminded him of Stockholm, which seemed odd, for I can hardly imagine a city more different from Stockholm. The similarity, to him, had to be that they were both big cities. I loved the atmosphere, the vaguely Portuguese colonial air, the 1950-ish aura, the dark yellow light of the street lamps which only partially pushed the darkness away, which was everywhere present anyway. But after ten minutes he wanted to go back to the hotel, he said the food there was good, and although I stopped in front of one restaurant after another, as run-down as they were beautiful, with mosaic floors and dim interiors, only the hotel would do for him, and I gave in, I wanted him to enjoy this trip as much as possible and had made up my mind not to correct him and, so far as I could, to let him do as he liked. So half an hour later there we were in the empty, sterile hotel restaurant, each eating our Brazilian steak with pommes frites and rice. Afterwards I lay on the bed and read a manuscript, Tore's latest book, but all the impressions and all the light during the day, followed by total darkness, had taken their toll, and I fell asleep with my clothes on. When I woke up a few hours later, your brother was asleep in the other bed, he had got un-dressed, brushed his teeth and crept under the sheets while I slept. The TV was on, he probably hadn't been able to find the remote control, I thought, and located it beneath the duvet, switched the TV off, opened the screen of the Mac and began writing this.

Wednesday 29 June 2016

After a seven-hour bus ride north along the coast from Rio, we arrived in Paraty late this afternoon. I have never seen so many trees in my life as during this journey. All the hills, which in some places rose steeply, in others stretched into the blue distance, were covered by trees, which I suppose they are at home too, but here the forest grows so densely as to be impenetrable, and this gave it a different air, it seemed a force of its own, greedy and formidable. On the outskirts of Rio we drove past slum areas, shacks, stray dogs, rubbish, a gaunt horse standing in the middle of the street, derelict industrial areas, overgrown and desolate, and then the concrete road ran over a river, and although the backwaters were full of piles of plastic and all traces of humans there were impoverished and ramshackle, it was still beautiful in its peculiar way. The dirty river glinted greyish-green in the sunlight, and the dark green vegetation, which managed to find a foothold everywhere in the landscape, was fresh and new, unaffected by the roads, the concrete, the fences, the rubbish. This gave the decay a different aspect than it has for example in Detroit, where it seemed irreversible, a destructive force impossible to conquer, one-sided in all its bleak greyness, or in the large industrial cities of northern Russia, like Murmansk, where everything is barren and hopeless. The poverty outside the bus window was grotesque, but the intense force of growth that surrounded it, this mighty abundance of green, pointed to something else. Or was it that the abundance, the immense wastefulness, also applied in the human realm?

I talked with your brother about what we saw, about how his life would have been if he had been born here, that he might not have been able to go to school, for instance. He wondered why there was poverty here and not at home. I said that Sweden and Norway are such small countries they were much simpler to organise. I said that the differences between rich and poor had once been just as great in Sweden and Norway, but that the workers had united, and since they were many, they had gained power and rights. And that now those advances were on their way to disappearing again.

I like talking with your brother, and I like seeing how different parts of the puzzle keep falling into place for him. The continents, the countries, the cities, but also the great empires of the past and the epochs of history. He knows quite a bit about the two world wars, since his best friend's father is interested in them. He knows about the Roman Empire, the Middle Ages, the Soviet Union and the Great Wall of China. He knows a lot about outer space and a lot about dinosaurs. After *Star Wars* that is maybe his favourite topic of conversation. Then, as the bus grumbled along the roads leaving the city, we gradually began talking about ostriches.

'They're dangerous,' he said. 'They can tear a person apart with their claws.'

'But do you know what the people who raise ostriches do to keep them from attacking?'

'No?'

'Ostriches have such a tiny brain. They don't understand very much.'

'He-he!'

'So if you bring a stick and lift it over your head, the ostrich thinks you are bigger than it is and doesn't dare to attack.'

'He-he!'

'And if you pull a black bag over its head, it thinks it's night and falls asleep.'

But mostly he is the one telling me things and I am the one listening. At home he doesn't always say much, there isn't so much space for him, his sisters take up a lot of space, but when you're alone with him, he starts to talk. He is almost always in a good mood, and he can talk non-stop for an hour if there's nothing to prevent him. My mother, your grandmother, says that I was just like that when I was his age. Just talked and talked about everything between heaven and earth. That changed abruptly when I reached puberty and ran into a wall of shame. I hope he never encounters it. But even though he maybe resembles me when I was his age, it's not like I recognise myself in him. I see him from the outside, an eight-year-old boy whom I like very much, whom I often feel like hugging and cuddling, but to see him, who he is and how he is doing, demands an attitude which everyday life doesn't allow many opportunities for, it is as if my machinery is coarser and geared towards larger movements, while his is more finely tuned and therefore often escapes my notice. That's fine, really, I don't believe that adults should be close to their children all the time, on the contrary, children need space of their own, but after that bicycle ride, when I saw my own coarseness so clearly and the distance that separated me from what was important to him, I decided to spend more time with him. So this journey was just the ticket.

After perhaps an hour's driving we had exited the city, and for the rest of the trip the landscape presented variations of the same theme, the ocean on one side with foaming waves breaking upon beaches or striking against cliffs, and on the other the forest with a built-up belt that was rarely more than a kilometre wide. We were driving on the very rim of the continent, which was so vast that thoughts couldn't grasp it. I read on in Tore's novel and became completely engrossed by it, while your brother sat looking out the window. Now and again he played games on his new iPad, but the battery was running low, so he was rationing it. I had forgotten where I was and that Tore had written what I was reading, and disappeared into it completely.

Paraty lay on a plain resembling an estuary between the mountains and the sea, the town dated back to the 1700s and the outermost part still looked as it may have looked then, roughly cobbled or sand-filled streets, white brick houses on both sides, little churches like those of southern Europe, a park – and alongside all this ran a river, while at the end, towards the ocean, lay a somewhat swampy area. The ocean extended out like a fjord, with land on both sides and a few islands here and there, and at a distance, from the road at the back of the hotel, beneath an overcast grey-white sky, the surface of the water dark grey, nearly black, what I saw reminded me of western Norway. When I turned and looked at the white colonial-style buildings, I seemed to be in a dream, a place where everyday logic was suspended.

It is pitch black outside now. I am sitting at a table on the ground floor, writing, while your brother is lying upstairs playing computer games. Outside the door there is a large patio, with palms and green shrubs, around which the rooms of the hotel are located, and in the middle there is a pool, with a bar and a restaurant. We had a swim in it when we arrived, the water was freezing, it can't have been more than sixteen degrees. That was the first time I was reminded that it is winter here. Now we are going out to eat, there is a pizza restaurant right around the corner, and then we are going to sleep through our third South American night.

Thursday 30 June 2016

We woke early this morning, as we have done every morning
here, and had to wait for nearly two hours before the breakfast room opened. We were the first guests and had almost
finished when I heard a familiar voice say hello behind me.
It was Henry Marsh, the British neurosurgeon whom I had
met in Albania the previous summer. When I asked him
how he was doing, he said that he was still in shock after
Great Britain had voted to withdraw from the European
Union, and we talked a little about that before we agreed to
have dinner together here one evening. I met him again half
an hour later when I went out to the pool to have a smoke,
and we sat chatting for a while. Henry Marsh has a round
face with soft wrinkles from age, the eyes behind the round
glasses are kindly or distracted, his lips are thin, and there is
something sharp about his mouth. He is of average height,
thin, with powerful hands, which are often covered in small
cuts. His character is decidedly British, pleasant and cul-
tured, and he understands the art of conversation. I don't,
and perhaps that is why we spoke so little about general matters and so much about personal ones. It has been like that
every time I've met him; he has confided in me. Yet we are
not really familiar, there is a distance of both age and culture, it's something else. This year several people whom I
don't really know have confided in me, people have told me
secrets which they haven't told anyone else or only the persons closest to them, it is as if they skip a link in the chain.
Sometimes it is difficult to receive their confidences, to
know how to deal with them, should I be just as confiding in

return? Are they telling me because they have come to identify with me through my books? They have all been public figures, some of them in positions which preclude them from trusting many others, rumours might spread if they tell the wrong person, while at the same time I have sensed that they have felt a great need to tell. Intimate things, often. Or things that are unheard of. What they see when they see me must be something completely different from how I see myself. Something in me would like to write about what they have told me, it would make a text full of tensions and with great drawing power, but the tensions and the appeal would not stem from the text itself, but from the aura that these persons have for the reader. It happened earlier too, before I made my debut as an author, I remember one time in particular, I was taking the sleeper train to Bergen from Oslo and shared a compartment with a young man, he was a few years older than me, we got talking, and while the train rolled across the mountains through the summer darkness he told me the most intimate, private and dramatic things from his life. I was a stranger and that was the point, he knew we would never see each other again. After maybe two hours he looked at me and said, What about you? What's your life like? I hesitated, I said there was nothing to tell. But there has to be something? he said, I said no, there isn't. He sighed, or maybe it was more of a snort, and shook his head. *You can't do that*, he seemed to be saying, *here I've been telling you all this, I've been totally open with you, and you won't tell me anything about yourself*? So I gave in and told him about my life as openly as I could, that is without consideration for the people involved, since that is the price of openness. It didn't matter, we would never meet again, but as always when I had transgressed a boundary, I still had a bad conscience when later that morning I left the train station and went home to sleep. Now I can't recall anything of what he said back then, only one episode remains in my memory and even that is fragmented. He was an anaesthesiologist, that I remember, and he had worked for a helicopter ambulance service, I remember that too, for he told me how it had been to land in tiny communities, along the shores of a fjord or on one of the islands where a fjord opens towards the sea, the mood of despair and panic they would sometimes encounter. And then he told me something I no longer remember fully, only a part of it, which therefore no longer makes sense. But in one of the houses they had visited, with the helicopter standing outside, one must assume, in the rain in autumn, perhaps, a person had appeared who didn't exist. Whether this person had appeared in a photograph but not in reality, or the other way round, in reality but not in a photograph, I don't remember. I only remember him sitting there, on the floor of the train compartment, surrounded by a pale summer-night light and holding a beer bottle in his hand, while I lay on my side in the upper bunk with my head supported on my hand, looking at him. He didn't look at me, he gazed straight ahead while he told the story. *Duh-dunk, duh-dunk, duh-dunk* sounded from the wheels striking the joints between the rails beneath us, the feeling of rushing headlong across the landscape. The rain and the darkness which he spoke about, the helicopter coming in for landing, the speed with which everything happens. And then the dead person who was there, seemingly alive.

The things he told me about his life, which shook me so,

I have completely forgotten. But I have a notion that I wouldn't have been as shocked if I heard them today; back then I was in my early twenties and almost unpardonably naïve.

Perhaps I still was, in the eyes of Henry Marsh?

He was sitting on a sun lounger with a computer on his lap, dressed in a light blue shirt, the sky above us was pale grey, almost white, the water in the pool in front of us as transparent as glass. He had just written a new book, he had sent me the first pages, they were from Nepal, where he had worked for a few months at a time in recent years, as far as I understood. Once I received an email from him while he was there, he wrote that several of his patients had died. The darkness contained in that sentence, the medieval aspect of cutting through people's skulls and sucking out brain matter, was completely gone from my mind when I was with him, then I never thought about the fact that patients had died while in his hands, nor was death ever present when I watched him operating in Albania, it wasn't in the room, and if death had occurred there, amid all that light and surrounded by all those instruments and screens, it would have been more like a mechanical error, a car that refuses to start. Only in language, in that one sentence from Nepal, was the darkness that death brings. It is as if death in itself is nothing, merely a notion we have, which is wakened in various ways, and which perhaps also takes different forms, from the lightweight and near-insignificant at the surface of consciousness, in use almost daily, to the heavy, earthbound screaming at the very depths, which only rarely rises, perhaps no more than once or twice in a lifetime.

After about half an hour I went in to your brother again. We were going boating and packed our backpacks with swimwear and a jacket each, met one of the hotel employees at reception, she walked with us the five hundred metres to the jetty where the boat was moored. It was still overcast and no more than nineteen or twenty degrees; not unlike a Norwegian summer day, in other words. The boat was of the kind one seems to find in practically every seaside holiday resort, and in fact the jetty was packed with them, from the biggest, which could carry large groups, to the smallest, which had room for no more than five or six people. A cabin roof one could sit on, a music system, cool bags with soft drinks and beer. Our boat was fairly small, piloted by a man in his early thirties, he was friendly and helpful, spoke good English and gave your brother plenty of attention. So had everyone we had met so far in Brazil, actually, they tousled his hair and asked him various things, often jokingly. He would look down then, or over at me, after all he doesn't know very much English. But he is trusting and quickly got used to it.

We sat down on the cabin roof, it was upholstered in some sort of synthetic leather, and the captain, if one could call him that, gave us a map and a pair of binoculars, loosened the mooring rope, started the engine and propelled the boat out by pushing against the neighbouring craft with his foot. The fjord which opened up before us was magnificent, for the sea was a smooth grey, the sky milky white, all the islands and the shoreline dark green, almost black. We might have been outside Bergen. But fifteen minutes later when we passed one of the islands, the trees were palms, the forest a jungle. And the dark thing drifting over the sea floor in the little cove ahead of us was a turtle.

Your brother peered at the shoreline through the binoculars. On an overhang, maybe twenty metres up, lay some old fortifications, the cannons were intact. The captain poked his head up and told us there had been a lot of gold here and that there were several small forts in the area which had protected the seaward approach to the town. The slave trade had continued longer here than anywhere else, he said. It had been financed by the sale of spirits; that's why there were also plenty of old distilleries here.

After about an hour we anchored in a bay. The beach at the far end of it was white and fine-grained, but narrow; everywhere the forest grew almost down to the edge of the water. The captain brought out diving masks and snorkels for us and tipped the ladder at the stern into the water. He said there were turtles here. I asked if they lived here or were just passing, he said that this was their regular hangout. No sooner had he said it than a narrow neck with a small, aged face on top poked out of the water. There's one there, the captain said.

We changed into swimming trunks, I dived in, your brother clambered down the ladder. The water was cold and fresh, maybe eighteen or nineteen degrees. We put on masks and swam along, the pale sea bottom glimmered maybe four metres beneath us. After just a few metres I saw a turtle, it was as big as a child and glided slowly along right beneath me. It looked like a stone that had come to life and developed flippers and a small head. I looked for your brother, but he was heading in the other direction. I swam over to him, got him to join me, but by then the turtle was out of sight and your brother hadn't quite mastered the use of the snorkel, he just wanted to swim the regular way. So we did, and it felt strange, since the bay was perfectly quiet except for the occasional cry of a bird, the water was green and cold, and along both sides of the bay the tropical vegetation grew so densely it seemed one unbroken growth.

Our next stop was a small island, the captain tossed bananas on to the land, and soon the narrow rock slope was full of animals: four or five rat-like creatures, four or five light-footed birds that didn't seem to use their wings much, and finally, after hesitating for a long time up in the trees, six little monkeys. They were lion-coloured and had a mane around their manlike, gruff faces, they were the size of cats and had long tails. We threw bananas at them for a while and observed the myriad of events that occurred on the overhang, before we dived back in again and I swam in to land with your brother clinging to my back. Our final stop was in some shallows beyond another island, where the water was clear and full of tropical fish, which we swam among wearing our masks. I fell asleep on the way back, by then the sun had come out and the temperature had risen. At the hotel we met the babysitter, since the publishers had ignored my message that we didn't need one, or perhaps it had never reached them, she was Swedish, in her early twenties, and it turned out she lived here. I thought that might be best after all, so your brother wouldn't have to tag along with me at every literary event, where in any case I wouldn't be able to look after him. They went into town to eat lunch, while I followed the publishers' representative to a press conference. When I had seen this item in my programme, I had imagined that it would consist of a couple of journalists whom I would talk to in a reception area, but it wasn't like that, he led me into a large conference room full of people seated around a long horseshoe-shaped table. There were maybe thirty people in there. I was introduced to the interpreter and the questions began. I remember only one of them, from a woman at the end of the table, she said I wrote like a woman and wondered why that was.

When the press conference was over, I changed into trousers and shirt in our room before I strolled through the town, across the river and over to the festival hall, where Henry Marsh was speaking. There were maybe twelve hundred people there. On every seat lay a headset in which Portuguese was translated into English and English into Portuguese by three interpreters who sat in a booth at the head of the room. Henry Marsh was supposed to discuss the brain with a Brazilian scientist, but they were on separate planets, so it was more like two separate dialogues than a conversation. Marsh was of the view that we hardly knew anything about the brain, that it was a mystery, one of the greatest in the universe, while the researcher seemed to believe that we knew almost everything worth knowing about it. I don't think she even understood the underlying question, how mind and consciousness and everything that is us, everything we have been and can be, everything we believe in and perceive, can arise out of a lump of matter.

I am sitting and writing this on the ground floor of our hotel room while your brother is sleeping upstairs. It is completely dark outside, and quiet except for the few times when someone walks past on the road, and it sounds as if their voices are coming from inside the room, since the window behind the blinds is open. It is the first time I have been south of the equator at this time of year, and it feels strange that it is winter here, for in my mind it is summer.

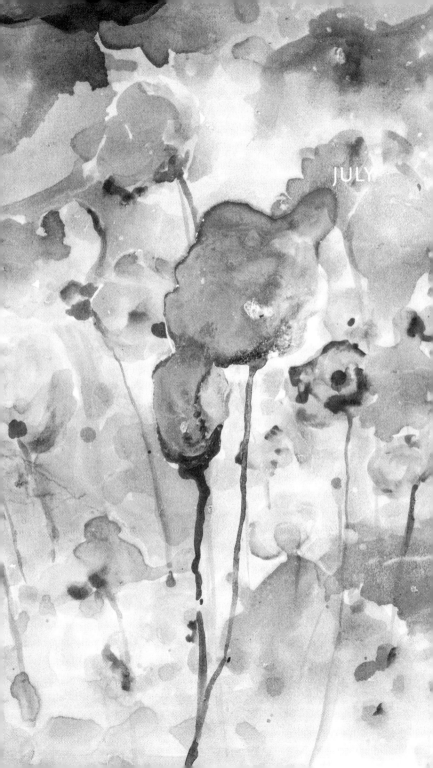

JULY

Grass Lawn

Grass is one of the most widespread plant families on earth. The vast grass-covered tracts of prairie and savannah cover more than a fifth of the earth's surface, and when you realise how densely the blades of grass grow and how many of them there are in even a relatively small area, such as the garden beyond the room where I am sitting and writing this, you come to understand that in terms of numbers, blades of grass are on a level with raindrops, grains of sand and stars. Indeed, number is a part of the essential nature of grass, rarely do you find a single blade growing by itself, and where one plant ends and another begins is usually impossible to determine, since below ground they are interconnected in a dense and intricate system of stringy roots that extends in every direction and, as it were, sews the grass fast to the soil, not singly in blades but like a carpet. Thus the grass spreads out, conquering ever greater territories. What makes it do this? Nobody knows, for plants are infinitely removed from us and the only thing we really have in common is the will to live, the will to expand. That this will is found in grass, which has no brain, no bone marrow, no nervous system, no heart or lungs, and neither nose, ears nor eyes, and which accordingly has no clue where it is, who it is, what it is nor why it is, this makes the same will within ourselves seem equally alien. Fill the earth and subdue it, the Bible says, thus opening up a lasting ambivalence, for when it is written down it no longer seems obvious, and not to subdue the earth, not to expand, suddenly becomes just as much of an option. And perhaps that ambivalence is as typical of humans as non-ambivalence is of grass. In any case, grass is closely connected with the expansion of humankind, it was with the help of grass that we subdued the earth when, thousands of years ago, we became sedentary and began cultivating grass near our dwellings in the form of cereals, which belong to the grass family, and as pastures for our cattle and small livestock. It was an alliance, for humans cultivated the soil, cleared away trees and rocks and made room for the grass, which in return was cut, dried, crushed, ground and eventually eaten, or perhaps more of a symbiosis, in which humans lived as near to the grass and were as dependent upon it as certain tiny fish are on the whales they live on and off. The same holds true today; this very moment, in the house across the lawn there is bread, pasta, flour, porridge meal, muesli and other breakfast cereals, and just beyond the bigger circle of houses the grain fields stretch out for kilometre after kilometre. The lawn has no part in any of this, it stands in the same relation to grain as the circus horse once did to the workhorse, and grows outside the house as a pure and pointless product of surplus, a feast of green, of which the grass itself is of course wholly ignorant, it simply grows, covering ground where there is ground to be covered, blade after blade. And even here, on this small lawn of roughly a third of an acre, the striking thing about the grass is its number and the greatly varied ways in which it grows. When

I mowed the lawn yesterday afternoon, pushing the droning and puttering machine in front of me through fields of light and shadow beneath the blue summer sky, this is what I was thinking about. I have mowed the lawn so many times that I am familiar with every square metre of it. Between the willow and the wall of the house where I am sitting now the grass is always a deep green, moist and luxurious, and always taller than the rest of the lawn, while along the southern fence, near the hedge, it has never really taken root and only grows in scattered clumps that spring from the naked soil. On the opposite side, beneath the trees, it has been nearly supplanted by moss, over which it lies like a layer of thin wispy hair over a scalp. By the brick wall to the east, which I seeded the autumn we moved here but which I rarely mow, since there are so many trees and flowers growing there, almost unchecked, the grass grows knee-high and the blades are as thick as reeds. This little world of grass is large enough that I can lose myself in it, and the satisfaction of knowing it so well I can only compare to that of knowing intimately the work of a painter or poet, when everything about it is familiar and yet nothing is ever exhausted.

Ice Cubes

Ice cubes are small, hard and shiny cubes of frozen water which are used mainly to cool drinks. The ice cubes produce a rustling or clinking sound when the glass they are floating around in is moved, and for many that is one of the most distinctive and joyful of noises. Glasses are generally moved with smooth gestures, from kitchen to table, from table to mouth, but when it comes to glasses with ice cubes in them, one may often observe that the hand holding the glass jiggles it a little, often without the holder paying much attention, it is done distractedly, the underlying purpose being to wrest from the ice this distinctive sound, which is like a swishing when the pieces of ice are small, more of a tinkle when there are large ice cubes in the glass. Since the ice slowly melts and turns into water, ice cubes are usually used in drinks that are already a mixture of liquids, such as water and fruit squash, gin and tonic or vodka and juice, or drinks that don't really matter, like Coke or Solo, in which the slowly melting water causes no particular damage to either taste or consistency. In organic drinks, whose taste is finely balanced and produced through considerable effort and which consequently have an air of exclusivity about them, ice cubes are rarely used – this goes for white and red wine, but also for port, champagne and beer. Since beer is less exclusive than wine, it is not a sign of poor taste to put ice in your beer, it's merely odd, and in fact I don't think I have ever seen anyone do it, while putting ice cubes in a glass of good wine is considered vulgar and a sign of low breeding. For writers the clink of ice cubes in a glass is an abiding topos and an ever-present possibility when the text requires the description of a summer scene, because precisely that sound is so evocative and seems to contain the very essence of summer – the afternoon sun in the sky, the warm air, the well-dressed people on the veranda, their tanned faces and white teeth, the hum of their voices, the smell of grilled meat, the hostess who takes a quick sip of her glass and sets it down on the sideboard to go inside and check on something, while the man she was just speaking to also takes a sip of his drink, which he then continues to hold in his hand as he looks out over the garden and then in across the veranda, at all the naked shoulders and bare arms, all the routinely smiling faces. The cubes in the glass give off a tinkling sound as he jiggles it distractedly. It is as if the sound brings him back, for he looks down into his glass, ascertains that it is nearly empty and goes over to the sideboard to refill it. As he stands there waiting for the woman in front of him to finish, the hostess comes to the door and their eyes meet. She quickly averts her gaze. A little too quickly, he thinks and grips the bottle of gin, pours some into his glass, fills it up with tonic and two or three ice cubes and watches them slowly capsizing in the clear, fizzy liquid, rather like icebergs, he muses, and without thinking takes another cube, which he closes his fingers around as he walks over to the place where he was standing before. At first the ice is dry against his palm, as if it is burning, but then it becomes slippery and wet, and the nature of the pain changes and becomes insignificant. Each ice cube is a tiny triumph, a tiny piece of winter that has been transported into summer, where its coldness is no longer something unpleasant that one has to protect oneself against but rather something pleasant that one opens oneself up to with relish. The opposite of this, a tiny piece of summer which is stored and taken out during winter, does not exist, for heat speeds up processes, cold causes them to stop, and this is so because everything comes from nothing, and because nothing, the void, is also void of warmth and empty of motion. That is the starting point, which all heat and all motion defy simply by existing. If the motion and the heat cease, they become nothing. Motion and heat cannot be preserved, only reborn, only projected ever further, which gives life its hysterical and manic aspect, which the ice cubes are also given their share of when they are introduced into summer, for in them too speed increases, they are transformed, they turn into water, which trickling or sloshing, splashing or streaming, lapping or purling, burbling or billowing is caught up by the great wheel of nature that turns slowly between earth and sky and keeps everything going.

Seagulls

I have always lived near the sea, so gulls and their squawking have been a part of my life for as long as I can remember. In the housing development where I grew up, they sat on chimneys or rooftops or lamp posts with wings folded close to the body, which was shiny white on the underside and ash grey on top. They were larger than both crows and magpies, weighing maybe a kilo, and their wingspan was considerable, you realised that when they stood up and unfolded their wings, taking to the air with a couple of wingbeats. On days when a strong wind was blowing, they would hang like pennants over the sound. Their characteristic squawks, with their long-drawn-out descending tones, which grew shorter and shorter like the rhythm of a wobbling coin coming to rest on a tabletop, seemed sad somehow and filled with loneliness. From my early childhood I have associated the squawking of gulls with the emptiness of summer, that sunlit void which we try not to sense by keeping busy. Back then the mood I perceived in their squawking probably mirrored my own loneliness, but later on I heard something else in it, almost a condition, as if the cry of a seagull articulated the very meaninglessness of life's struggle. A shrill and unpleasing noise, deeply melancholy, emitted by creatures who would gather in huge flocks at landfills, where they tore plastic bags with their beaks and snatched up whatever scraps of food they could find, who trailed behind tractors ploughing the fields as well as fishing boats out at sea, who sat on rooftops gazing down at outdoor restaurants, ready to swoop down on the tables as soon as anything edible was left behind, who balanced on rubbish bins and jabbed their beaks into whatever was in them, or who attacked other birds and took whatever morsels of food they had got hold of. Yes, maybe that was it, that the sound of their squawking was transplanted back into a time when there were no people, when life was blind and mechanical and living things were like automatons driven by hunger and thirst and the desire for reproduction, confined to a small space for action under impassive stars, greedy, brutal, primitive – a colossal lizard lying on a wave-swept rock, a maw crushing an egg as the gooey white runs down its jaw and the tiny body within crunches between sharp teeth – and that all this is still present today, on the periphery of human life and visible in seagulls in particular, as they hang over us like a pall, observing our every move, always prepared to force their way in should an opening appear with something to eat in it. This is the gap, between us and them, between the prehuman and the human, that is bridged by their squawking. And their alienness is terrible, because it makes clear to us that we too are alien to ourselves and to our own presence here. Not that I thought about this on the summer nights when we would go ashore on the islets beyond the island where I grew up and gulls on the wing would come screaming, flying straight down at us, when the fear I felt was as primitive as the instincts that made them protect their young. But many years later, when I was at my father's mother's house, which lay on a small heath with a view over the harbour and the town, and I saw the gull she was feeding, what struck me was its terribleness. It was enormous, we could see it coming from several hundred metres away, a tiny speck that grew larger and larger as it approached the veranda. It braked with its long broad wings, and when it landed on the balustrade or on the cement floor, it took possession of the whole veranda as if it owned it. If there wasn't any food there, it rapped its beak on the window. Grandmother found it comical, and so it was, for the bird was like a sailor standing there waiting for the door to his onshore lodgings to open; it glanced away, as if with arms behind its back; it knocked again. But when she went out to it with a scrap of food in her hand, it was the gull who brought out what was bird-like about her. Bent nearly double she quickly laid the food on the veranda floor, and the big gull snatched the morsel up with its beak, jerked its head back and swallowed it whole, all the while staring straight ahead, as if it had no connection with its surroundings. And thus the difference between them, the old woman and the large bird, who met there every day, became manifest too, for as the bird flew out over the harbour, now growing smaller and smaller, she turned to me with a look in her eyes of warmth and amusement, the two evolutionary advances represented by humans, and which I believe have come about to help us bear the burden of consciousness.

Banana Flies

In the summer our house is full of tiny insects. They gather wherever there is food or the remains of food; if I lift a tomato from the bowl on the kitchen windowsill, a swarm immediately takes off, if I take an apple from the fruit tray on the living room table, the same thing happens, if I leave the used cups and saucers in the sink for a few hours before I do the dishes or am slow to clear the table after a meal, the dishes soon acquire a faint, shadowy tinge where these microscopic creatures congregate. Only a few minutes ago I saw just that, one of my daughters had made French toast with a friend before they left to go swimming, they hadn't cleaned up afterwards and a cloud of tiny midges rose from the burned, egg-soaked slices of bread. I carried them into the kitchen and threw them in the bin. Shortly after, as I was putting crockery into the dishwasher, her elder sister shouted from the dining room, 'Where's my food?' I went in and told her I had thrown it away. 'You threw away my food?' she said. 'I haven't had breakfast! How could you throw away my food?' 'It's nearly two o'clock,' I said. 'It's not my fault that you slept through breakfast.' 'But it was on the table,' she said. 'You can't just throw away my food!' 'It was covered in flies,' I said. She snorted and went back to the living room, where she stayed watching TV while I came in here and googled 'small flies'. They were probably banana flies, I gathered, and I sat there looking at a greatly enlarged image of one specimen, which with its big glowing red eyes looked like something from hell. One of my brother's girlfriends did some work on banana flies, I remembered, she was a biologist and used them in her research, primarily because they reproduced so quickly, and there was also something about their genes being very uncomplicated. I haven't seen her for nearly twenty years, and since then I haven't heard a single person talk about banana flies, which isn't so strange, a banana fly is the king of insignificance, a mote of dust which has crossed the boundary from matter to biology and which even in the company of hundreds of its fellow genus members is unable to create anything more substantial than a shadow in the room. They are so tiny, their lives are so brief, and there are so many of them that their existence seems to take place on the fringes of life, albeit not to them, who see the glowing red eyes of their fellows everywhere about them through unconscious days long as years filled with orgiastic feasting on juicy rotten fruit, spoilt meat and fermenting sugar, and with egg-laying, which occurs all around them when it is hot and humid. In *The Circe*, a book from the Renaissance, Giambattista Gelli wrote dialogues between Odysseus and the people whom Circe had turned into animals, she had given him the power to change them back, but only if they themselves wanted it. Odysseus spoke with ten different animals, none of them want to be changed back; human life was the punishment, animal life was freedom. This must be so also for the banana fly. If it had been capable of complaining, it would not have, for it has everything, and it neither reflects upon the meaning of what it is doing or on the death that awaits, it just sits there on the sun-warmed overripe tomato, helping itself to its delights. Just beyond it, on top of the wood stove, some cat food has stood untouched for three days, and in the summer heat a large gathering of white worms has made its way there, they are crawling around in the brown meat sauce looking like tiny live cigars, and they don't seem to lack for anything either. On every wall and glass pane houseflies are sitting, in every corner spiders and harvestmen are crawling, and at regular intervals a wasp or a bumblebee strays in through one of the open windows, or some ants or small beetles cross the threshold. In the summer the house is not only a dwelling place for all this life, in some cases it is also the place where it is generated and hatched out, in the wake of our lives, as it were, in everything we don't want or have no use for, like the rubbish bins, lukewarm with the remains of food, or the cool dusty cellars, or the warm spaces between the damp clothes in the laundry basket. That I have just filled a glass with vinegar, which the banana flies will seek out and drown in, thrown the cat food into the rubbish, rinsed the bowl and placed it in the dishwasher, tied the tops of the bin bag and put it in the dustbin out by the road, loaded the washing machine with laundry and turned it on, as well as throwing away all the fruit that had gone soft, this doesn't change anything as far as the flies are concerned. To a banana fly, life is like a duty watch. When its watch is over, someone else takes its place. What the banana flies are watching over is what once brought them across from the other side, that shadow of life which they possess and which lives on in others when they themselves are swallowed up in vinegar and return to being motes of dust.

Cherry Tree

The cherry tree is relatively modest in size and has an unspectacular shape, little about it attracts attention, and to me, who is unable to recognise and name trees other than pine, spruce, birch, oak, rowan and aspen, the cherry trees that grow in the forest are almost wholly anonymous, merely trees among other trees which I pass without noticing, not unlike the quiet pupils in class, those who were neither very clever nor very dull, neither very beautiful nor very ugly, and whose faces and names it could be difficult to remember in later years, at least if one moved away and didn't see them again. Nevertheless, to this silent childhood flock anything can happen, of course: suddenly you see one of them on TV, she has distinguished herself in one way or another, become the head of a non-profit organisation or been appointed to a political office, or you run into them on the street in one of the big cities, and it isn't you who recognises them, for they have changed beyond recognition, it is they who come over and say hello, self-confident and smartly dressed, the kind of people one notices, and since you can't immediately place them and this is visible in your face, they say, *You probably don't remember me, but we were in the same class in primary school*: *Annlaug*, they might say, or *Helge* or *Frode.* That's how it is with the cherry tree, only there it is more acute, for when the cherry tree blooms in the forest, some time in the late spring or early summer, it is so magnificent, so resplendently beautiful that everything else around it fades and vanishes. Yet there is nothing ostentatious about it, for its blossoms, white or pink, are so sheer and so fragile that apart from immense beauty they also radiate a kind of bashfulness, which makes the cherry tree hard not to like. There it stands, radiant, a feast of light amid the suddenly coarse and primitive green. And once you have seen that, a cherry tree blossoming in the forest, you won't forget what kind of tree is standing there when you pass its modest shape in autumn or winter. In the place I grew up there were two cherry trees in the woods, both of them close to the road, and although I did think they were lovely when they flowered, still it was their fruit that made them stand out in my mind, for when the cherries arrived in July we could sit in the trees for hours, eating and talking. More often than not we were unable to wait until they ripened and became dark red and soft, but instead began eating them while they were still hard and sour, with merely a hint of sweetness. That the cherry tree probably originated in an area that now lies within Iran and Iraq, and that it spread to the Mediterranean region and was highly valued in both Greek and Roman antiquity – the Romans introduced it into the countries they conquered, bringing it with them, for instance, to Great Britain – this we knew nothing about as we sat there gorging ourselves on an island in southern Norway in the 1970s. There was also a cherry tree in our garden, I remember now, it was planted when we moved in, and when I looked at it through the window, it sometimes struck me that the cherry tree and I were roughly the same age, that it would have been in the class below mine if trees had gone to school. The last time I saw it, I was twelve and it was eleven. So now it is forty-six years old, if it is still alive, and no doubt considerably taller than the house, whereas compared to the tree I myself have grown hardly at all.

Mackerel

The Atlantic or Norwegian mackerel is a streamlined, strong and swift fish without a swim bladder, which has to keep moving in order to get enough oxygen. It is relatively small, up to forty centimetres long, and it swims in shoals, which can comprise several thousand individual fish. There are two separate populations of Atlantic mackerel, one lives in western Atlantic waters, the other in the eastern Atlantic. The eastern stock migrates as far south as the Mediterranean Sea and as far north as Iceland. Mackerel prefer water warmer than six degrees, and move closer to shore along the Norwegian coast in summer. There the arrival of the mackerel is a major event, since it is a sure sign of summer, as the return of migratory birds is a sign of spring. But also because mackerel fishing is so different from other forms of fishing. Most of the fish along the coast of Norway are relatively solitary, each on their own they rest near the sea floor close to shore or swim alone in deep waters, and even in areas that are rich in fish a long time can pass between one nibble on the line and the next. The fish hook hangs suspended in the water down below, rather like a beggar standing on a little-visited street, and the few fish swimming by ignore the hook just as people ignore the beggar.

Now and again a fish will bite, as the occasional person will stop and toss a coin into the proffered cup. With the mackerel things are different. It arrives in such huge numbers, the sea begins to boil around the shoal, and it will take any bait at all, rather as if the gates of a sports arena were to swing open near the beggar and thousands of people suddenly came pouring out. Although relatively speaking there are no more people giving than there were before, perhaps fewer, the number of people is now so huge that money pours into the cup. And with the mackerel, number is everything. Nearly a billion tons of mackerel are caught every year around the world. And yet the mackerel is not an endangered species, on the contrary stocks are increasing, in large part because its natural predators, such as sharks and whales, have been decimated, and because climate change favours the mackerel. A female mackerel in its prime can spawn up to half a million eggs a year, the mackerel's lifespan is up to twenty years, and it can travel in shoals as long as nine kilometres. Fishing mackerel is therefore a feast, a fever, a frenzy. When you are out in a boat trolling for fish on a sunny summer afternoon, or standing on shore fishing with a rod, sometimes you can see the mackerel moving in, the water begins to boil as if a crew of divers were down there. And at once the nibbles begin. All you have to do is to pull up long chains of thrashing fish, unhook them, toss them in the bucket and drop the line out again. At other times the mackerel arrives without warning: suddenly there are urgent nibbles. But the excitement is the same, and it is impossible not to get caught up in it. When you have been trolling out in a boat for hours without getting more than a few fish, perhaps none, and fishing consists of waiting and hoping for something that is rarely if ever granted, when one is used to waiting for nothing, then pulling up fish after fish becomes something almost unreal, as seeing all one's wishes fulfilled nearly always is. The boundless is a joy, the inexhaustible is a miracle. But also a curse, at least that's what I thought, or rather sensed, on those occasions during my childhood when we were out in the boat fishing and happened upon a school of mackerel. First came the excitement, for we hadn't felt a nibble in a long time, and since the mackerel is strong and agile, the line jumped and jerked. The mackerel has a greenish or blueish back with dark vertical stripes, while the underbelly is all white, so when you pull up the line, you suddenly see them gleaming whitely down in the deep, or glowing greenly, and it is beautiful, for the ocean is impenetrable and full of secrets, the sky is blue and deep, the coming of the afternoon breeze breaks up the surface in choppy waves, and back on the shore the trees are rocking back and forth, flickering in the glare of the sun, which now hangs high above us. We can taste the salt sea-spray on our lips, and the fish are glinting and gleaming down below, growing bigger as they are pulled towards the surface, no longer small gem-like stones, but living creatures with large empty eyes. When they are pulled over the gunwale – there are five – I tear out the hooks quickly and carelessly, there's no time to coax them out, or so I am thinking, for the line has to go out again at once. Then it changes and the excitement turns to nausea, for there are now so many fish in the boat, many more than we need, and yet we don't stop, we just go on and on, pulling in fish after fish, we are past utility, we are past reason, we have caught the fever of the inexhaustible, we are intoxicated by overabundance. I probably felt this way because I was so young, I was only twelve and wasn't able to handle the sense of the over-whelming very well. For in Dad's face I couldn't find even a shadow of unease, he was happy, and I now think that boundlessness corresponded to something within him, and that during that hectic hour out at sea he was free.

Wasps

Wasps lead brief and intense lives within an intricately constructed society in which every individual has a precisely defined role and specific duties. There is no room for doubt or hesitation among wasps, nor is there a place for improvisation or individual considerations, and I suppose that is why wasps and wasp societies are often thought of as robotic: within their nest everything occurs with automatic precision, functioning like the parts of a machine or a clock. It is presumably also why we have such a general idea of wasps; a wasp settling on the edge of a glass of squash is seen as a representative of the species, and to us it is really the same wasp whether the glass is in a garden in Stavern in south-eastern Norway or on Funen in Denmark, in Löderup in south-eastern Sweden or on Karmøy in south-western Norway. Naturally, that's not how the wasp sees it. It knows only its own community, its own nation, which is located in a precise spot nearby, under the eaves of a house, in a garage, beneath an uprooted tree, on a branch or in a small burrow in the ground. One such nest may shelter as few as ten wasps or as many as five thousand. These individuals have grown up together and live their brief lives together, tight-knit and closely packed yet untroubled and conflict-free in a system which at all times ensures the common good. If one were to compare their nests with anything from the history of human social organisation, the Greek city states would perhaps represent the closest fit: each town is self-governing and has its own characteristics, but the same language is spoken in every town and they all share basically the same culture. So if the wasp on our glass for one reason or other were to fly off to some other nest, everything would seem familiar to it yet it would still be a foreigner, rather like an Athenian in Sparta. Of course, this doesn't make the wasps either democrats or philosophers, we shouldn't expect to find a Heraclitus or a Sophocles among them, and it is precisely the difference between their sophisticated social machinery and their great intellectual limitations which makes wasps so interesting, for how can they construct something like that when they themselves are obviously incapable of either conceiving of or understanding it? This thing which none of them has ever taken charge of and yet every spring it is recreated, everywhere in the world, and has been for million of years? They follow their instincts, that is true, but who put together the various instincts so that this magnificent whole, this feat of social engineering, could develop? Good fortune? Trial and error? Or are they following a plan which God has given them? In autumn, when all the wasps die, their queen goes into hibernation, like the sole survivor of a great catastrophe. She wakes up again in spring, begins to build the nest, lays eggs, gathers food for the larvae, defends the nest against hostile intruders, until the larvae are fully grown, then they take over her duties so she can concentrate on producing more of them. Therefore the first generation of wasps in a nest never comprises very many individuals, being limited by the queen's work capacity, while the second generation is much more numerous, and also physically larger, since it is better fed. The first generation dies off, the second brings forth a third. The average lifespan of a worker in a wasp society is around six weeks. During this time it builds cells, flies out gathering food for the queen and the larvae, feeds them, cleans and guards the nest, sometimes posted at the entrance, like a soldier or a sentinel. Owing to all these activities, which so resemble our own and which we use the same words for, practically every description of the inner life of a wasps' nest will have an element of familiarity about it, as if wasps were not fundamentally that different from us, whereas in reality they are probably infinitely foreign, infinitely removed from the human world. But are they automatons, are they like little machines that have no soul? When on an early summer morning a wasp crawls out of the nest and flies through the forest, through which the rays of the sun fall in broad shafts of light, and where there are shadowy niches, green and mild and warm, heading west towards a garden it knows of, is it then perfectly untouched by the world, is it like the hand of a clock, moving mechanically? There lies the garden, and there are all the orange poppies, their flowers as big as cups. It lands on the edge of one of them, crawls down along the soft wall and sucks the nectar up with its proboscis, and is soon nearly completely covered in pollen. When it has had enough, and it always knows when it has had enough and needs to return home, it takes off and flies back, very low over the ground, almost touching the tall dry blades of grass that rise above the meadow, and then in between the tree trunks, where the rays of sun cannot reach and it is dim and silent, and at last across the final open stretch to the nest, which is built out of material from a dried-out bog, past the wasps guarding it and into the warm humid nest, where there is creeping and crawling everywhere and where all is familiar and nothing foreign exists. The wasp will have seen all this, but probably won't have experienced any of it, the world will have seemed much nearer to it, indistinguishable from itself, since it lacks that contemplative space which always lies between the world and us. So if one wanted to compare the wasp with anything human, the human being as a whole wouldn't do, it would have to be its separate body parts. The heart no more knows the reason it is beating than the wasps' queen knows why she begins to build a nest. The signals that pass between brain cells know no more about the kind of thoughts they are transporting than the wasp knows what the nectar it is carrying really is. The human body is also a community, within which all the different parts have specific tasks and roles which they perform continuously without being conscious of either their tasks or of themselves. And if consciousness could arise in this community, out of its separate parts, uniting it, as it were, under one single thought – *This is me* – then it isn't inconceivable that it could arise out of the wasps' community too. Perhaps it already has. But in a form so alien to our own consciousness that it is impossible for us to recognise as such.

Stunt Show

The stuntmen wore crash helmets with visors, which made their heads look big compared to the rest of their bodies, and in a paradoxical way this made them seem more vulnerable; their heads looked like eggs. For the rest they were dressed in full leathers, the kind that racing drivers and motorcyclists wear. The leathers were not black but red or blue with bands of white. Even though their names were presumably announced over the sound system each time they were about to perform a stunt, they were still anonymous, similar to how circus artists are anonymous; whatever breakneck feats they brought off belonged to the show, not to them. Where they came from I don't know, nor where they were going; all I know is that they were at Bjønnes in Arendal one summer in the 1970s, and that I was among the audience. I have no idea whom I saw the show with, nor am I sure of what I actually saw and what I have added later. The stunt show belongs to the circle of my early memories and really consists of only a very few vague images. A motorcycle driving straight ahead across the gravel to gain speed, the sputter of its engine rising to a whine, the whirling dust, and then it drives up a ramp and flies through the air, over a row of parked cars, landing on the other side. The number of cars was gradually upped, I remember. And therein lay the excitement: would he make it this time too? Or would he land on the car? What would happen then? I also remember fire but can't really understand how they could have used flames in the show, did they jump through something that was burning? Or was it the stuntmen themselves who were on fire? In the kind of suits they used in films? My final mental image definitely can't be an actual memory, for it involves a man diving from a tower into a tank of water. Or can it?

A big open space a bit outside the town centre, right among the wooden houses, between which plenty of green plants and leafy trees grew in summer, one early evening in which the sun still stood high in the sky yet the town was already quiet; the few streets that made up the town centre must have been nearly deserted, and all the shadows long, with only the occasional tourist strolling down them past the closed shops.

There must have been a couple of hundred spectators at the venue, perhaps more, the mood excited and a little giddy prior to the show, one of cathartic release when it was over and people began to leave.

What did the attraction consist of? Why did images from the show lodge in my memory when nearly every other image from that time has vanished?

So much of the 1970s came together in the stunt show. Especially the aesthetics of the decade, that part which had to do with Formula 1 and racing cars, the full leathers, the crash helmets, the carelessness, the rock-star-like appeal of the drivers, who sometimes died in burning car wrecks, whose style we recognised in the motorcyclists who stopped at the Fina petrol station in the summer and also in the coolest boys, whose mopeds may have merely looked almost like motorcycles but whose crash helmets, on the other hand, were just as frightening as Niki Lauda's or Ronnie Peterson's.

But the most important element was the presence of death. While the tightrope walkers and circus acrobats merely toyed with death and always kept well on the safe side of it, which I understood intuitively, the stunt show seemed to entail something different and more dangerous, since the death within it was motorised. That too brought it closer to us, who were surrounded by motors of every description, from boat motors to those of cars, motorcycles, bulldozers, trucks and articulated lorries. At the circus death was a tightly controlled pantomime, and the stunt show too was a pantomime, but not as controlled; once the engine was started, anything could happen. Death was in the speed, and death was in the petrol, which in an accident might catch fire and explode.

Although I don't remember it, I must have gone to bed that night too, lain down in the warm room which the sun had heated all through the afternoon and evening, closed my eyes in the dim light and felt my own thin body lying there beneath the duvet, while ever-changing images of motorcycles, cars and violent flames kept gliding across my mind, connecting me directly to a distant but glorious and fantastic reality.

Playgrounds

Playgrounds are demarcated areas with apparatuses especially built for children and intended for play, such as swings – or *ronser*, as we called them in our local dialect – slides, climbing frames and sandpits. I don't know the history of playgrounds but I assume they originated in cities at about the same time that childhood was set apart from the rest of life, while simultaneously the state began to assume responsibility for all its aspects, that is in the early post-World War II period. For in fact there is nothing spontaneous about playgrounds, they show none of the signs of things that develop organically, but look rather as if they have been planned from above and then lowered onto society, in accordance with overarching notions of public health, welfare, well-being. In cities, with their countless roads, cars and houses, the creation of restricted spaces where children could play safely represented a rational and adequate solution, but the idea was also exported to the countryside, to smaller and more rural communities which of course already had large open spaces and plenty of room for children to play in, and there playgrounds came to have a rather contrived and uniform air, as if the objective were to force children's play into these ready-made forms. In the place I grew up too, a 1970s housing development, a playground had been laid out. It consisted of a tall swing constructed from metal pipes with paired chains with a wooden board between them suspended from the crossbeam, a wooden box with sand in it, a boat-like construction, also made of metal, with two seats facing one another in which one could sit rocking back and forth since the seats were fastened to two rounded runners, and finally a see-saw, consisting of a long plank mounted on a small block of cement, where two could sit facing each other and bob up and down. The playground lay at the foot of a steep slope below the road near the supermarket, as far as I remember it was already there before the supermarket was built, bounded by a small wood on one side and a marshy area on the other. It was never maintained; the municipal authorities, whose decision it had been to construct it, must later have forgotten that it existed, and left unattended it gradually fell into decay. The chains rusted, the planks bleached in the sun and cracked in the rain, grass grew up along the boards of the sandpit and little by little erased the distinction between the pit and the surrounding nature, paint flaked from the rocking boat, and after only a few years it was no longer a clearly defined place but rather a few dilapidated playground apparatuses rusting in a forest glade with a faintly post-apocalyptic aura about them. Just thirty metres away stood a wrecked car with broken windows, surrounded by slender young willows and small birches, and another broken-down car stood in a copse of trees on the far side of the wood lining the playground, maybe a hundred metres away, and somehow or other all this belonged together, we would just as happily climb into one of the wrecked cars as onto the swings or the see-saw, for children don't care whether something looks nice or not, the important thing is what you can do with it and whether it frees up your imagination. Not so long ago I spoke to an acquaintance who told me about his father's childhood in a German town after the Second World War, they would play in the ruins, where they found weapons and occasionally also dead people who had not yet been removed. It made me think of the bunkers we used to play in, they were also from the war and the most exciting place to play of all. We too had vague expectations of finding weapons and dead soldiers, although the war had ended more than thirty years before. Other places we played were construction sites, full of large mounds of recently blasted-out rocks where we gathered bits of blasting wire and bulldozers we could climb around on, piles of cement pipes which we balanced on or crawled into, and those bobbin-like contraptions with wire wound around them, which were the height of a man. These places represented a principle that was the polar opposite of the playground, whose order and formulaic reason is a kind of bureaucratic utopia and essentially foreign to children's imagination, which thrives best amid things that are broken or have not yet come into being.

The Bat

Only once have I seen a bat close up. I have seen them from a distance many times; in nearly every place I have lived, there have been bats. But they move so fast and their flight pattern is so unpredictable that I have only caught sight of them in glimpses. From when I was thirteen until I was eighteen we lived in an old house on a hillside above a river, at the edge of the forest. If I stood at the window in my room on a summer evening I would often see them, they appeared abruptly against the pale sky and vanished just as quickly into the dark of the trees. My mother and father got divorced during this period, and when I was eighteen and about to leave home, my mother moved to western Norway, so one day in July a huge removal van drove up the gravel road to our house and took away everything it contained. I re-member it as a chaotic period – while they were getting divorced my mother found out that she had a tumour in her stomach, so when the removal van pulled up a few days later outside the new house she was renting, which also lay by a river, in a valley between Jølster and Førde, I was the only one there to receive it, since she was in hospital having an operation. Some hours later, packing cases and furniture crowded the rooms on the ground floor of the new house. I was used to being alone, but being alone in an unfamiliar house was different, and all those packing cases didn't exactly make it more homely. I hunted around for the coffee maker and unpacked it, found some pots and plates, cutlery, glasses and cups, placed them in the kitchen cupboards, ate a few slices of bread, drank coffee and had a smoke while I looked out at the rain pouring down, the luminous green colours of the landscape. It felt chaotic and I was anxious, but at the same time I was filled with a strong feeling of freedom: everything I had had up to now, all that until now had been my life, I was putting behind me. I began carrying the packing cases into the rooms, placing them against the walls for the time being to free up more space, and then I provisionally set out the furniture. A number of paintings and framed pictures leaned against each other beneath the window. I took the outermost one, a reproduction of *Marsh Marigold Night* by Nikolai Astrup which had hung on our wall for as long as I could remember, intending to carry it upstairs. On the back of the canvas hung a little bat. When I caught sight of it, I was terror-stricken and set the painting down at once, with the bat to the wall. I don't know why I became so frightened, the sleeping bat looked like a little black pouch, there was nothing threatening about it. But I felt panicked, my heart was beating fast. I put on a rain jacket and went outside, down to the river, which flowed green and swollen, foaming in places, past the slender birches that grew densely along the bank and shimmered in the evening light. I sat down on a stone. The sound of cars driving by was nearly indistinguishable from the rushing of the river. I had to get the bat out of the house. And it wasn't difficult, all I had to do was carry the canvas outside and maybe give the creature a little poke with a broom handle or something, then it would fly away. But as soon as I thought of the bat, my body reacted as if I was standing in front of an abyss, everything rose within me, and the tips of my fingers and toes tingled. How ridiculous, it's just a little mouse with wings, I thought, and went back in to remove it. The painting stood as I had left it. Carefully, I lifted it up. There was a scratching sound. I resisted the impulse to throw the canvas down, instead I ran towards the doorway holding the painting in both hands. The next instant the bat flew up in front of me and began flitting around the room. Bloody hell! I hurried outside and closed the door behind me, crossed the road and walked over to the same stone. The pouring rain, the heavy grey sky, the shimmering white birches, the dark green moss, the water gliding rapidly past me. Who could be afraid of a little bat? What kind of person allowed himself to be driven out of his house by it? Sitting there like that, out in the open, my sense of proportion returned, and I told myself that I had to remember this when I went back inside, how small and insignificant and harmless the bat really was, it was merely within me that it was overpowering. I had to get it out of there, I couldn't sleep with a bat in the house. After a while I went back inside. It was hanging on the living room wall now, not moving. I located the red plastic bucket among the packing cases, the one which had once melted a little on one side and looked like a face, tiptoed over to the wall holding the bucket in front of me. Took one step, stood still, took another step. When I was standing right in front of it, I lifted the bucket carefully, and then I slammed it against the wall as hard and fast as I could. The bat flapped about inside, beating against the sides of the bucket. Pressing the mouth of the bucket to the wall, I slowly moved it downwards. When I reached the skirting, I waited until I was certain that the bat was well inside before I plonked the bucket against the floor. The bat struggled to free itself, its wings striking against the smooth plastic. I left the room, closed the door behind me, went upstairs to the bedroom and closed that door too. Even though I was separated from the bat by three walls that it would never be able to pass through, I had trouble falling asleep, the awful sound of its flapping was hard to shake off, but at last I drifted into sleep. The next morning I avoided the living room, and after I had eaten breakfast in the kitchen I took the bus to Førde and visited my mother in the hospital. She told me the tumour was nearly the size of a football and that for a long time she had been in denial of its existence, that she didn't know how things would turn out. When I got back to the house in the afternoon I found a spanner that had been left behind in the shed, went into the living room, lifted the bucket carefully. The bat lay motionless on the floor, and I closed my eyes and struck it as hard as I could with the spanner, set the bucket down over it again just in case, fetched a towel from the bathroom, lifted the bucket, caught a quick glimpse of the bat, closed my eyes again and placed the big towel over it, opened my eyes, folded the towel so that the bat was inside it, carried it outside, shook the towel and saw the little black creature tumble out onto the grass. After putting the towel in the washing machine I went back outside, crossed the road and sat down on the stone by the river once more in an attempt to regain the strong feeling of freedom I had had in the preceding days, the sense that my whole life lay ahead of me, that I could do whatever I wanted with it. But it was impossible, the guilt I felt was too strong, everything within me gravitated towards it. And this is how it has been whenever the gates of freedom have opened before me later in life, I have never felt guilt-free enough to walk through them. To kill guilt, as a free life demands, is something I have never had the strength for.

Barbecue

If you walk in a residential area outside the centre of a Scandinavian town on a sunny afternoon or evening in summer
from early June to late August there will always be a smell of
grilled food coming from one or several places. The smell and
the accompanying sounds, the chink of cutlery, shouts or conversation, often make me think that each family is a separate
unit, for they each live in a house of their own, in a garden of
their own, enclosed by their own hedge, in the driveway or the
garage they each have their own car, and at regular intervals
during the summer half of the year, when the weather per-
mits they each gather around their own barbecue. Barbecuing
may be seen as the spearhead of the family's activities, the
pinnacle of their joint achievement, for not only does it require coordination and cooperation, it also takes place in that
zone of family life which is the closest to other families and
therefore the most visible. The potential for failure is greater;
a teenaged son screaming at his parents, a mother who gets
drunk, children who are out of control, or the opposite, a
family grilling their food silently and eating without exchanging a word, might be seen by someone outside the family, the
neighbours, a child who comes by to play at the house, casual
passers-by. That outside gaze, which one is protected from

within the walls of the house, is of course harmless in itself, it doesn't matter what other people think, but it can leave an indelible mark on some or all the members of the family, so that whatever is dysfunctional within the family unit, which they may have repressed or made excuses for, suddenly becomes apparent. That regardless of this, most families still get the grill out of the garage or the basement at the start of the summer doesn't mean that all families are happy and well-functioning units but rather that barbecuing has great symbolic effect, and that preparing food outdoors over burning coal contributes something more than merely the smoked flavour it gives the meat or fish. A kitchen stove is an integrated part of the house, an inconspicuous element of everyday life, and there is also something machine-like about it which, together with the way foodstuffs are packaged in supermarkets, makes the food's origins and connection to the world nearly invisible. The barbecue isn't machine-like, it seems more manual, more subject to physical forces, it is mobile and belongs outdoors, under the open sky. A barbecue is made of metal, often shaped like a sphere, of which the upper half serves as a lid and has a handle, while the lower half functions like a bowl or pit and contains the charcoal. Coal consists of carbonised plant matter, millions of years old and brought up from underground mines, whereas charcoal is made synthetically, by slowly heating wood in the absence of oxygen so that all moisture is removed, in an imitation of processes occurring naturally below ground. Lumps of charcoal are light in weight, dry and completely black, and pouring them into an empty barbecue affords a very particular pleasure, for they make a rustling sound as they strike against each other and tumble out of the bag with a lightness seemingly belied by their size – they ought to fall with heavy thuds – and as they fall they raise a little puff of ash particles, which the sun, if it is shining directly on the grill, causes to glitter in the air. The charcoal, archaic and evoking the world below ground, is then soaked in lighter fuel, which at first makes the lumps shiny and wet and may cause the air above them to quiver for a few seconds but is then absorbed by them. The charcoal is then ready to be lit. Charcoal doesn't burn in the same way a campfire does, somehow or other it is as if the flames have a more tenuous connection to charcoal than to the logs of wood in a fireplace, they seem to dance above the charcoal, at times even darting nimbly over it, apparently almost wholly uncon-nected to it. It's enough to make you think the flames know they are not the lead actors here, that their presence is merely a guest performance, a warm-up act, for the actual barbecu-ing can only begin when the flames have done their job and the charcoal is glowing. And what a transformation it is! The lumps of charcoal, black and underworldly, in half an hour turn red and darkly luminous. Then you place a gridiron over the barbecue's bowl-shaped lower half, which is by now so hot from the glowing coals that you can't move your hand through the air above it without feeling a burning pain. While the charcoal is slowly progressing towards this intense state, the barbecue chef can prepare the food, sprinkle salt and pepper over the meat, thread the vegetables onto skewers, wrap the fish in aluminium foil, make salad, lay the table. This part of the grilling process is interesting, since the plates, the glasses, the wine and soft-drink bottles, the napkins and the bread baskets all belong to the life of the middle class, a modern carefree existence geared towards consumption, while the grill standing beside the table radiates only archaic and elemental forces: the flames, the coal, the heat of glowing eyes. The cooking pit is a primitive invention, so is the gridiron. Yes, next to the stylish bottles of olive oil and the beautiful wine glasses the grill looks like something from the Cretaceous, a three-legged fossil with fire in its depths. And that of course is why we barbecue, it affords us a glimpse into the fundamental conditions and depths of existence, which yawn open in the middle of a suburban villa garden but in controlled circumstances. Personally I love to barbecue, it feels wonderful to lay the big slabs of meat on the grill, see how the pores close and pearls of juice immediately begin to form on the surface as the steaks slowly curl at the edges, as if they were still alive, and when you turn them over see the black burn marks made by the gridiron against the golden-brown meat glistening with fat, while the smell of smoke and seared meat fills the air. We usually barbecue behind the summer house, where there is a wooden platform with an overhanging roof covered in vines, below it are tables and chairs, next to which I have placed the barbecue, against the wall of the house where I am now sitting and writing this. We are the kind of family that doesn't bring in garden furniture for the winter, so every other year the barbecue is so rusty that we buy a new one, of the cheapest kind, knowing that it too will spend the winter outdoors. Now there are three barbecues out there. This summer they haven't been in use, the wooden platform is completely overgrown, some of the weeds come up to my waist, and although it wouldn't take more than a day to fix it, I have left everything as it is, for this summer I have no longing for either middle-class security or the archaic, something in me just wants to let it all grow freely and manage on its own.

Sting

In the glove compartment of the car I keep about seventy CDs lying about, and I always pick them without looking, so as to leave something to chance. Today, driving to Malmö with the afternoon sun in my eyes, it was Sting's first solo album, *The Dream of the Blue Turtles*, that fate wanted me to hear. It was just long enough since the last time I had played it that the first chords and the chorus 'free, free, set them free' unleashed every mood I had experienced in the months when the album was new, the summer when I was sixteen and had just finished my first year at the *gymnas*. For a few seconds my soul seemed to tremble. I was filled with the most fantastic feelings. Then they retreated like a wave on a beach, one that has washed high up on the shore and left the normally dry rocks there wet, one might imagine, and I was back in the everyday, in a run-down Volkswagen Multivan, a forty-seven-year-old father of four whose death in a road accident might have made it into the daily paper, with uncut hair, straggly beard, the beginnings of a paunch and nearly a whole life between myself and the person I was thirty years ago. Life feels much better now, I know what I can do and what I can't do, but I still felt a jab of unhappiness sitting there, for placed side by side fullness of life can never compete with intensity, and my life has never been more intense than the summer I was listening to that album. I have powerful memories of every album by the Police, produced during what for Sting must have been one continuous period of his life, from when he was twenty-six to when he was thirty-three, but which to me represented different stages, infinitely far apart. *Outlandos d'Amour* – I am lying in the bath with the cassette player set on the floor, listening to the first song on Side 2 of the tape, 'Can't Stand Losing You', the autumn darkness is like a black wall against the window and the wet black tarmac glistens beneath the street lights outside. I do this every time I take a bath, I love that song, it shuts me up in a place where nothing except the song exists, its headlong-rushing energy. It drives me nearly wild with joy. *Reggatta de Blanc* – I am about to enter the sixth grade, it is summer and I am in Oslo playing football in the Norway Cup, and when I hear two older boys on the team above mine bellowing 'Message in a Bottle' in the street I feel so proud that they, who are so cool, like my music, that I almost begin bellowing along with them. *Zenyatta Mondatta* – I listen to 'Don't Stand So Close To Me' in the basement recreation room at Dag Magne's house in the spring, on the way home I see the pines tossing in the wind as I walk down the path with pine needles trampled into the soil and crooked roots spreading across bare wet rock, singing 'de do do do de da da da' loudly in my mind. *Ghost in the Machine* – I play the single from that album, 'Every Little Thing She Does Is Magic', again and again, it is the best song I have ever heard, I can't understand how not everyone shares my opinion. The rest of the album is darker, and I am hypnotised by it. *Synchronicity* – that's the first record by the Police that I don't care all that much for, but I hear 'Every Breath You Take' being played everywhere that summer, for example on a radio someone has brought along to the bathing spot below the waterfall, where we dive from the rock into a deep pool, in the new place I have moved to. When *The Dream of the Blue Turtles* is released, in 1985, I am attending a new school, in town, it's a different life, and the album too is a different album, lighter, more playful, with elements of jazz, Caribbean music, reggae, and I am in love, shut up somehow within my infatuation and the music, as if I am making use of it to light myself up. The other stuff that is going on, my parents get divorced, my father starts to drink, takes place outside me. That autumn I go to Drammen to see Sting live in concert for the first time, and I do it alone, take the train alone, stand in line alone, stand in front of the stage alone, see Sting and the fantastic band he had then, alone. When I listened to the opening track, 'If You Love Somebody Set Them Free', this afternoon, Linda was sitting in the seat next to me and our youngest daughter was in the back, we were going to Malmö to buy wallpaper, and I wondered about that peculiar variety of joy, a happiness that is closed off to the world, and what it really is, that intensely shining inner light which for a few seconds had been turned on again? It had obviously been a form of defence, something that made me invulnerable. Throughout the years of my childhood and youth I had shut myself up within my emotions, shut myself up within the light, and if music was a key, then I had used it to lock the door, not to open it. A shield of elation, that is as good a description as any of the manic state.

Rosebay Willowherb

I am sitting here behind my desk trying to understand what
memories are or what it really feels like to remember something. It is nearly ten o'clock in the evening, early July, and
the nights never get really dark, there is always a faint light in
the sky. Now it is white. The trees up by the churchyard are
dark, while the leaves on the trees in the garden just beyond
the window are green. I look at all this, at the trees outside
and the sky above them, while at the same time I see before
me the landscape I grew up in and to which I am still emotionally attached. I see before me the pebble beach at Spornes,
the colour of the pebbles washed by the sea, which seem a
shade darker than the pebbles further up the beach. I see before me the grassy field above the beach where we would lie
on towels after swimming, the sand between the blades of
grass, the pit with rocks around it which someone had used
for a campfire, charred bits of wood, other pieces nearly intact, merely singed on the sides. And I see before me the dog
roses and the thickets of blackthorn which grew further up
among the rocks, and the low, bent trees. It is as if these
images lie far inside me, while the images of the trees and
the sky are outside. It is the latter that I *see*, through my eyes,
but what do I see my memories with, and how can they be

there inside me, so clearly visible, at the same time as I am looking at something else? When just now I happened to stare down at the tabletop as I stubbed out my cigarette in a cup, in my mind's eye I simultaneously saw a black bag on the floor of a dressing room. These remembered images feel transparent, it is my concentration that gives them form, and when it lets go of them, they dissolve and merely the external image, the tabletop with black coffee-cup rings and a thin layer of grey ash, remains. Rather like a dirty windowpane, which can stand out if one focuses all one's attention on it – somehow dimming the view of what is on the other side – and which disappears completely when concentration lets go of it. Not only is there something a little vague and difficult to hold on to about remembered images, they are also and always encumbered by distance, they rarely fill one's consciousness entirely, appearing instead somewhere in the middle of it like a red deer standing in a large field: it only occupies a small spot, yet it is the only thing you see. I began thinking about memories because this morning I remembered something which I haven't thought about for many, many years. For some reason or other, the word 'willowherb' popped up in my mind. The name was familiar to me but didn't evoke any visual images, so I googled it. When images of rosebay willowherb appeared on my screen, an avalanche of memories swept through me. For it grew everywhere in the place I lived as a child! Especially by the roadside, in ditches, where the roads were new and the ditches were full of blasted-out rocks. And on newly laid-out plots, those craters in between the rows of houses, there too there would be rosebay willowherb growing. There were always many of them together, and they grew so densely that they rippled over the stony slopes and the steep hillside in waves of pink and green. They had spindly stems, and the pink or pale red flowers rose in tiers, so that the tops resembled slender pyramids, broader at the base – presumably because the flowers lower down bloomed first – and narrow at the top, where for a long time the flowers were merely buds. Rosebay willowherb is known for rapidly colonising plant- and tree-less areas, it roots easily and spreads quickly. The roots are long and each plant yields vast quantities of seeds. It prefers areas rich in nitrogen, such as roadsides, riverbanks, burned-out ruins and forest land that has been swept by fire, around outside lavatories and large open spaces in the forest, logging areas for instance, but also meadows and plains. There is something primitive about the willowherb, something a little coarse and primeval, it is not at all refined, though it forms beautiful and intensely coloured carpets wherever it grows, and in a strange way it made sense that it did so well precisely on the large developments, which although they were modern then and represented a new era, also had something simple and brutal about them – hillsides were blasted out, forests were cut down, machines roared and shook – and amid all this, the piles of blue and angular rocks, the fresh-laid black tarmac, the heaps of gravel and yellow loaders and bulldozers, the simple, fast-growing and robust willowherb shot up, containing no other secret than the most obvious of all, shared by all ancient and primitive creatures, namely that the world is ever new. Greed for the new is old, and history merely a series of flickering see-through images seen at a great distance like the red deer in the meadow; it lifts its head and stands perfectly still for a few seconds, then vanishes into the forest.

Dogs

Dogs have never interested me, perhaps because we didn't
have a dog when I was growing up and because I was afraid
of those there were in the neighbourhood, even of Alex, the
good-natured and kindly golden retriever which belonged to
the Kanestrøms and followed the children of the family
when it had to but obviously preferred their father, whom
I often saw it gazing up at with a devoted and expectant
look, tail wagging. The problem was when I encountered it
alone, for then it barked at me, and I couldn't handle those
barks, they overruled everything I knew about the dog's temperament, and I would remain standing on the gravel path
in front of the house, unable to walk past it and ring the bell.
Dag Lothar often found me in that position, frozen to the
spot outside their house while the nice dog stood there barking at me. It didn't help that as a human being I was
intellectually and presumably also emotionally superior to
the dog, that I knew how to read and write, draw and paint,
tie my shoelaces, butter my bread, buy sweets at the shop
and take the bus on my own, for the loud, aggressively monotonous sounds it made trumped all that; when I stood there
facing it only those sounds mattered. The dog's barks were
like a kind of law, they marked a boundary I couldn't cross,

and it was the dog which enforced it. The kinship with my father's law was obvious, since the feelings his loud voice wakened in me, all of them connected with an inability to act, that paralysis of fear, were the same as those produced by the dog's barking. Defying the law wasn't just unthinkable, it was impossible. That this was so made me a subordinate, which was something I knew even then, that I had the character traits of a subordinate, and more than anything else this has marked the forty years I have lived since then. A subordinate does what he is supposed to do for fear of reprisal, which in my case has meant fear of anger and loud voices. Although I have sought out arenas where anger and loud voices are considered unsophisticated, first university, later the literary establishment, I have still been behaving as expected of me, for I have always had within me that same fear of doglike aggression, and whenever I have encountered it, for example in the form of an angry motorist or an angry girlfriend, every time I have yielded to it and become paralysed. The only area where I have defied it has been literature. At times I think that is what literature is for, that literature is a place where one can express oneself freely without fearing the law of the father, the law of the dog. That literature is the arena of the cowardly, the Colosseum of the fearful, and that authors are like pathetic gladiators who freeze up when a dog barks at them but retaliate and assert themselves and their rights as soon as they are alone. Speak for yourself, I hear other authors protesting. But I think I am right. Has a single good author ever owned a dog? Flaubert didn't. Rilke, who described dogs more beautifully than anyone else, didn't have one either, he would start in alarm if anyone coughed nearby. Kafka didn't have a dog. Hamsun didn't have a dog. Sandemose didn't have a dog. Tor Ulven didn't have a dog. Did Duras have one? I find that hard to imagine. Ibsen, did he have a dog? No. Faulkner? I believe he did. In that case perhaps his position in the literary canon ought to be reconsidered? Virginia Woolf also had dogs, but only so-called lapdogs, which are too small and pet-like to cause fear in anyone, so they don't count. As for me, I had a dog for two years for the sake of our eldest daughter, who wanted a dog from the age of three, and whom I finally gave in to. The dog was infinitely kind but also infinitely stupid, and I completely lacked the strength and authority to teach it anything at all, so it jumped up on everyone it met, ate all the food it could find, including the food on our dinner table, it pulled on the leash as hard as it could whenever we took it for walks, it dug holes in the lawn, it was never properly house-trained, and it was so submissive and humble that I could hardly look at it without a feeling of irritation or even rage rising in me, the way it often is when one recognises one's own least attractive traits in others. It never let me out of its sight, tagged along after me over to the house I write in, lay down at my feet when I was working, and if I put on some music it would sometimes begin to howl, often in the same pitch as the vocals. When we got a new baby in the house, it all became too much, the dog had to be walked several times a day, and it had to come with us every time we left the house – we eventually had a fence erected so that it could stay outside in the garden when we were away, but after a couple of months the neighbour came over and told us, in his circumspect way, that it had barked and wailed every time we had left it alone during all those weeks – so in the end I gave it away to a family that loves dogs and knows how they should be treated. Only afterwards did it strike me that in the two years we had it I didn't write a single line of literary prose, merely articles and essays, and although I'm not blaming the dog, and certainly don't want to claim that I belong among good authors, I still think that in a certain sense owning a dog undermined my literary project, which, since it is so largely autobiographical, somehow dissipated in a way I don't fully understand but presumably had to do with the dog's character being so like my own, something I actually knew even before we got it, for the original title of my first autobiographical manuscript, which was later changed to *Argentina* and eventually to *My Struggle*, was *The Dog*.

Gjerstadholmen

The islet of Gjerstadholmen lies in the Tromøy sound, right by the bridge to Tromøya island, perhaps twenty metres from land. It is a couple of hundred metres long, hilly, full of bluffs and crags, those closest to the water worn to smooth rock, with a ridge running down the middle. The hollows are covered with grass, and trees grow there too, on the south side, most of them low, with dense foliage that rustles when the wind blows and flickers when the sun is shining. The islet is so small that no one has built anything on it, there are neither houses nor cabins there, but in summer small boats will occasionally moor there and people come to spend the day, bringing blankets, swimming gear, towels and picnic food. I grew up in a house just a few hundred metres away, and I remember it always seemed strange to me that people would moor, for not only does Gjerstadholmen lie in the sound, with a view of the bridge, but also so close to shore that nothing of what I associated with islets and archipelagos – the whole point of boating to me was the freedom of the open sea – was to be found there. I remember feeling a little sorry for them, and I also felt a little sorry for Gjerstadholmen it-self, which was in possession of everything an islet should have but never really had a chance to demonstrate its worth in the only arena that counted, which never managed to get out into its true element, the world of islets, to show what it stood for. It had lain there since the last ice age, I knew that much, perhaps for as long as ten thousand years, so that I sensed in it something melancholy, a kind of mild hopelessness, was maybe not so strange. But I never sensed any bitterness, Gjerstadholmen had reconciled itself to its fate and its place in the world, and it did sometimes happen that the waves in the sound broke into whitecaps and rose in great walls of water that smashed against its cliffs, just as they would have if the islet had lain where the sea opened out. To us who grew up nearby, Gjerstadholmen was nearly invisible, a little like Atle, one of the boys in class, who never tried to distinguish himself in any way, never drew attention to himself, he was someone who neither took nor gave anything and was therefore neither disliked nor liked, he was just there somehow. He kept to his room a lot of the time, where he would sit drawing, and he too seemed without bitterness, it was as if he didn't demand anything more of life. He lived at the other end of the housing development, which to us was like living in a different country, and I never saw him anywhere near Gjerstadholmen. One of our swimming places, the closest one, was known as Nabben, a smooth rock that protruded into the fifteen- to twenty-metre-wide channel between the shore and Gjerstadholmen, from which one could dive into the deep, cool, blue sea, which we would generally do in the afternoon and evening, since the point wasn't to lie in the sun and bathe all day – for that there were better-suited places – but just to have a dip. It felt natural to swim across to the islet on the other side, perhaps climb up on the rock there and dive into the sea again, but not to stay there. On the rare occasions when we did, it was as if we were discovering the islet, as if we were seeing it for the first time. I remember one winter when the sound had frozen over and we walked across to the islet on skis and spent the whole day there, the snow glittering in the sharp winter sun, the air still and cold as ice, and how exciting it was to make tracks down from the central ridge between the bare crags and ski all the way down and onto the ice. I also remember one day in summer when we swam across to Gjerstadholmen from Nabben and this time didn't just lie there like seals on the smooth rock to warm ourselves, but walked away from the shore and kept discovering new places, finally having a swim on the far side of the islet, which we had never done before. We told each other we had to do it again. But we never did, Gjerstadholmen's potential for joy sank back into oblivion, not unlike what happened to Atle, for he too would sometimes be discovered, suddenly someone might turn to him and for a few days he was one of us, beaming in the rays of the attention he was getting, until just as suddenly it passed and no one gave him a thought any more.

Mosquitoes

What it is that determines the size of a species, which evolutionary law it is that dictates the dimensions of plants and animals I do not know, but I imagine it has to do with maximising potential and with marginal utility. Trees, for example, began their existence as small plants, but must have found there were advantages to growing so tall that they towered above other plants, not least as far as access to light was concerned. And that impulse – the form of which no one knows, for where in the tree exactly might the impulse to grow so drastically be located? – must in turn have been regulated by the purely physical limitations set by size, such as the need to distribute liquid out into every branch and leaf, which must become more demanding the more the tree grows, or wind, to which the tree will be more exposed the taller it gets. If not for this, trees would have grown into the sky. If one imagines that every living thing has its niche, in other words a space around itself, then everything alive will seek to become as big as possible, up to the point where size no longer provides advantages but rather disadvantages. And once a given animal or plant species has conquered such a niche, this reduces the space available to others, which are thus forced to worm their way in somewhere else, as it were, and if they find a form of existence there that works for them, they stick to it. Though we can't really be certain of the latter, since the development of species occurs far beyond our own time horizon. If, for example, the mosquito is getting larger, it is happening so slowly that neither we nor our children nor anyone within their immediate generation will be able to discern it. At present the mosquito is characterised by its negligible size, its spindly legs and puny body, its two wings and its dual existence, during which it is first a larva and then, after a brief stay inside a sort of tent, called a pupa, begins its life as a flying insect. The fact that there are more than two thousand species of mosquito in Norway alone, over fifty thousand species in the whole world, and that two hundred and forty million-year-old fossils of mosquitoes have been discovered, none of them significantly larger than today's species, would seem to suggest that mosquitoes have found their form, that they find their lives satisfactory. Whether they actually enjoy flying around in the summertime is of course impossible to say, but certainly nothing about their current situation indicates dissatisfaction or distress, unlike bees, which as we know are disappearing. The mosquito's method is working, it is reproducing and keeps spewing forth new swarms of individuals into life. As for the stinging mosquito, the females have become dependent on fresh blood to provide enough proteins for their eggs, so they swarm around animals that to them must be so large that they likely don't even realise they are animals, the mosquitoes probably perceive them simply as warm sites, which they covetously – for these sites give off a powerful scent of something they desire – seek out and settle on. The surface of the site is firm, but beneath the surface, which the mosquito punches its proboscis into, liquid is flowing, all that delicious blood which it sucks up. Then, full and dizzy with satisfaction, it lifts off and leaves the site, which as it happens moves around in unpredictable ways, being found now here, now there. Part of the explanation for the mosquito's success is that it only needs a little blood, due to its size merely a few drops are sufficient, which these skin-upholstered sites can easily afford to lose. Had mosquitoes been bigger, say as big as cats, and had a corresponding need for blood, they would have lost all their comparative advantage, they would no longer be able to sneak in through open windows at night, settle on those delectable sites and turn dizzy with pleasure, but would have had to develop other strategies; most importantly they would have had to drastically diminish their numbers, perhaps down to as few as there are now wolves, merely a couple of hundred individuals in all of Scandinavia. They would have had to obtain considerable quantities of blood, perhaps so much that the creatures they fed on would not have allowed themselves to be relieved of it without putting up violent resistance, and if the mosquitoes were to win that struggle, the creature would die, so that they would continually need to find new victims, while at the same time their size would now require them to conceal themselves in places where access to blood would be much more restricted. Oh, the giant mosquito would find life troublesome indeed. It isn't hard to picture it, perching on the branch of a tree, as big as a wolf with its proboscis dangling in front and its compound eyes the size of tennis balls glinting in the twilight, unable to maneouvre properly in the air, so that a few tens of millions of years later it is permanently grounded, its final pair of wings having turned into clubs. As big as a horse it stands there between the trees, with a huge need for blood that has turned its front legs into organs for penetrating and gripping, and a proboscis so large that it sucks a body dry within minutes. The mosquito is now feared but also hunted, so there aren't very many individuals left, and the journey back – to become smaller and smaller so as to finally be able to fly in and out of windows, settle on delectable surfaces and get dizzy from just a few drops – is by now far too long and arduous to be feasible. And in some way or other that knowledge must be biologically stored within the mosquito, since the species doesn't grow any bigger, not even at the slow rate of evolution, it has found its niche, and the price exacted for the blood, that a few thousand mosquitoes meet their deaths every year in the form of a slapping hand, is so small to them that they aren't even aware of it.

Fainting

The day before yesterday I was in a large room full of people, it was in London, a publishing house was celebrating an anniversary. Mounted heads of large animals hung on the walls, of elk and deer and roe deer, waiters dressed in black and white walked around with trays of canapés and white wine and champagne, the floors were wooden and there was a stage at the end of the hall, where speeches were being given. There were somewhere between two and three hundred people present, dressed in party finery they stood talking with sparkling glasses in their hands. Except for a couple of people I have worked with, I didn't know anybody. Just before getting there I had been in my hotel room getting ready for the party, showered, put on a light blue shirt, a grey-brown suit, dark brown shoes, filled with the particular pleasure which these almost ritual acts provide, the anticipation of a party contained within them. As I walked up the two carpeted flights of stairs in the old theatre building and heard the buzz of voices, however, reality caught up with me and I realised how it was going to be, I wouldn't know what to do with myself, wouldn't know what to say, and the faces of the people who addressed themselves to me would not be able to hide their rapidly arising feeling of awkwardness, their desire to get away from me. A woman who was standing by the entrance turned to me as I came in, she had fair hair and blue eyes, was in her thirties, she said that she had once interviewed me at my home, I nodded and smiled with my mouth closed, my teeth look terrible, they are completely yellow with black bars running down the sides. I remember, I said, it was nice. But I won't disturb you, she said, and I walked slowly through the throng of people, packed as densely as in a bus. Suits, dresses, jewellery, smiles and laughter. I caught sight of a woman who works for my publisher and walked over to her. There's someone I want you to meet, she said and led me further through the crowd to a group of people to whom I was introduced, they were heads of publishing companies. They asked if I was staying in London for long, I told them I was going home tomorrow, they said in surprise did you come all the way here just for this party? I realised that this signalled an undignified eagerness and said that I like London, that I take every opportunity to come here. I smiled with closed lips, they continued talking among themselves. She led me further into the room, there was an author who wanted to meet me, but when I went over and stood next to her, she was engrossed in conversation with someone else. I took a glass of white wine from a tray, she turned to me, I shook her hand, and when I met her gaze I saw that she was very neurotic and uncomfortable, not necessarily with the situation but in her life. She said that what I had written about living with children had made an impression on her, I asked if she had children herself, 'Two,' she said. 'But I suppose they're older,' I said, realising too late that this was an insult, she was someone who with her whole being wanted to be young still. I moved away towards a corner of the hall, it wasn't easy, the crowd was so densely packed. The air was hot and full of voices reverberating against walls and ceilings. Several groups of people came up to me, often it was the women who took the initiative while the men looked away, demonstratively uninterested. Most of them were authors, so that must be how it is, I thought to myself as I leaned forward in an attempt to hear what they were saying: the men feel they have to safeguard their integrity, whereas the women don't think like that. I didn't know what to say anyway, mainly I just nodded and smiled, so obviously uncomfortable with the situation that it affected even the people who had approached me, suddenly they didn't know what to say either and turned away or resumed their previous conversations, exactly as I had known it would be. If only I could sit down somewhere, I thought, but there were no chairs anywhere. Two women came over, they were in their fifties and their eyes shone. As I stood listening to them talk, I suddenly felt unwell, I could hardly stand, a wave of weakness rose within me and I said abruptly, Sorry, I have to go. I walked slowly down the carpeted staircase, steadying myself against the banister all the way down, saw that there was an outdoor restaurant on the pavement by the entrance, made my way there and sat down. A few minutes later I felt fine again, and I stood up and went back in, up the staircase and into the hot crowded rooms to find the two women, I had to apologise to them. As I re-entered the hall the feeling of physical malaise returned, as if it was in the air and passed from there into my body when I breathed it in, spreading out like a carpet of something faint and soft. Luckily the two women were still standing in the same spot. I went over to them and said, I apologise, but

I suddenly felt ill and had to get some fresh air. I could hardly stay on my feet. They laughed and said they had begun to wonder, had they said something terrible, or maybe I just didn't like them. No, no, really, I could hardly stand, I said, so I just had to get some fresh air. As I said it, the malaise came back, only much stronger. I had to get out and took a few steps towards the exit, and a black wave rose within me, and that is the last thing I remember.

I can see maybe ten faces, they are all staring down at me. Even though they are quite close to me, it is as if I am seeing them from a great distance. They are surrounded by darkness. I don't understand what it is I am seeing. It is as if I am looking into another time. That I am in a different place from them. And yet they are standing in front of me, they seem to be glowing in the darkness. I don't know who I am. I don't know who they are. And it is a truly terrible feeling, for I am no one, at the same time as the faces before me are clearly concerned about the person they are looking at. Is it the past I am looking into? For I seem to be in a very different place, in another dimension, or somewhere else in the universe, surrounded by darkness, and from there I am looking down on these faces, which at the same time seem unnaturally close to me.

'Don't get up, stay where you are,' a woman is saying. 'It could be dangerous if you stand up too quickly.'

I sit up, and that movement somehow makes me whole, I am suddenly myself again, I am who I have always been. I don't know what my name is, but I know who I am. A man supports me as I get up on my feet, he guides me down the stairs, says I can sit there, someone brings me water, and I realise what has happened, finally grasp the situation in its entirety, I simply fainted, fell to the floor and was gone for a few seconds. I must have struck my head against something hard for there is a big bump on it, and I must have bitten the inside of my cheek, since there is blood in my mouth. After I have sat on the stairs for a few minutes while the man questions me a little, whether this has happened before and so on, has anyone ordered me a taxi, I am led over to the cab, get in, close the door and in this manner leave the party. In the taxi, driving slowly through the glittering city streets, I feel fine and light, as always after being ill, but also happy in a peculiar way, for I feel certain that this is what it is like to die. When death comes, it comes as an instantaneous nothingness, an abrupt absence from oneself. It is nothing to fear. What was alarming was what I saw while I was still no one in the darkness, the image of the staring, anxious, faintly glowing faces. Alarming because I had absolutely no connection to them, nor they to me, nor to that in me which saw them. If, once dead, one doesn't remain in the empty void but returns in the darkness, I thought as I sat there in the back of the taxi, gazing out at the evening streets in the pale light of summer, it is without comprehending the living.

Giant's Cauldron

Along the smooth rocky slopes on the outer side of Tromøya there are many giants' cauldrons, some of them lying at the very edge of the sea and so close to the water that waves often wash over them, and because of their depth and shape, the sounds of the water's movements inside them are quite different from other shoreline sounds, they resonate in the cauldrons' interiors, producing a hollow ring, what is ordinarily hissing becomes slurping, slapping turns into gurgling, and sometimes faint booms can be heard from them. When I was small, I would sometimes lower myself into one of them in the summer. It was almost as deep as I was tall, and to glide down into the bubbling water as if into a big pot, right next to the sea, felt both fantastic and terrifying. On still and sunny days there was no contact between the sea and the cauldron, then the water inside it was stagnant and warm, almost like a tiny lake, except that the water came from the Atlantic Ocean and was salty and constantly renewed. Further up the slopes there were more giants' cauldrons, but none had the dignity of this one. I had also seen them in the mountains, for at that time we often went for car rides at weekends, and once a year we crossed the Hardangervidda plateau to visit my grandparents on the other side. What makes these often bowl-shaped hollows in the rock remarkable are their smooth and even and well-formed walls. Rock is often smooth and even, having been worn down in the course of time by the weight and movement of glaciers, rivers or oceans, but this applies to large surfaces, which seem to merge unresistingly with the structure of the landscape, consisting of plains, valley floors, river mouths, marshes, meadows and open country. The giants' cauldrons break with this overall visual impression, they have a very different form to the surrounding landscape, and like all geological exceptions they look artificial. Inside giants' cauldrons the same eroded smoothness that characterises the surrounding rock looks as if it had been made by giant people. Which of course is how they got their name. But the spiral – the form followed by the stone as it hollowed out the rock – belongs to nature's standard repertoire, it is found in tornadoes, in water flowing down a plughole, in conches and galaxies. It is like the fold, found in garments, in the brain, in landscape formations on Mars. And like the sphere, which is found on pebble beaches, in dandelions gone to seed, planets, stars. That matter tends towards and shapes itself into precisely these forms is due to a few fundamental premises that were laid down when the universe was formed, I have read somewhere – at the very instant when the universe expanded at a greater speed and more violently than anything else has ever moved, and then gradually slowed down and evened out. Nearly all advanced theories of physics end up with a conclusion that we can never either confirm nor disprove, namely that there are a myriad of universes, and that their beginnings must have been different from that of ours such that the fundamental premises underlying their formation have caused matter to coalesce in ways which we, who are confined to this universe, can't even begin to imagine. But if this is so, that not only are there other universes besides this but that their number is infinite, then there must also be some that are identical to this one, down to the smallest detail, such as the little boy who, filled with fear and exhilaration in equal measure, lowers his body into a giant's cauldron filled with surging salt water while the white ferry to Denmark is sailing into the archipelago, towering like a cliff above all the islets and small boats, and who forty years later has sat down to write about it.

Hildegarde de Bi...

Gertrude d'Anfgro...

Jeanne Chanal

Jeanne Marie Gug...

Diary, July

Sunday 24 July 2016

It is a few minutes past eight in the morning. The sun is shining and the outside temperature is twenty-three degrees, we are in the middle of a period of high pressure, the weather has been fine for a long time. A few days ago I picked up German radio in the car without trying, suddenly two channels appeared after the usual Swedish and Danish ones, and I remembered how it had been during periods of high pressure when I was small, when our TV began to receive Danish television, how wonderfully strange it seemed. Signals from a foreign country had made it all the way into the television set in our living room. Even Dad was excited. The picture was unstable and flickering, as if it had been worn down during its journey across the sky, or it was restless because it didn't belong here and was tearing at its moorings inside the TV set, wanting to move on, up into blue space again. Or was it the TV set that was trying to get rid of the alien images, like a body seeking to expel alien organs that have been transplanted into it? At times the picture stabilised and calmed down for a few minutes, as if it had resigned itself or got comfortable, or as if the TV set had accepted it. Then it would be deep and clear, and we could look into the TV set like a wizard gazing into a crystal ball, for we had got used to the miracle of television, but these unexpected foreign images come from far away brought it home to us again.

The German radio channels in the car weren't quite as exciting, but I listened to one of them for a while anyway while I drove towards Brantevik to pick up your sisters. The musical they are acting in is showing three times a week throughout July, and every Thursday they perform in the evening, so that I get to watch the entire sunset when I go to collect them. It is magical when the colours fade from the sky and from the sea to the east, and the fields of grain glow in the vanishing light as if illuminated, while broadleaved trees line the road like the shadows of large figures. This week I have been alone with the children, so you have come along for all these trips, sitting in the back seat with your face turned towards the road ahead, watching the flaring light in the western sky and the gradual fading that follows, until the sun is no more than a disc just above ground in the far distance, glowing orange, and then the darkness coming on. What you think about all this I naturally don't know, but you are interested in the different times of day and night, and if there is light in the sky, all of a sudden you will say, The sky is shining, it's morning. Or, as you said early this morning, It's morning in the sky. If I stop the car, for example at a red light or at a busy crossing, you shout, Drive now, Daddy! If I open the window so that a draught blows through the car, you shout, It's blowing! And if I glance in the mirror then, I see your hair flying above the seat. It is something I look forward to every day and which I still haven't started taking for granted, that language has come to you. Not merely that you are able to make yourself under-stood, as when you say you need to pee, and we go to the toilet together and I place you on the seat, and a few seconds later you say, gripping the seat, that you're done, but also all your descriptions of things you see, such as a bird flying from one tree to the other, for then it flies twice, once in the air and once more in language. Or like the spiders which you are afraid of; if you see one, you come running to fetch me, I have to take it away, you say, and at the same time you remember what I always tell you, that spiders aren't dangerous, they're kind, and then you say it yourself, thereby creating two levels in your language: an emotional one from within, which you counter with a rational and reasonable one from the outside.

We have had a good but somewhat unfulfilled week during this period of high pressure: Sunday evening I got the copy-edit of the short texts in this book, on Monday I went through it while you were with your babysitter, and on Tuesday morning I finished it just in time to receive two friends, Thomas and Marie, who came by for a brief visit. I sent your younger sister down to the shop with her friend who had spent the night here, they bought ice cream, which we ate together with the strawberries our guests had brought. When they had left, I put you in the car and drove to the shop, since my cousin was arriving with his family that evening, and I thought we could barbecue for the first time this summer. A bag of charcoal, a bottle of lighter fluid, hot dogs and pre-marinated meat, tomatoes, cucumber, onion, feta cheese and olives for a salad, more ice cream, more strawberries, soft drinks and some bottles of beer. You enjoy putting items into the shopping trolley, sometimes on your own initiative; occasionally we take home the most outdated items. It had been a long time since I went shopping for a meal with guests, it had been a long time since I felt that particular kind of stress, when time is short and everything has to be done quickly and for some strange reason one always manages. The last time we had guests was last summer – not counting your grandparents, since they help out when they are here and are a part of the household, nor all your sisters' and brother's friends – and as I placed all the food in the fridge, cleaned the strawberries, made the salad, filled the grill with charcoal, squirted lighter fluid on it, set the table and prepared the meat while you sat in front of the television, where I had put you to free up my hands, I thought to myself that there had been a decline, that life too could become overgrown, fall into decay and even rot, like a forgotten and neglected part of a property, for even though it required a bit of effort beforehand, and perhaps also during the meal, the act of preparing food for others and eating it with them was something which opened up, brought some light and air and life into things, it was an event in an existence which ordinarily was uneventful, in the sense that it was totally predictable and monotonous.

My cousin's mother, my mother's youngest sister, died some years ago, and it seemed almost unthinkable, she was young and full of life, of a lighter disposition than her two sisters but also obviously one of them. They stuck together their whole lives, called each other often, were interested in each other's children and knew each other's friends. When I turned forty I received a long email from her, she told me in detail about the day I had been born, what happened, what was said; she had been living in Oslo then and was close to my mother. No one had told me any of this before, and I was touched, not by what she told me but by her gesture. She was a psychologist and worked with children, and when we had your older sister and were inexperienced parents, it was her we turned to for advice when we were at a loss. She had three children herself, and it was the youngest of them who was coming to visit. I hadn't seen him since he got married. They had been on the Danish island of Bornholm and were travelling on next day. They had two children, four and two years old, and the elder one had been looking forward to meeting his second cousins, they said, but he must have been a little disappointed, since your brother was holidaying with another family on an island up near Strömstad, while your elder sister was visiting her cousin in Copenhagen, she had taken the train there by herself for the first time. So, besides me, it was just you and your younger sister who were at home.

I heard a car stop and walked round to the front of the house with you on my arm just as they took the other path round to the back. The house has three front doors, since it was originally three houses, it confuses most people who haven't been here before. I walked back and met them in front of the actual entrance. You pressed your face into the hollow between my neck and shoulder, as you usually do when strangers come too near. While they fetched their baggage, we walked over to the patio behind the summer house, where the barbecue stood and the table had been laid. I had tried to clean the grill before they arrived, it was covered in a thick layer of rust, and I had managed to scrape off the worst of it. You were sitting in a chair when I lit the barbecue, and you shouted Fire, fire! when the flames rose high, so high that I was afraid the grapevines which dangled from the rafters of the open roof would catch fire. I moved the barbecue a little, but then it came dangerously close to a shrub. Our elegant and always well-dressed neighbour glanced over the fence and asked if we were going to barbecue, I nodded and said yes, I just hope I don't set fire to the house first, he probably didn't understand what I said, since he looked quizzical for a few seconds before he nodded, said Bon appétit and vanished again. The flames calmed down and I went into the kitchen, carrying you with me – it was impossible to know what you might do if left alone with a lit barbecue – brought out the meat, the salad, knives and forks, beer and soft drinks. When we ate half an hour later, you put all the olives, the feta cheese and all the onion on my plate, while you yourself ate meat, tomatoes and pieces of cucumber. The patio had been totally overgrown earlier this summer, the weeds had completely covered the flagstones, the flower bed that ran alongside them had been one jumble of green, as big as a car and full of stinging nettles, even a couple of trees that had taken root and grown half a metre tall, while the grass on the lawn beyond came up to my knees. The patio lies behind the garden, out of sight, and has been given the lowest priority for quite some time. This summer the babysitter, who lives in our house across the road, has had two Italians visiting, and in return for them being allowed to spend their holiday there, we agreed that they would spruce up the garden that belongs to that house, as well as this patio. Which they emphatically did. When they had finished, the patio looked like a parking space. The amazingly beautiful silvery shrub, as big as a small tree, had been razed to the ground, along with all the other plants and flowers in the flower bed except for the boxwood, which for some reason or other they had thought worthy of saving. I didn't say anything to them about it, the poor souls had done their best, they were only twenty years old and hardly spoke English, instead I thanked them for their earnest efforts. At first I was afraid even to look at the garden around the other house, but earlier that day I carried a garden table over there, and it looked just as I had feared: like a parking space. That garden had been overgrown in a deeply romantic, almost Gothic way, and even though it was hardly bigger than an eighth of an acre, one could almost lose one's way in there. Now it was just empty and full of light.

After we had eaten and the children had gone to bed, we sat out in the garden drinking beer and talking in the dark. My cousin and his wife are thirteen years younger than me, almost a generation, and he told us how big we had seemed when my brother and I came to visit during his childhood, while I told them that he had taken pistols and rifles to bed with him at night, which he didn't remember. He began to talk about the place where our grandparents had lived, which he too of course has many memories of. And without me having said a word about the fact that I had written about it this summer, he began to talk about their cellar. He said they had slaughtered pigs there. His mother had told him about it, how the pigs began to scream when they realised that they were being taken down there, as if they knew what awaited them. And how terrible the cellar had smelled then. 'I've never heard about that before,' I said. 'They only had cows when I visited,' he said. 'So it must have been when she was growing up.'

When I think back, I did know that they slaughtered animals on the farm, I have been told in detail about how the blood was collected in tubs and used for blood pudding or blood sausage, for example, or how the intestines were rinsed and used as sausage skin, but I had never thought about it in concrete terms, it was as if these things took place in another department of my mind. That pigs and cows were slaughtered in the same cellar I spent time in during my childhood, always cold, dim and damp, where the freezer stood, where the fishing nets hung, and where the vats of redcurrants, blackcurrants and gooseberries stood before they were taken away, this I had never imagined, but now that I know, it makes sense, it was a transitional space, not quite inside but not quite outside either. A place where what came from the outside was stored for a while, such as tools and equipment, but also a place where outside things were refined so that they could be brought all the way inside, into the kitchen or the dining room, like fish, berries, animals.

The Second World War took place in that world, a world that was more manual and closer to physical reality, but the war also changed that world; it was during the 1940s that the first computers, as big as assembly rooms, were constructed, that aeroplanes became effective, that nuclear power became possible, that rockets were built. But despite this I still imagine that life wasn't so very different, that if I had been flung back into that time now, I wouldn't have felt a stranger to it. One has only to read books from that time, like those of Malaparte, Céline or Hamsun – to take those writers who all at one point or another were on the wrong side – even read in a time which rejects what they stood for, what they describe is familiar and possible to relate to. Perhaps this is because I grew up in the 70s, a time which in many ways was a prolongation of that epoch, in which the life lived on my grandparents' farm, with its roots going back to the 1920s, which in turn were planted in the soil of the second half of the nineteenth century, was still accessible, and in which the wartime bunkers were still there, abandoned merely thirty years earlier – a leap in time which to me today would correspond to the world as it was when I was seventeen – while those who are growing up now, in what is probably a new epoch, separated from the old one by a mental chasm, will not be able to grasp what is at stake in the writings of Malaparte, Céline or Hamsun, or quite simply won't be interested in it? Or is everything always the same?

Not everything, perhaps, but everything essential – I suppose that is why the word 'essential' exists: the essential is the unchanging. The old woman in Malmö whom I have written about earlier in this journal and who is a fictionalised version of a real woman that my mother's father, and presumably also my grandmother, once knew, this woman experienced something which few people experience but which is not unusual in wartime, and to her it must have been as if the world yawned open in an infernal light, and even though it closed again afterwards – as it did for the whole of society and always does when a war has ended, sealing up secret, unspeakable places – it must still have pained her for all the years she had left to live. The question I let her ask herself – do we all die happy? – was linked to that, although she didn't necessarily think that way, for that's how people are: what we think comes more often from places we ourselves are unaware of than from places we know. When her 'I' takes the place of mine in the next sentence, she is sitting by the living-room table in the apartment in Malmö, the sun is on its way down, and she is writing to her husband about what happened that day: the journalist who knocked on the door and wanted to interview her, and about everything it brought back, such as the time she fell down in the street during a heart attack and, sure that she was going to die, felt an intense happiness. The happiness surprised me. So something in me was in fact happy and grateful. That gave me something to think about! I hope you won't be offended to learn that it was the years before we met I was thinking of then. The years before you came and saved me, like an Austrian prince. The years before the war, the years before Ivar. Then I was a girl with scratched knees and laughter bubbling in my chest. I haven't told you very much about that time. We never did talk very much about the place I was from. Nor will we do so now, my friend, it has been a long day and I am too tired to write any more. Not that I will be able to sleep, I hardly ever do any more, but at least I can lie in bed and rest for some hours and think about what I should do about that journalist. He will return, I am certain of it. He has come all this way to speak to me. But I will think about that alone. So goodnight to you wherever you are, Alexander . . .

The most terrible thing about getting old isn't that death approaches, or that one's health deteriorates and what used to be simple and easy becomes laborious. Those are things one is prepared for. The most terrible thing is that one disappears. I think that is especially so for women. Nothing had prepared me for that, that no one would look at me. Early this morning I went to the supermarket to buy some groceries. On my way home I walked through the park. I sat down on a bench. A young man, he was maybe around twenty-five, sat down next to me. He had curly hair and a moustache which didn't suit him. He didn't see me, even though his body was half a metre from mine. He was leaning forward, with his hands on his lap, gazing up above the trees. He was dressed in a pair of very short shorts, red with a white stripe down the side, and he had a white T-shirt on. He looked like he had been playing football or tennis, but he wasn't carrying any equipment with him, so it was probably just the way he dressed. Well, he saw me, of course. He saw an old woman with wispy grey hair and a face full of wrinkles. She caught his attention about as much as a pigeon on the gravel in front of him would have done. It is this lack of interest I am talking about. If he had only known what I was thinking! I looked at his hairy ankles and his compact powerful body, and I thought, oh, to be able to lay one's hand on his chest. My thoughts are not dry and old, they are as young as when I was sixteen, they are just as alive. But when I look into the eyes of a man, I am no one. That is the terrible thing about getting old.

He went on his way gazing down at the ground in front of him, I thought he might be suffering from unrequited love. And then I thought, what wouldn't I give to be twenty-five years old again and have my heart broken!

I remained there on the bench, in the shade of the big trees. The water in the canal shimmered between their trunks. I thought of Gro, Henning and Solveig. That I had exchanged them for you.

Today I have cleaned the cupboards and drawers in the kitchen, it took me several hours. Then I sat on the balcony in the heat, gazing out over the city. I like Malmö, I am glad we settled here. As I sat there, the idea came to me that I should go home. The thought was a sudden one, and it made me feel shaky. For it would be so easy. I could walk to the station and take the night train to Oslo, take another train to Bergen, and then a boat from there tomorrow evening. Or I could fly and get there even faster.

I fantasised about what would happen there.

What they would look like.

How they would receive me.

I fantasised about them letting me stay there for the last years of my life.

Not even in my weakest moments have I thought anything like this before.

I snorted with indignation at myself and went into the kitchen to make a gin and tonic – I bought tonic this morning at the grocery shop, you see, I had a feeling I might need some soon – and went back out on the verandah, shaking my glass a little and listening to the wonderful tinkling of ice cubes.

That's when I decided to talk to the journalist. If he contacts me again. As I'm sure he will.

Your past, Alexander, I don't know very much about, other than that you were an orphan and that you were in Norway one summer as a child together with other orphaned children. That's why you loved Norway. It was paradise on earth, you used to say. Later, when we were living here and I was going through my slow awakening, I began to wonder whether I was a part of that calculation. That you simply transferred your love for the white glaciers, the green mountainsides, the deep fjords and the winding gravel roads to me. But by then I was sufficiently awake to understand that it really didn't make any difference. One ends up with something other than what one fell in love with, anyway. For you don't think that the stooped, resigned man who every morning sat on the edge of the bed with his head bent, sighing deeply, was the man I wanted back then, do you?

I was born in 1916, during a world war which was hardly felt at home, to Håkon and Halldis Myklebust, as the fourth of their six children. Daddy was a short and powerfully built man, he was strong as a bear and known as such. His hands were unbelievably coarse, that is almost what I remember best about him, when I sat on his lap as a little girl and he would stroke my head. It was like sitting on a rock! He smelled of tobacco and the cowshed, and he hardly ever said anything. Mummy was small and slight, she talked all the time, and later in life I have come to realise that she must have been nervous, as it was called then. Her nerves were upset, and she was always scolding us, we were impossible, especially me. I think it was because I was so beautiful. Am I allowed to say that? Because I was. And I was daring. I was still a small child when I realised that she didn't have any power over me, that I could do as I liked. I had only to scream back at her and act violently, that made her afraid, she couldn't take it. It was a very pleasureable feeling, but also painful.

When I saw Ivar for the first time, I was seventeen. It was the seventeenth of May 1933, at a dance at the local youth club. He was almost thirty. He was strong and dark, and among all the the others he saw me. It was only a brief look, but it made my blood sing, and I thought, it's him, he is the one I want, she might have written, this woman who had such a strange life, whom I know hardly anything about except a few events in which she played a part, which must have marked her in fundamental ways. For that's how life is – at least if one is open to it – at any time something unpredictable and fateful can happen that will determine who or what or where you will be for the foreseeable future. Everything that happens has this element of unpredictability, but normally the events are minor and their consequences so unnoticeable that we hardly think about them. As when you get a call from a cousin who would like to stop by, and the ensuing visit, which just a few days earlier no one even knew would come about, in fact does. Or as when you meet a new person, perhaps peripherally in another setting, during which the encounter seems to both of you insignificant, or at least inconsequential, until you meet again, in another context, and perhaps also in a third, and you suddenly think, I want to be with this person for ever. Our small lives are traversed by momentous movements, avalanches in the depths of the everyday. War brings them to the surface, it heightens one's feeling of being alive, and the things that normally attach a person to his or her own reality are more easily cancelled out. Parents are more alert to unpredictable events than other people, they are more familiar with them, or with the fear of them. First while their children are very young, when everything is a potential danger – I am filled with dread when I think of the father who forgot his infant child in the car last summer and found it dead upon his return, or of the mother who went into the living room for a moment to do some chore while her daughter was having a bath and found her drowned when she returned to the bathroom – then later when they grow older and life's real trials begin: few parents want to see their children become entangled in the wheels of great events, most wish for predictable, safe, reasonable and harmonious lives for them. I do too. You are only two years old, so for the time being it is only a question of keeping you dry, warm, well fed, safe and reasonably stimulated, but a day will come when you have to go out into the world and live your own life, and I for one certainly don't want you to take great chances, to risk failure, or expose yourself to danger or end up in exposed positions within society.

Just as I was writing this, you came running at full tilt across the lawn, barefoot and with your hair flying, chased by your youngest sister. It is ten minutes to eight in the evening, the rays of sunlight have vanished from the garden, except in one place at the top of the chestnut tree, where it is reflected by the leaves and glows bright green. Besides working on this text, I have also driven your sisters to the venue of the musical today, that was at eleven thirty, I have slept for an hour in the summer house, which is so cool and where I sleep wonderfully well and deeply, and I have driven your sisters back again, that was at five o'clock, and on the way I first had three German radio channels, then one, finally none – while the golden grain fields stretched out in every direction beneath the deep blue sky, with the sea as a rim of darker blue to the east. In some places the grain is almost white, in others yellow with hues of red, and everywhere it is dry and rich, while towering up from it are not only broad-leaved trees but also wind turbines, slender and white and on this windless day perfectly motionless.

Now it is thirteen minutes past nine and the sunlight has disappeared from the chestnut too. There is no longer any trace of it in the landscape outside, except indirectly, in the grey-toned air which becomes lighter the higher up in the sky I look, and which at the centre of the vault still has a tinge of blue in it. A little while ago I took a break out in the garden, and above me, with the deep sky as background, a flock of swallows flew back and forth in the air. Some of them were so far away that they appeared as tiny dots, while others darted about perhaps twenty metres above me. Whenever they happened to be at a certain angle in relation to the sun, which was out of my sight where I sat, their wings turned a glowing orange. It happened again and again, it was as if the little birds caught flame. I tried to count them and arrived at fourteen. Between them and me hung swarms of insects, also clearly visible against the backdrop of the sky. Everything was still, not even a breath of wind stirred the leaves around me. From the neighbouring garden came a number of shouts in the same voice and laughter which at times sounded almost hysterical. For a while I thought the voice belonged to a woman, but then I realised that it must belong to a man, perhaps in his late twenties. 'Come on!' the voice shouted. 'See how strong your daddy is!' the voice shouted. 'Ha ha haaaa haa haaaaaaaa!' said the voice. It went quiet for a moment, and a sound as if of someone farting sounded faintly from the other side. But surely it couldn't be that quiet, could it? There was at least twenty metres between us, and two hedges separated me from the people there. The sound came again. 'Ha haa haaaaaaa!' the voice shouted. Then there was a belch, and this time I was certain what it was. While this was happening, I read a *Guardian* article about William Eggleston, the American photographer who has an exhibition in London right now, and looked at his pictures. I had seen some of them earlier and been hyp-notised by the colours in them, I had never seen anything like it. The first time I heard about him was in an office in New York, someone who knew him well got out some of his books and showed me while he told me stories from the pho-tographer's life, which was colourful in the way the lives of alcoholic artists can appear when they are given anecdotal form. Half a year later a photographer visited me here, Juer-gen Teller, and I told him the stories I had heard about Eggleston, until I noticed that the expression on Teller's face had changed ever so slightly, as if a shadow had fallen upon it, even though we were sitting indoors. 'William is a friend of mine,' he said. 'We have travelled together. I have taken many pictures of him.' I thought of this as I sat scrolling down the article and looking at his photos, which the small screen of my phone of course did not do justice to, but which were still striking. Colours can have a depth to them which can make surfaces seem dizzying, something which often happens in paintings but almost never in photographs. I have a book by the Danish photographer Keld Helmer-Petersen, some of the colour photographs he took during the 1940s achieve the same effect, colours that leave me greedy for something though I don't know what, but in a very differ-ent way, for he is interested in forms, in geometry, patterns and systems, whereas Eggleston is interested in people and sees them, in my eyes, from such a long distance that it is as if he were photographing animal species, tropical birds or animals of the African savannah, while at the same time what is particular to them, to each individual specimen, shows through.

The father who was playing football with his son in the

neighbouring garden will presumably forget this moment of this evening sooner or later, and the same goes for his son, and also for me – unless of course I wrote it down, I thought and stood up to go in here and do just that, not without a tinge of sadness in my heart, for the moment had no apparent meaning, and its meaninglessness would increase the moment I wrote it down, and even more the moment I die, it would be in a book somewhere, alone and unwitnessed: why did this moment in particular need to be saved, of all the things that happen?

You have gone to bed after being read to by your mother, who came home yesterday evening. The two of you have been together all day, you have been in town with the babysitter, shopping and eating pancakes, you have slept for an hour in your cot, and when you got up from it, still sleepy, you didn't want food, you just wanted to sit on my lap and watch the rest of us eat outside in the garden. When a butterfly landed on my hat, you laughed and waved your arms so that it flew away. When you made a 'p' sound with your lips, spraying saliva everywhere, and I asked you to stop, you slid down from my lap and walked over to the fence with an offended pout and your arms crossed over your chest, then stood there with your back turned to us while your younger sister laughed because you were so cute. That made you even more cross, and as you turned your head to watch my reaction, you reached out your hand towards a large leaf intending to tear it off, since only yesterday I had told you not to do that; then it was one of the still unripe plums on the plum tree that you plucked. When I merely smiled, you withdrew your hand and padded over to the table again.

Just now your mother is walking down the flagstone path

alongside the house with a bottle of mineral water in her hand, looking shadowy in the twilight, she is heading over to the wooden stoop where she usually sits when she is smoking. I imagine you are already asleep, normally it takes only a few minutes from when you are put to bed until you fall asleep. I am tired myself, but I have to sit here for a few more hours, for the plan is to hand in this final part of the manuscript tomorrow. I went through the first part on Wednesday morning and left our guests to their own devices – they were going to the beach before their plane left in the afternoon – sent it in around one o'clock, and since it was too late in the day for me to mobilise enough energy to start something new, I took the lawnmower out from the porch of the summer house and cut the grass instead. As I pushed the mower around in ever-diminishing circles on the lawn, I thought of the previous evening, fragments of the conversation surfaced, and I was suddenly overcome by a paroxysm of shame, for I had sat there boasting. My cousin had asked me how Brazil had been, and I had told them how many people came to my event. He had asked me whether I travelled a lot, and I had said that I could travel every day of the year if I wanted, but that nowadays I turned everything down. India, I said, Argentina, Bali, Chile, South Africa.

Why had I said this?

It wasn't necessary information, it was just boasting.

I passed into the long shadowy stretch along the fence where hardly any grass grew, just weeds and moss in between areas of bare earth, and I blushed. They were fifteen years younger than me and yet I still felt the need to mention that things were going well for me.

It was like I was twelve years old. Twelve-year-olds

couldn't be expected to control such urges. But a forty-seven-year-old? A father of four?

Instead of following the stone border of the flower bed on the shorter side of the garden and mowing the lawn in one big shrinking circle, I swung round and so divided the garden in two as I thought of Dad, who had once said that the Beatles, who were the band I listened most to at the time, had copied all their best-known songs from unknown classical composers, and that he had discovered this when he took piano lessons in his youth. He was going to show me next time we went to visit Grandmother and Grandfather, they had a piano. The next time we were there, I asked him to play me those songs. I didn't disbelieve him, he was my father, and I assumed that everything he said was true; I asked because I was genuinely curious and interested. He said they were in some old sheets of music, he didn't know them by heart, and he didn't have time to go rummaging through a lot of old stuff now. I believed him then too; I didn't understand until many years later that he had made it up. But why? Maybe he was jealous of the Beatles, who meant so much to me, and wanted to bring them down and at the same time elevate himself?

But that was lying, not boasting.

Still, they were related.

I felt deep remorse, finished one area of the lawn, started another one.

But so what, I thought. That's how it was. There was nothing to be done about it.

And my mood rose slightly, for soon the lawn would be mowed and in the evening my brother was coming to visit.

Oh no, no.

Another episode emerged from the recesses of shame. Our band was playing in New York, which was bad enough in itself, but during the whole trip I had talked about myself in just that way. Especially to the bass player. It was because I liked him so much and somehow felt I could let myself go with him, I could be as I really was, namely immensely self-centred.

While we were in a recording studio this autumn, in Gothenburg, I had flown back and forth to Stockholm to take part in a talk show, and my shame at what I had said during the programme was so unbearable that on the return flight I thought about taking my own life to escape it. It sounds like an exaggeration, but that's how it is with me at times, small insignificant matters can suddenly take on gigantic proportions and become almost too much to bear. When I got back to the studio, it was all I could talk about. Talking about it was an attempt to cut it down to size, to restore it to its just proportion. Then the others could say, surely it wasn't that bad, and it would be as if a breath of cool air wafted over the fire. The next morning I sat on the sofa talking to the vocalist, still racked with shame, and when the bass player came and stood in front of the coffee maker to make coffee, I said, by way of excusing myself and showing some self-insight, 'Can you guess what I'm talking about?' I had expected him to reply, The talk show, but he didn't, he merely said laconically, 'Yourself?'

That comment has burned in me ever since.

Since I am aware of this perception of me I always try to talk about other people, ask them questions, in a mechanical way, and on those occasions when I forget and say some-thing related to myself, shame comes rushing in, what must

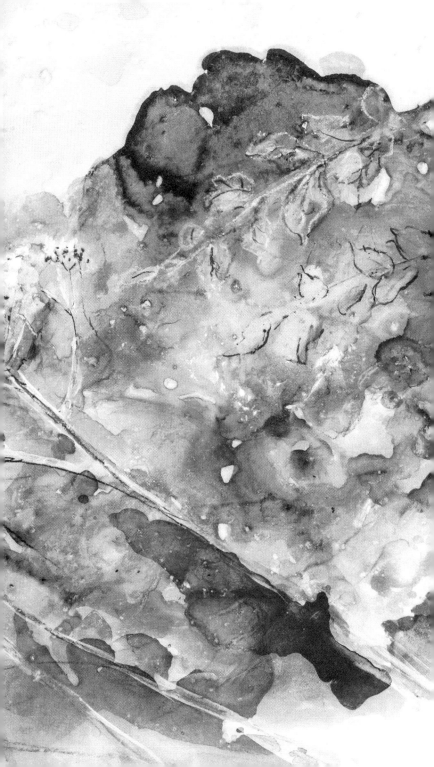

they think of me, and I try as hard as I can to think of something else to say.

Narcissism is an infantile state, but so is trying to get out of it.

The other circuit with the lawnmower was more troublesome, it involved areas more like forest than garden, and twice the blades struck rock with a grating noise, which brought me back to physical reality with its abundant sunlight and wealth of plants in every colour.

The struggle against shame is old, I have been battling it since I was thirteen, but part of the problem with shame is that it is always new, that it always comes as if for the first time – and that, I suppose, is something it has in common with the other emotions that take control over us, desire or infatuation, jealousy or shyness, they are pure, in the sense that they contain nothing but themselves, they are devoid of self-reflection or experience. One has to have a system to counter them with, one has to fence them in somehow to be able to stand outside them. The only insight that helps me to overcome shame's total ascendancy is that it will pass, that one day it will reveal its true proportions, which are almost always minor. The important thing is not to do anything stupid while it is raging, not to act on it but ride it out. Same thing with anxiety, jealousy, desire.

When the grass had been cut, I went upstairs and woke you – you had slept ever since the babysitter left at around two, and now it was three thirty. I put a new dress on you and, sitting in the hall with you on my lap, your pink sandals, before we left to pick up your elder sister at the railway station. She had both called and texted during the journey, anxious that no one would be there when she arrived alone, and then we went shopping for almost exactly the same groceries as the day before, hot dogs, meat, vegetables, feta cheese, olives, hot-dog rolls, soft drinks, strawberries and ice cream, for my brother and his friend were coming at around six, on the same ferry from Bornholm that our cousin had taken, but they were staying one day more. I had also invited some friends who live in the area and their two children, so we would be ten for dinner. I put two tables together, laid tablecloths over them, set the tables, filled the barbecue with charcoal, soaked it in lighter fluid, sliced the meat and made the salad, a rerun of the previous day. Then I picked up your brother and his friend from the dock just beyond the railway station and drove them home, while you sat as if paralysed by the company of strangers sitting right next to one of the places you are most familiar with in the whole world, the child seat in the back of our car.

Next day, in the evening around nine o'clock, I saw one of the most fantastic sights I have ever seen. We were driving along the road between the grain fields, and when the sea opened up before us it was as smooth as a mirror, with a strange silver-blue colour closest to the shore. The colour gradually blended into a slight haze, erasing entirely the divide between sea and sky. The fantastic thing was that there were so many big ships out on the sea that evening, and it looked like they were floating in the sky.

A shiver ran down my spine looking at it.

But that wasn't all.

On the way home with the girls in the car, the eldest one next to you in the back seat, the younger one next to me in the front, we saw the moon rise behind us in the east. It was enormous, and it hung just above the ground, bright yellow against the faded blue of the sky with the endless grain fields stretching out below it. All colour seemed to have been sucked out of the landscape, except the pale yellow of the grain and the moon's rich reddish-yellow. 'The moon!' you shouted. 'See the moon!'

It was a magical evening.

Next day I woke you early, we had to drive to Gothenburg to pick up your brother, and we couldn't be late, since he was being given a lift by a neighbour down to a place called Onsala, where there was a McDonald's we were supposed to meet at. It was over twenty degrees when we set off and it had risen to nearly thirty by the time we joined the motorway from Malmö. It was the most beautiful day of the year, and we were spending it in the car. You were not pleased, but there was nothing I could do about it. When we stopped at a large lay-by outside Helsingborg and I took you to the toilet, you were so offended that you refused to use it. Or else it was the horror of the dry toilets outside the musical venue the previous evening – where you had made yourself as stiff as a board so that I couldn't set you down on the toilet seat, which I quite understood, what was down there wasn't a pleasant sight – that still held sway over you. Either way the result was the same, you peed yourself in the car seat. I had brought a change of clothes for you and a towel that I placed over the seat, but in the heat the smell soon became unpleasant, which didn't improve matters. Four hours later we drove into the car park outside the McDonald's, and while you slept in your seat I stood outside, smoking two cigarettes in rapid succession. Then your brother came out of the restaurant, together with the neighbour, and I woke you up. Luckily you were in a good mood, and we all had lunch together. The neighbour said that your brother had told him all about Brazil and all about *Star Wars* during the two hours the trip had lasted. I was glad to hear it, it meant your brother had felt safe. And I was glad to see that you were so happy to see him. He had also told him about our cat, Amaga, the neighbour said. That it had even killed a fox. I looked at John. 'Did Amaga kill a fox?' I said. He looked down guiltily. 'Yes, I saw it,' he said, 'it killed a small fox.' 'Really?' I said, but I let it drop, I didn't want him to lose face, he didn't realise that the neighbour had known he was making it up. This was unlike him, or at least I hadn't noticed anything like this in him before. But I recognised myself as a child in it and wasn't surprised.

He was tired from the trip, had gone to bed late and got up early, but he was pleased with the visit, they had caught crabs, they had gone climbing in the mountains, they had driven a boat.

On the way home we stopped at Thomas and Marie's summer place at Höganes. You two got fruit squash and buns, I got coffee. I showed them the book dummies, which had arrived the day before, so that they could see the Kiefer paintings, hoping it wouldn't strike them as self-centred on my part. Once when they were visiting us I had shown them the pictures from the Munch exhibition, and the thought that they might think I was doing it to receive praise didn't strike me with enough force to dissuade me. For in fact I could have not shown them either Munch or Kiefer.

After a total of nine hours on the road we came home to a warm sunlit quiet garden full of birdsong and buzzing insects. Your sisters had managed fine on their own and the babysitter had come over to make lunch for them, so everything was all right.

The next day we drove back and forth to the venue of the musical three times, all in all two hundred and twenty kilometres, I saw on the odometer. In the evening your mother came, and today I have done practically nothing but write. When I was getting ready to drive your sisters, you were quick to say that you didn't want to come, you wanted to be here with Mummy. I can understand that: even for someone who likes riding in a car as much as you do, there are limits.

The shame I feel so strongly occurs only on the surface of the soul, it is a bit like the flame over charcoal, it is fuelled by lighter fluid and dances above the blackness, lightly and almost non-committally, whereas the glow within the charcoal is something quite other and deeper. I haven't killed anyone, even though it sometimes feels as if I have, and the things I anguish so much about are inconsequential in the bigger picture, they have to do with superficial matters in the world of social interaction, what others might think or believe, and the anguish is inconstant and flickering, not embedded in anything essential. Shame really belongs in puberty, when the curtain goes up and you understand that you are part of a larger context, but if something goes wrong then, it can persist. The woman whom I have fictionalised experienced something quite different and deeper, namely guilt. Whether she really felt guilt I have no idea, it may be that she suppressed it or didn't have sufficient self-insight to understand the full extent of what she had done. The woman I am writing about knows what she has done and reflects upon it; while she has forgiven herself, she has not been able to prevent it from ruining her life.

Though, how can a life be ruined? In relation to what? An imagined sequence of actions, an alternative fate, nothing more, but all that is hypothetical, those are fictions. If a person falls, he falls, or she falls, and while it is possible to think that it could have happened differently, it cannot be different. Only what happens happens. Only the life that is lived is lived. I don't think I have ever written anything more obvious, yet it is still difficult to grasp, since we make so many choices, and each choice excludes so many other possibilities, which continue to exist in the shadowy regions of our selves. If Dad hadn't begun to drink, he might still have been alive and have met all of his grandchildren. But he did begin to drink. If the woman in Malmö hadn't fallen in love with the German soldier, she wouldn't have abandoned her children, wouldn't have battled against guilt for the rest of her life, and wouldn't have had the feeling that she had lived only half a life. But she did fall in love with him, she did abandon her children, and she never saw them again. To reconcile oneself with one's fate, the expression goes, and it means just this: understanding that life turns out the way it does, that nothing can ever be redone, that there is no other path to be taken than this one, which ends the moment you die and, as it were, draw the ladder up after yourself. It is a thought I find comforting. We do the best we can. Even the people who don't do the best they can are unable to do differently. Few among us can point to one event, one choice, and say, it changed everything. Swedenborg could, and this woman could. My maternal grandfather's brother, who left for America and made a new beginning, he could. I can't. My life is the result of many small and perfectly common-place choices, good and bad, some of them consciously made, most of them not – in decisive moments I let myself be ruled by emotions, and what motivates our feelings is something consciousness knows little about, at least to begin with – though if given a little more time and an experien-tial space, it may come to see and understand what lies behind them. And we are used to considering life in this way: to have insight into life is good, by understanding what we are doing we can do the right thing, so that life turns out the way we want it to. But if we know what we are doing, there is a big chance that we won't do it. If we stop to con-sider the consequences, we don't rush headlong into something, we stay where we are. 'And thus the native hue of resolution/ Is sicklied o'er with the pale cast of thought,' as Hamlet puts it in his famous soliloquy, to be or not to be. Life's irony is that it is made up of two parts, one part in which one isn't able to think, only to act, and another part in which one is able to think, but not to act. For this woman, who will take over as the 'I' of this text in the next sentence, it was like that: she made a choice once based on her feelings and spent the rest of her life wondering how it might have turned out if she had chosen differently, or whether she really had a choice at all. I don't know what was more important to me that evening at the youth club, that he saw me or that I saw him. When we became engaged, I told myself that I had followed my heart. I gave myself over to that thought, I was almost as much in love with it as I was with Ivar. And then there were the other girls, the thought of them lifted me too. It was him I saw, but what gave what

I saw such force, what made me dizzy with joy, that is a different story.

Mummy didn't like him. She made her displeasure clear. But by then it was already too late.

Nothing happened that evening at the dance. He looked at me a few more times, that was all. And yet I thought of nothing else when I woke the next morning. I found out that he had asked about me. And I asked about him. He came from one of the villages further up the fjord. He built houses in spring and summer, when there were houses to be built, sometimes as far away as Bergen. In autumn and winter he helped crew a fishing boat. They would lie out near the Bulandet archipelago. His mother was dead, he lived with his father and two brothers, and it was with them that he built houses and jointly owned and manned the fishing boat. He had been engaged once, but the engagement had been broken off. He was known as a carouser. That he had looked at me and asked about me was almost unbearable, that's how exciting it was. He was a grown man. I had been confirmed only two years before.

Weeks went by without anything happening. But I knew what he would do, how he would come for me. It wasn't hard to figure out. In June, when the cows were led up into their summer pasture, I moved to the mountain farm along with my eldest sister. The farm lay at some distance up the mountainside at the end of the valley. There were other mountain farms nearby, and other girls. And where there were girls, boys would come. If he wanted to meet me, and I was certain he did, that's where he would go.

Summers in western Norway are completely different from summers here. Not only do the mountains give a depth to the days of summer and seem to close them in, while summer days here are stretched out, open and wide, but the summers at home are also greener, in a wild way, if one can put it like that – here on the plains of Skåne the green is dry and surrounded by yellow and beige and white, whereas in western Norway the green is moist, lush, dark. And while nights here are dark, the nights there are light.

I still long for those light summer nights when we would sit on the hillside above the mountain farm and gaze out over the valley, with the fjord at one end and the mountains on the other side. When the sky would be so light that the stars were almost invisible, and we didn't have the heart to sleep.

And I long for the rainy days when we would sit inside the mountain farm with a fire burning in the fireplace while the rain pattered on the roof and we played cards or knitted or just peered out at all that green.

And afterwards, the days of fine weather when we bathed in the deep pool down by the river and gazed up towards the snow-white mountaintops beneath the dark blue sky while insects danced in the rays of sunlight. That summer it was him I thought about every time I saw something beautiful or experienced something fine.

After we had gone to bed I would lie awake for a long time, listening for sounds that he might make. But all that could be heard were the bells worn by the cows and the sheep, tinkling forlornly between the mountainsides, and once in a rare while the call of a bird. And on some evenings distant voices or music from an accordion or a fiddle far away.

To myself as I lay there, I became the one who waited for him, she who would receive him.

That was my identity.

It was a big identity, bigger than the one I normally had. Perhaps because it was non-specific and not divided into parts; everything that was me flowed into that notion of myself and was swallowed up by it.

Of course he came.

He had brought a friend with him, I heard their voices from a long way off down the hillside, it was one of those nights when sounds travel far. So when their footsteps too became audible, I heard one of them hushing the other outside the house.

I smiled.

In the bed across from mine my sister turned her head and looked over at me. I put my finger to my lips. She tittered, I shook my fist at her.

Now they were inside the room below us. I heard someone climbing the ladder.

'Come on, let's go back,' one of them whispered.

The other, who was standing on the ladder, laughed out loud. It was Ivar.

He took a couple more steps, and then I saw his head appear over the edge of the loft.

'Johanne?' he said.

'I'm here,' I said.

And my heart hammered in my breast. Oh, how my heart hammered in my breast!

We walked up to the waterfall. He didn't say much. He embraced me there, abruptly and passionately, I felt his hard body against mine, and the feeling didn't leave me.

Dark and silent and dangerous, that was how I thought of Ivar.

I gave no thought to why I needed darkness, silence and danger.

On long sleepless nights at the mountain farm I longed for him to press himself against me. Sometimes I would get up and go out, filled to the brim with the thought of him I would walk up to the waterfall, shining whitely in the greyish night.

He came again, this time he kissed me. He had been drinking, the sweet smell on his breath excited me.

On Midsummer Eve we were gathered around the bonfire on the flat stretch down by the river. He grasped me by the hand and led me off, away from the others, and I laid myself down and received him. Afterwards I felt both joy and shame burning within me.

I was sullied, but I wanted to be, it gave me joy.

I married him the following summer. He built a new house next to the old one, and we lived there. We had three children together, with one year between them. He lost interest in me, and he was never interested in them.

There were many whose lives were like that, I wasn't the only one. But I was so young, had the door really slammed shut so early?

He drank, he had no pride, he flew into a rage if I suggested he do something during the periods when he didn't have work. I knew that he flirted with others, perhaps he even had others. With his light eyes and dark complexion and the wildness that came over him when he was drunk, he attracted many. But at least he had enough tact to keep it out of the village we lived in.

I had no one I could go to, no one to talk to, I was totally alone. I had the children, but I lacked the strength to keep the lightness up, I scolded them as my mother had scolded me.

In the beginning I tried to understand him. Then I made excuses for him. That was while I still wanted something from him, and sometimes I got it, there were times when things were good between us, but later I no longer wanted even that, he became someone who was just there, someone I put up with.

For more than ten years that was my only experience with love.

Then the war came, without life changing noticeably. There were Germans staying in the village and a camp for prisoners of war some distance outside it. Ivar chauffeured for the Germans, there was nothing unusual about that, several local men worked on the roads they built, and the Germans bought milk, vegetables and meat from the farmers, fish from the fishermen. The language barrier meant that he didn't have any close contact with them, he wouldn't bring Germans home with him or go drinking with them, with one exception.

One of the officers, an Austrian, spoke Norwegian quite well, he had been here during the summer in his childhood, and he became if not a friend then an acquaintance of Ivar's.

Once Ivar invited him to have dinner at our house. It was the first time I saw you, Alexander. Through the kitchen window as the lorry parked in the yard and you climbed out, a man of medium height in his early thirties, dressed in German uniform, peering against the sun, thin-haired, it turned out, when you removed your cap and greeted me a few minutes later. Thin lips, brown eyes, a friendly face. I wouldn't have noticed you in a crowd, you were not someone people turned to look at.

I was sceptical, I wanted as little to do with the Germans as possible, and that you had made Ivar's acquaintance didn't make me more favourably inclined. I hid myself away, I hid behind the cooking, the serving of the meal and the children.

Friday 29 July 2016

You didn't ignore me as some of Ivar's friends would do, but nor did you look at me with interest, as others sometimes did. You looked at me with curiosity. You looked at the children too with that same look. I noticed it because it seemed out of the ordinary, and I thought to myself that it was as if you had left yourself behind somewhere.

Actually I don't know if I really thought that then or if it came later, during my slow awakening after we came to Sweden and much of what I had experienced gained new significance. But I felt it: that you were curious about us, about who we were and how we felt, and I sensed that this openness was a part of your character, independent of whom you encountered or where you happened to be.

No, I didn't think it. For I was angry when this Austrian left. Why had Ivar dragged a soldier home with him, to our house? I brought my mother some food, I was irritated with her and impatient. I did the dishes, I milked the cows, I put the children to bed. I told Ivar not to invite him again. He asked why, I said he had acted superior, as if he thought he was better than us.

To be seen was not a good thing.

In any case he didn't come back, and I didn't think more about him. Mummy needed more and more care. She peered confusedly at me when I came, didn't know what would happen, what time of day it was. But she recognised me, and she expected to be waited upon. I don't know how she saw herself, but it seemed like she believed she was a queen. I combed her hair, I laid out clothes for her, she smiled gently and accepted my services. There was no trace of anger or despair left in her. Mild and gentle she sat there in her nightdress in the middle of the day with her thin grey hair loose over her shoulders, looking at me kindly and confusedly when I brought her food. At night, however, she would shout or scream in her sleep. Her bedroom was in the other house, but it was right next to ours and we could hear her, muffled as if by a pillow, how angry she was while she slept. Then that too ended. She died that winter, it was Henning who found her and who came running in to me, she sat cold and thin on the sofa with her hair loose and her eyes open in terror.

What kind of life had she had?

I cleaned the old house thoroughly, but other than that we left it as it was.

On the day she was buried the sky was grey and heavy and the cold winter rain fell from early morning on, drummed against the roof, settled in pools and puddles, pricked like thousands of needles against the still surface of the fjord. I walked up to the edge of the forest and cut some branches from the spruces there, laid them across the road leading to the yard. Got the children's best clothes out, set out the food I had prepared the evening before, put on my black dress. Ivar helped carry the coffin. She would have disliked that, and I disliked it too but didn't say anything. Six men wandering over the churchyard carrying a coffin between them in the rain. All was still except for the footsteps and the falling rain. We sang a psalm, the priest said a few words, he tossed soil on the coffin, it was lowered into the grave while we sang another psalm. Then it was over.

She was laid beside Daddy, and it wasn't until I thought of him that I cried.

That evening when everyone had left and the children had gone to bed, I sat in the living room with the window open, looking out into the darkness. There was a light on at the neighbours', shimmering through the fog, and a faint hush rose as the rain fell upon the fields. Ivar had gone out, but for once he had at least asked me if I minded. I didn't, I was only too pleased.

I was twenty-eight years old then.

I looked in at the children, they were all asleep, I took off my dress and hung it in the closet, and when I went to bed, I tried not to think about anything, just to listen to the rain falling on the roof and disappear into sleep.

A few weeks later Ivar asked whether I remembered the Austrian who had come for dinner at our house. 'Of course,' I said. 'It's not like we have visitors every day, is it.'

'He has been seriously ill,' Ivar said.

'He has?' I said.

'He is on his way to recovery,' Ivar said. 'But he's still bedridden.'

'And?' I said.

'We have room for him, don't we?' Ivar said.

'Have you gone mad?' I said. 'Are we to have an infirm person here?'

Ivar shrugged.

'We're being paid for it,' he said. 'I've already told them we can take him in.'

'We?' I said. 'We?'

He came to our house the next day, two soldiers carried him from the ambulance and into the other house on a stretcher. The sun stood above the mountains to the west, the light over the yard was faintly reddish. There was a strong wind blowing off the fjord, swaying the bare branches of the tree in the yard. The girls were standing over by the chicken coop and looking on, Gro with a few eggs in her hands. I had cleared out all of Mother's things from the bedroom and placed them in the loft; I was going to do that anyway. I had also made up the bed and put some flowers in a vase on the night table; if he was going to be here with us, I wanted him to think well of the place.

'Thank you,' he said when the soldiers had left and he was lying in bed looking at me. He was thin, his cheeks were sunken.

'Are you hungry?' I said, using the formal form to address him.

'No,' he said. 'But thank you anyway.'

His voice was low and faint.

'I'll look in on you again in a while,' I said, again using the polite form. 'If you are thirsty, there's water on the table.'

'Please, no need to be so formal,' he said. 'I am a guest in your house. And your patient.'

'As you like,' I said.

I left to do my other chores. I was a little uneasy, having

a stranger in the house changed it, suddenly it seemed as if everything was centred around the old bedroom.

'How is he?' Ivar said while we ate.

'He seems weak,' I said.

'They said he should be over the worst of it,' Ivar said.

'He is thin.'

'Well, you'd better fatten him up, then.'

When I had shovelled the cow dung down into the basement, fed the cows their hay and milked them, I stood close to Rosa's flank and stroked her. She turned her head and gazed at me with her deep, brown eyes. I laid my arms over her and stood like that for a while, feeling the warmth of her large body. Then I went into the kitchen, prepared a supper tray and carried it over to him.

He was asleep as I entered the room, but he opened his eyes when I set the tray on the table next to the bed.

'Here's some supper for you,' I said.

'Thank you,' he said, sitting up a little.

'You must excuse the smell,' I said. 'I was just now in the cowshed.'

He smiled.

'If you should need anything tonight, you can knock on the wall. Our bedroom is on the other side.'

'I don't think that will be necessary,' he said. 'If you could just . . . well, help me a little now?'

He looked away as he said it. Did he perhaps use a chamber pot?

'To the bathroom, I mean?' he said.

I blushed.

'What is it you need help with?' I said quickly.

'If you could just support me a little?'

He smiled.

'The rest I can manage on my own.'

'Oh, that way,' I said.

He sat up with difficulty, swung his legs down to the floor. I took him by the arm, he stood up slowly, and then we walked across the floor, out into the hall and over to the toilet. One step after the other, and pausing as he leaned against the door frame, and I thought he was going to fall. It was like helping someone ancient.

'I'll wait in the room,' I said when we were there. 'Just call me when you're ready to go back.'

He nodded, and I heard the door close behind me.

I drew the curtains shut, arranged the flowers in the vase, looked at the embroidery Mother had made of two red deer in a meadow, which had hung over the bed for as long as I could remember.

'Johanne?' came his voice from inside the toilet.

I went out to him and helped him back to the bed.

His face was pale and moist, covered by a film of sweat.

'That was kind of you,' he said. 'I'm sorry to be such a bother.'

'You mustn't think that,' I said. 'We're paid to do it.'

Why did I say that? I thought as I walked over to the other house. But it was true, after all. He was a German soldier, neither friend nor family, and we needed the money. Just as well he was clear about how things stood.

When I woke up early the next morning, it was with a feeling of expectancy. Something nice would happen today, something I was looking forward to. It was a feeling I hadn't had for years. But then I realised what it was, and joyful anticipation turned to disappointment, for it was nothing, merely the patient in the other house. So wretched then was my life that a sick man lighted it up.

After I had been to the cowshed, made a packed lunch for the children and sent them off to school, I went over to him with his breakfast. I wished him a good morning, placed the tray on the table and was about to pick up yesterday's tray and leave when I remembered that I had to help him to the toilet again.

He must have seen and understood this. Or at least I got the feeling that he understood what was stirring within me before I myself did.

I leaned over him, put my arms behind his back and helped him into a sitting position. He had done it by himself the day before, but it had cost him a great effort. Then I took him by the arm and helped him to his feet.

We walked slowly and wordlessly across the floor.

'You can come now,' he said when he was done.

That he didn't say my name settled like a faint shadow over my soul.

Outside, spring was in the air. The west wind died down and the warmth returned, the snow on the hillsides had melted and now remained only in patches, in ditches and on north-facing slopes. The children stopped using their winter boots, I rubbed fat into the leather and put them in the loft along with the winter clothes.

Caring for the patient soon became part of the daily routine. We didn't speak much the first week, I kept my visits to his room as brief and efficient as possible, tried to let him understand that I didn't have much time left over after the necessary chores had been completed. He followed me with his gaze as I bustled about him, often with a smile playing around the corners of his mouth. He likes me, I would sometimes think, but each time I did I told myself that he spent his days lying in bed in a room all by himself, it was only natural that my presence would seem a welcome diversion to him.

On the third evening I prepared a basin with warm water in the bathroom and carried it in together with a bar of soap, a flannel and a towel for him.

'I thought I should let you wash a little,' I said.

'Yes,' was all he said.

I laid the duvet to one side and unbuttoned his pyjama jacket, pulled it down around his arms, as I had done many times before with my children, wrung the flannel and laid it carefully against the back of his hand.

'Is it too hot?'

'No. It's fine.'

I soaked the flannel in the water again, rubbed some soap on it and began washing his upper body. He closed his eyes. I had been dreading this part and was glad he didn't look at me. I took his hand and lifted his arm a little to get to the underside of it. He lay very still. I dried his chest with the towel, took off his trousers, washed his thighs and groin, dried him. Not until I was dressing him did he open his eyes.

'Thank you,' he said. 'I feel much better now.'

'You will soon be able to do it yourself,' I said and straightened my back, carried the basin back to the bathroom.

Afterwards I felt the need to be alone. It was as if a space had opened within me which had to be protected.

'I'm going out for a walk,' I said to Ivar.

'Out? Where are you going this late?'

'Just for a walk,' I said. 'Up to the waterfall and back.'

'Why?'

'I feel like it. It's spring.'

He gave me a look. I turned and went out, saw the children playing by the barn bridge, there was a whole bunch of them there this evening, laughter and excited voices filled the air. I crossed the meadow, climbed over the fence and followed the river upstream. If he found my behaviour suspicious, that was his problem, I hadn't done anything wrong, I thought. But I didn't want to think about Ivar. I didn't want to think about the children or about the farm, about money or the future. I wanted to feel the spring and not think about anything. The air above the river, which wafted towards me, was colder than the air in the meadow. Patches of snow shone here and there between the black trees. The light of dusk lay on the mountains, lighter than down here where I was walking. Soon the birds would return. Soon the nights would get shorter and shorter until darkness would briefly cease to exist other than as a blue-grey veil over the sky in the hours after midnight.

I climbed up the mountainside along the waterfall, the way I had gone as a child, holding on to the slender trunks of the birches; I knew every single stretch of the path, at the top I sat down on a stone, in the place where the river formed a deep pool and seemed to swell before it plunged down the gorge.

I felt so happy.

He had been there for a week when for the first time we spoke more than just a few sentences to each other. I brought him his breakfast and was about to leave when he asked me if I was in a hurry.

'No,' I said.

'I am longing for someone to talk to,' he said. 'Could you sit with me for a little while?'

'Well, yes,' I said.

He asked me to tell him what I did when I wasn't looking in on him. What my days looked like.

I told him.

He asked whether I liked to read. I said that I hardly ever read anything.

He said there was a book by a Russian author that he had thought of. It was called *Faust* and was about a woman who doesn't read, and who one day is given a book by a man who is in love with her. She reads it, and she is so torn apart by it, it affects her so deeply that she dies.

'It sounds like a very silly book,' I said.

'Maybe so,' he said without smiling, as I had thought he would do.

'Would you like me to lend you some books?' I said.

'No, you needn't do that,' he said.

'Why did you think of that book when you saw me?' I said.

'I didn't say that,' he said. 'I just said that I had thought of it.'

Now he was smiling.

I stood up.

'You must rest,' I said.

He grasped my hand and pressed it lightly.

'Thank you for taking the time,' he said.

Saturday 30 July 2016

I was in a bad mood the rest of the day. The children were lying on their beds reading, all three of them, I sent them outside, changed their bedclothes and hung the duvets out to air, began to beat the rugs. Here he was, living in our home and with me spending my days taking care of him, and then he tried to play me for a fool with a book about a woman who hadn't read a single book in her life. He was lying in there laughing at us. But if that's how he wants it, that's what he'll get, I thought and went in again with the three long rag rugs, laid them in their places in the hall and upstairs in the bedroom, and carried the large rug in the living room outside. The sky was light blue and the sun was shining, but the wind blowing in from the ocean to the west was ice cold. A cloud of dust rose from the rug with every stroke. I didn't want to speak to him any more. Then he could lie there wondering what that meant. The dust clouds grew smaller and smaller with each blow, and when they were nearly gone I carried the rug inside, my hands red with cold. Where the rug usually lay the floorboards were lighter than the rest of the floor, and I scrubbed it with potash soap before I returned the rug to its place.

I reheated yesterday's soup for dinner. It was rich, smooth with oil and with big chunks of meat in it, perfect for a cold day like this. As Ivar parked the lorry outside, I laid the table and called the children inside. We ate without speaking. After a while Ivar asked how our patient was doing. 'Why don't you take him his dinner and see for yourself?' I said. 'Why yes, I can do that,' he said, laughing. 'And you mustn't forget to help him to the toilet,' I said. 'It's easier for me than for you,' he said and rose from the table.

I told the children to tidy their rooms, now that they had fresh bedclothes and everything. Then I went out to see to the sheep, some of them were about to lamb, but nothing had happened yet. I heard the lorry start up and drive away. I brought in the duvets, drank a cup of coffee in the living room, gazing out over the fjord. The mountains on the other side were blueish in the mist.

I wasn't angry any more. What did it matter if he looked down on us? He was an Austrian officer we were nursing for pay.

When I went over there with supper I greeted him without looking at him, set the tray on the table, picked up the dinner tray and went out again. The sun shone on the mountaintops to the south, they sparkled white with snow, and on the hills to the north, where the tops of the spruces shone as if made of gold. In the yard and over the meadow dusk was falling. The air was as cold as ice.

With my back turned to Ivar I lay in bed and cried that night, without a sound, the tears just welled up, ran down my cheeks and onto the pillow in the dark, it was as if I was unravelling.

The next day the wind had shifted, it came from the south and filled the valley with warmth. And it made the landscape seem milder, without the sharpness of the previous days. When I brought him breakfast, I felt silly for having wanted to punish him.

'Good morning,' I said. 'Did you sleep well?'

'Like a child,' he said.

'You look better,' I said. 'Would you like me to set the tray on the bed?'

'Yes, please,' he said.

He raised himself slowly, I took the pillow and set it upright against the headboard.

'There,' I said.

'I'm afraid I need to get up a little first,' he said.

I helped him to his feet and supported him as he walked across the floor. The upper arm I held him by felt sturdy. Although he was thin – I had seen how his ribs arched beneath his skin – there was nothing frail about him.

'Have the sheep lambed yet?' he said when he was back in bed and I had placed the tray in front of him again.

I shook my head.

'Not yet. But soon. I have a feeling it will happen tonight.'

'Why?' he said.

'It's much warmer out.'

'Does it make a difference?'

'I think it does,' I said. 'Do you have everything you need?'

'Yes, thank you.'

With his hand he stroked the back of my hand lightly and looked at me.

'You are an angel,' he said.

I blushed.

'I'm a peasant woman,' I said. 'And they pay me to look after you.'

'I am grateful anyway,' he said.

'That's good,' I said and went out without turning to face him.

*

No matter where I was, no matter what I was doing, my thoughts turned to him. That was why I had cried, I had realised that his presence had filled me with hope, and then, when I understood that there was nothing to hope for, everything within me emptied out. And it was a different kind of emptiness than the one which had been there before the hope.

What had I hoped for?

I didn't know, it was nothing definite. Just hope.

It had been such a good feeling.

Couldn't I simply let it be, bring him his food, speak with him when he wanted, and neither punish him nor hope, just be present in whatever it was I had wanted to immerse myself in that evening by the waterfall?

He slowly got better, soon he was sitting up in bed, soon he could walk to the bathroom and back again unaided, and one day he washed himself in there, seated on a stool in front of the basin I had filled with warm water.

His eyes were alive, I had never seen eyes that alive in any person before. I was used to eyes being closed off.

And I liked that he looked at me, it was as if when his eyes rested on me I became something more than what I was.

I also liked it when he touched my hand or my arm, always lightly and fleetingly, something lit up inside me then.

I began to wonder what he thought about when he lay there all alone.

Who was he?

He had transformed the room he lay in, it was no longer my parents' old bedroom. It was as if it belonged to another world, the door to which I opened every time I brought him food.

He was my first thought when I woke, and my last thought before falling asleep. But I never let on to him. How much I cared about him was my secret. In the mornings when I brought him breakfast, we would sit and talk, I sat on the edge of the bed while he ate and asked me all kinds of things about my life and this place. The only thing he didn't ask about was Ivar. He didn't say very much about himself. He liked to tell me about his childhood memories of Norway. He also liked to talk about books he had read, he spoke about the characters in them as if they were real people. Once he joked that Hitler ought to have read *War and Peace*, then he might have thought twice about invading Russia. No one had ever succeeding in conquering Russia, he said. Charles the Twelfth of Sweden had tried, Napoleon had tried, Germany had tried during the Great War and was at it again as we sat here talking.

'You do know that Germany is losing the war?' he said.

I shook my head.

'It's merely a question of time,' he said.

It began to rain, a cold hard spring rain, and it kept on raining for several weeks. The budding leaves and the grass that sprang up shone green and moist against the heavy sky, as if lit by a subterranean sun. The days with Alexander were coming to an end, I knew that, even though he hadn't said anything; his health was much better. They had been strange days, for nothing had happened, and yet everything had changed, it was as if everything within me had been set in motion. Feelings of all kinds passed through me. Joy, sorrow, anger, tenderness, despair, hope, desire. Sometimes the feeling was so powerful that I didn't know what to do with it, where to take it. On the exterior everything was as usual, I did what I had always done, and when I sat with him talking, our daily half-hour, I held it back. I came into the room, and he had heard me coming and sat up, I greeted him and drew the curtains so that the room was filled with the greyish twilight of the rain, I placed the tray in front of him, sat down on the edge of the bed and asked him how he felt today. If I met his gaze, I quickly looked down. If he stroked my hand in his friendly way, I withdrew it. Sometimes I also stood up, to show him who I was and who he was. At such times my heart would beat hard when I left. A rejection of something which might not be anything at all allows the thing that is rejected to emerge into sight and become a possibility.

I knew he liked me, and I was certain that he thought about me. For after some time he too would look down when our eyes met, and that told me that he too thought about the impossible.

Then one day I gave in. I had stood up, taken the tray, he stroked my arm with his hand.

'Thank you,' he said. 'You are an angel.'

I set the tray on the table, bent down over him and pressed my cheek to his. When I straightened up, we looked at each other. Then I hurried out.

It was innocent, I had given him a hug, it was nothing.

But I had been near him. I had felt the warmth he gave off, his smell. When I came into the kitchen, I sat down. It was as if I was overflowing, it was too much of everything, I trembled with emotion. I stood up again and went out into the rain. I knew that this was my last chance to stop something which would destroy me. I knew I should go inside, splash some cold water on my face and get on with the day as if nothing had happened. But I didn't want to. I wanted to go to him.

I opened the door to the other house, walked up the stairs knowing that he was lying there listening to my footsteps. I went into the room and straight over to him, bent down and kissed him.

When I straightened myself, it was as if I was somewhere else. I was suddenly calm, I was no longer in the middle of something, I was above it.

It was a wonderful feeling.

'I want you,' I said, looking at him.

I moved the duvet aside and slowly undressed him. He lay perfectly still. Then I undressed in front of him, he lifted his hands towards me, I smiled at him.

Afterwards neither of us spoke, I merely snuggled up close to him and rested my head upon his chest. Not even when I was about to leave did I say anything. 'I have to go' would have dispelled the magic, flung us into that which existed beyond us. I dressed, stroked his breast and kissed him, went out silently. Outside the air was streaked with rain, the ground soggy, the tracks of the lorry's wheels filled with greyish-yellow water. I didn't know what would happen when Ivar came home, how I would react, if it could all be read in my face, whether I would be afraid or filled with guilt. Cross that bridge when you come to it, I thought and went upstairs to the bedroom, opened the window and lay down on my back on the bed. It was as if parts of me I hadn't known existed had sprung to life.

So *this* was happiness.

So *this* was pleasure.

I closed my eyes and fell asleep as I was, to the sound of the rain that rose and fell in the wind outside.

There was no trace of fear in me when Ivar came home, nor of any guilt. He didn't notice anything different in me, everything was as usual. The children didn't notice anything either. I was entirely open with myself, I hid nothing from my own thoughts, and I could do this because what I had done wasn't wrong. This too was something new. I had no shadow. There were no dark corners where otherwise manifest truths were hidden away.

But I felt apprehensive about going back to him. What we had together still didn't have a form. Nor did I know what he was thinking, only what he felt.

What if there was a gulf between us now?

I went up to him with his dinner while Ivar was still sitting in the kitchen, to show clearly that nothing was going on up there that couldn't withstand the light of day.

My heart hammered in my breast as if I were a young person as I walked up the stairs thinking of him up there waiting for me.

'I was longing for you,' he said in a low voice as I entered the room.

I stopped in front of him.

'Come to me.'

'Not now,' I said.

'Yes, come.'

'He is down there,' I said.

Alexander stood up.

'Then I will come to you.'

He stood behind me, put his arms around my waist, kissed the nape of my neck.

'You are so good,' he whispered.

'I love you,' I whispered. He lifted up my dress, pulled down my knickers and entered me. I leaned forward and supported myself against the windowsill. My whole body was trembling, and when I heard the front door slam shut down in the main house, it seemed a sound from another world, far, far away.

'Harder,' I said. 'Harder, harder, harder.'

'You're so good,' he whispered.

'Ah,' I said. 'Ah. Ah.'

Nothing can take those days away from me. Every morning I woke up happy, and the happiness was strong, it protected me against everything, it made me invincible.

We hardly spoke to each other while those days lasted, the excitement was too great, we wanted only each other.

The happiness was a shield.

'The day after tomorrow I am going back,' he said one evening.

'You can't do that,' I said.

'We'll find a way to be together,' he said.

'Promise me,' I said.

'I love you,' he said.

'Do you know that no one has ever said that to me before?'

'I hope no one will say it to you later on, either,' he said.

'I love you,' I said.

There was Ivar, there were the children, there were the neighbours, there were the other soldiers. There were stolen trysts in the evenings, but it wasn't enough, not for him, not for me.

'I don't have anyone else,' he said. 'I have no family and no friends who mean anything to me. I am totally free. It doesn't feel that way, but I am. Sometimes I think about what that really means. That everything is open, that I can go anywhere I want in the whole world, do exactly as I like. Do you understand what I mean?'

'Yes.'

'Come out into the open with me.'

'I can't.'

'But do you want to?'

'Yes.'

Never before had I thought that the world was open. I knew it was out there, but I had never thought that it was there for me. But that isn't why I did what I did. I thought about him all the time, in my mind he was with me every minute, every feeling I had was directed towards him. It was unbearable to be parted from him. Unbearable. It was a kind of madness. Something tugged at me, it was so powerful that I was unable to resist.

Something within me also wanted to go under. Something within me wanted me to be destroyed.

The children wouldn't be destroyed. They would manage. They were already self-sufficient. And they belonged here. They weren't mine, they were their own.

I packed a rucksack in the morning when I was alone in the house, set it in the barn. That evening, when everyone had fallen asleep, I fetched it and walked along the fence to the edge of the forest at one end of the farm where he was to wait for me.

We kissed across the fence before I climbed over it.

'This is your last chance to pull out,' he said.

'I haven't changed my mind,' I said.

'I have deserted,' he said. 'If I'm caught, they will execute me.'

'Come,' I said, taking him by the hand, then began walking down towards the fjord in the pale June night.

The boat came for us about an hour later, a fishing boat owned by two brothers who were both on board and who had been paid by Alexander.

I had known them since we were children. They hadn't realised that I was coming too, and I could see that they weren't happy about it.

The smell of petrol and the roll of the sea made me nauseous, but I still slept a few hours that night, resting my head in Alexander's lap.

We got there at around twelve noon the next day. It was overcast and cold, the fjord was almost completely black beneath the mountains. They steered the boat as close to the rock as it was possible to get, and I put on the rucksack and jumped ashore onto a ledge.

Then the terrible thing happened. Even today I still can't believe that I saw what I saw, that it really happened.

Alexander was bending over his rucksack, and when he stood up and turned round, there was a pistol in his hand. He first shot one of the men in the head at close range, then he shot his brother in the chest, and then, when he fell down, in the head.

I must have screamed.

Alexander looked up at me with his mouth gaping open,

as if he himself didn't understand what had happened. With the two dead bodies lying on the deck, he went into the cabin and backed the boat out a little before he turned it and steered out into the fjord.

Inside me everything had stopped. There wasn't a thought in my head.

I leaned forward and vomited.

The boat was drifting about a hundred metres from the shore. I could see that he was doing something on the deck. So he hasn't left me, I thought.

From his movements I realised that he was pushing the two corpses overboard.

I squatted down and took a few deep breaths. My legs were trembling, my hands and upper body were trembling.

The boat came back towards land. The sound of the engine echoing against the side of the mountain was unbearably loud. He went below, how long he was down there I don't know, I had no notion of time, everything seemed to happen in an instant and yet it went on for ever.

He came back up, put his rucksack on and jumped across to the stone ledge as the boat slowly keeled over. He stood for a while watching the boat sink, then he looked up at the mountain.

'They would have informed on us,' he said. 'And even if they hadn't done it of their own free will, they would have given us away under interrogation.'

I couldn't look at him when he turned towards me.

'We would have been caught, I would have been executed, and you would have had to live with your shame for the rest of your life, there in the village.'

'You planned it,' I said.

'We have to go,' he said. 'Come now.'

Sunday 31 July 2016

We followed the valley inland. It was dark and damp, large unmoving spruces grew along the mountainsides. I walked without thinking, mechanically, absent from myself. Once in a while I glanced at the back of his neck and shoulders. This man to whom I had given myself blindly and whom I knew nothing about. I had had all kinds of feelings for him, but not fear, which was what I felt now.

We stopped by a brook to drink.

'I'm not a monster,' he said, wiping his mouth dry with his jacket sleeve. 'If that's what you're thinking.'

'I'm afraid of you,' I said.

'There's a war on,' he said. 'In war people get killed.'

'They weren't at war,' I said.

'I love you.'

'I don't know who you are.'

'I am the one who loves you.'

We walked up the side of the mountain all afternoon. When we got to the top, the sky had lightened, between the clouds to the west the sun was shining.

'Are you able to walk for a few more hours?' he said.

'Yes,' I said.

'Now you are free,' he said. 'Be in it while you can.'

'I don't understand what you mean,' I said.

We began walking again.

'No ties to anyone or anything,' he said. 'And no way back.'

He wept as we lay together that night, I bent down over him and rubbed my cheek against his wet cheek, kissed it and felt the taste of salt. 'I love you,' I said, grasped his hands and pressed them to the ground, he was lying on his back looking at me, and I didn't know what he was thinking, but I knew what he was feeling, and a wave of joy and grief bore me up.

Afterwards I clung to him, and we fell asleep like that.

When I woke up the next morning and saw him sitting on his haunches and slicing off pieces of the cured mutton sausage I had brought along, then laying them on slices of bread he had cut, I realised what he had meant the evening before. I went over to him and put my arms around him.

'There really is no way back,' I said.

He shook his head.

'And we are free, entirely free.'

That evening we sat outside a mountain lodge, the landscape around us glowed reddish in the light of the setting sun. We had knocked at the door a few hours earlier, told them the story we had agreed upon, and we had eaten with them.

I didn't know whether they believed us, probably not, but it didn't really matter. I had been talking and laughing all evening, a powerful feeling of happiness was tugging at me, and now, as we sat outside in the light from the evening sun, I began to laugh again and was suddenly unable to stop.

AUGUST

Clothes

We are six people in our household, four of them children, so if we are not careful, the house overflows with clothes. Then piles spring up beside their beds, where they undress in the evening, and on the sofa, where they occasionally pull off a sweater or a pair of trousers while watching TV, and on the bench in the hall, where the two older girls try on clothes in front of the mirror, not to mention in the front porch, especially in the winter when instead of hanging their jackets and waterproof trousers up nicely and putting their caps and mittens on the shelf, they fling them on the floor or on the bench beneath the window. These piles, which need to be washed, encounter another pile – of already laundered clothes – which also grows if we don't pay attention, for it is so easy to leave the clothes from the dryer on the guest bed in the room beyond the wardrobes, so that they sometimes form a pile the size of a small car. These two types of pile represent opposite poles in the circuit followed by the clothes, and it is easy, at least for someone who is easily swayed by their emotions, to think of the piles of dirty laundry as evil and the piles of clean clothes as good, or as hostile and friendly, or as belonging to darkness and light. Once in a while cases of doubt arise, a garment may look unused but be lying in a heap of used clothes, and then one has to do what I saw my mother do countless times when I was growing up, and which then I found monstrous, namely to lift the garment to her nose and sniff it, even if it happened to be a pair of underpants. Now I do the same thing myself, bend forward, press underpants to my nose and snuffle up their odours, like an animal. My relief when the underpants are dirty and smell faintly of urine is almost greater than when they are clean and smell of laundry powder, for then they are going to be laundered and become clean. Even though dirty laundry is simply clothes that have been worn on a body for a day or two, it feels almost like spiritual cleansing to put them in the washing machine, pour in the detergent and start the machine, to say nothing of the feelings that fill me when I remove clean clothes from the dryer and they feel warm against the skin and smell faintly of laundry powder, when the darkness I am in, or the narrow nooks and crannies that block the flow of thoughts or obstruct their passage, can vanish for a few seconds and make me suddenly not guilty but the opposite of guilty, which is not innocent but happy. It is because I want to prolong that feeling that in summer I sometimes hang washed clothes out to dry on the clothes line when the weather is fine, rather than run them through the dryer, for shirts hanging on a line above a lawn, beneath a blue sky, gleaming in the sunlight and gently swaying in the light breeze, are a beautiful sight, and also good, for although strictly speaking hanging up laundry is neither moral nor immoral, I must have imbibed something of the air-and-light moralism of the 1950s, according to which darkness was dirty and dirty meant poor and poverty was immoral, so that old dwellings were torn down and replaced by new, white and light-filled houses, and working-class kids were sent out of the city in the summer so they could get some fresh air and sunlight and thereby become good people. I have no idea how those attitudes have been transferred to me, presumably by way of my mother, who for as long as I can remember once or twice a year would air all the duvets outside and hang up rugs and bed linen and all the clothes we had on lines and drying racks, as if subjecting them to treatment. There is also an element of prestige in this, and I imagine that her mother, my grandmother, was even more vigorous in her efforts, and that no one could say about her family that they were lazy, unclean or immoral. That they were poor, however, there was no denying, but that was less shameful, for they had enough to get by and most people where they lived were no better off than they were. In our home no one works hard enough for their clothes to get either dirty or sweaty, and we have a washing machine, a dryer and a drying cabinet and enough money to buy new clothes every time a garment gets a hole or a tear in it or a button comes loose or a zip gets stuck, so the threat of the unclean, which I feel so strongly, isn't rooted in anything real, it is like the behaviour of a caged animal when the cage is removed but the animal for no reason stays where it is, inside no bars.

Ice Cream

Every year at the start of summer the ice cream manufacturers launch new kinds of ice cream, and the same law applies to them as to all plant and animal species, the survival of the fittest. If a new kind of ice cream is sold in sufficiently large quantities, production will be continued the following season; if it doesn't catch on, it is discontinued and never reappears. All these new ice cream sticks, bars and cones have to compete with old ones that for decade after decade have proved competitive, and in this way a manufacturer's assortment of ice creams is continually honed, and includes niches and pockets which only the fittest can fill. In this sense, Norway's two long-standing ice cream cones, the Kroneis – plain, milk-based cones which got their name at a time when they cost one Norwegian krone each, one strawberry-flavoured and the other chocolate-flavoured – can be seen as survivors, which isn't so strange, since their taste is uncomplicated and at the same time they are easy to hold, they are neither very small nor very large. When they come straight from the freezer the ice cream inside the cones is hard, with sharp edges around the circular plane on top, and one can choose whether to lick them – thus rounding the edges and slowly making the ice cream more plum-shaped, a process that is speeded up if the weather is warm and the ice cream melts, often dripping down the sides of the cone, which then has to be assiduously licked off – or to bite into them, which is quicker. But since for many the whole point of ice cream is to prolong the experience of eating, the latter provides no obvious advantage – except for avoiding the stickiness and mess which a prolonged eating session often entails, especially in the case of the chocolate Kroneis, since the chocolate also melts. Another way to attack the Kroneis is to – halfway through the licking process, by which time the ice cream has become soft and yielding, in some places almost like cream – simply bite off the bottom of the cone, thus creating a hole, through which the ice cream can be *sucked* out. The other long-standing survivor beneath Norwegian ice cream counters is the Gullpinne, the gold stick. As the name says, it is an ice cream stick. It is milk-based and covered with chocolate, with bits of *krokan*, caramelised sugar with butter and almonds in it, sprinkled on the coating, and there is also a layer of chocolate in the ice cream itself. This particular combination – ice cream, chocolate covering, *krokan*, stick – also has something basic about it, an air of solidity and unostentatiousness which I believe many parents select for their children to dampen the sense of extravagance that buying ice cream is fraught with, since it is an unnecessary luxury, unhealthy and devoid of nutritional value, which the Gullpinne, by virtue of its functionality and basic simplicity, in a certain sense tones down. My problem with ice cream when I was growing up was simply to choose the right kind. We didn't get ice cream very often, so making the wrong choice was, at least when I was around seven, eight, nine years old, downright catastrophic. Did I dare to pick a new kind of liquorice ice cream, for example? I liked liquorice, but did it taste good with ice cream? And the new kind that was called Kirsebærpinne, cherry stick, and was Gullpinne's brother, exactly the same except for the ice cream being cherry-flavoured, would it taste good *enough*? I did taste it, and for a long time it was my favourite ice cream, but then it disappeared, it was withdrawn from the market, and its brother, the solid and sensible Gullpinne, was alone once again, along with the two other survivors, Båtis (ice cream in a boat-shaped wafer) and Sandwich. But the most difficult choice of all was the one that had to be made in places where they sold soft ice cream, which is to say in town, for there they also had ice cream by the scoop, and who can say what is better, soft or scooped ice cream? They each have their big and obvious advantages. The strong point of scooped ice cream is the number of flavours. A well stocked ice cream stand can have as many as twenty different flavours. You can choose one, two or three scoops, which the salesperson shapes with a scoop and places in a cone-shaped wafer (or in a paper cup, but is anyone really stupid enough to choose carton over biscuit?), and the possible combinations are legion – one chocolate, one pistachio and one rum and raisin, for example; or two chocolate and one pistachio; or one pistachio, one strawberry and one vanilla; or one chocolate, one vanilla and one *krokan*; or one pistachio, one rum and raisin and one *krokan* – which is a difficult decision in and of itself, not least because the choice must at times be made on the spot, within a fraction of a second, something I still, with the benefit of more than forty years' experience, find rather challenging. Then add to that the possibility of

choosing soft ice cream instead, which isn't an uncomplicated matter either, for soft ice cream can be dipped in
melted chocolate or rolled in chocolate powder or *krokan* or
chopped nuts or chips of Daim chocolate or multicoloured
sugar balls. To me, soft was long the king of ice cream, it is
the only ice cream that is almost like whipped cream, but
with its quality of being ice cream intact. And my preferred
solution to the problem of all the different toppings is usually to ask for two, namely chocolate powder and *krokan*.
What sometimes happens then is that they roll it first in
chocolate, then in *krokan*, so that I get two layers, at other
times they press one side into the chocolate powder and the
other side into the *krokan*. One might think that my children
would follow in my footsteps, that they would understand
that the choices I make are the result of long years of experience, but they go their own ways. My son, for example, often
selects sorbet as one of the flavours of his scooped ice
cream – which he prefers to soft – something I have never
once done in my life, not even considered. My middle
daughter is not above asking for soft ice cream in a paper
cup and eating it with a spoon. What I choose is of no consequence to them. Often they say, 'But Daddy, didn't you say
you weren't going to eat ice cream and sweets any more?' 'I
did say that,' is my answer then, 'but the weather is so nice
today.' 'You ate ice cream yesterday too, and then it was raining,' they say. 'It's just an excuse you use.' 'Oh well,' I say.
'Why shouldn't you eat ice cream and goodies?' the youngest
one asks. 'Because it makes you fat when you get to be as old
as I am. You lot can eat as much as you want, but I can't.' 'It's
true that you've become fat,' the eldest one says, she is as
thin as a rake no matter what she eats. We were sitting at a

table outside the kiosk at Borrby beach, a wide, fine-grained and almost pure white sandy beach, it was perfectly still, the sky was luminously blue, the glare of the sand was so strong one could hardly look at it, and the sea was as smooth as a mirror and calm. 'So can I have another ice cream, then?' the youngest said. 'Since I can eat as much as I want?' 'No, you can't,' I said. 'Why not?' he said. 'Because you are a child, and because you are under my control. But I can eat two ice cream cones,' I said. 'No, you can't,' the eldest said. 'Oh yes, I can,' I said, stuffed what was left of my wafer into my mouth, stood up and walked over to the kiosk, bought a pistachio cone and walked back to where they were sitting. They looked on in shock and consternation as I proceeded to eat it. Two ice cream cones in a row, in their world that was something totally unheard of. How come I never thought of that before? I thought as I sat there eating and gazing out at the sea with the children's eyes fixed on me. Why have I never eaten two ice cream cones in a row before?

The children still remember that time, even though it was three years ago. To them it was a demonstration of force, since they didn't get another ice cream no matter how much they nagged me. To me it was a joke, although the joke also had a hint of seriousness to it, since it made me understand that I really could do whatever I wanted. That I used that freedom to eat two ice cream cones in a row also gave me a thing or two to think about.

Salt

Salt consists of small white granular crystals that look not unlike sugar but are very different from it as far as taste and properties are concerned. Salt is first and foremost a catalyst, an agent which makes things happen, such as causing meat to dry without rotting by drawing the moisture out and absorbing it, or keeping roads free of ice by lowering the freezing point of water, or enhancing the taste of various food dishes. In this sense salt is more sophisticated than sugar, which has something brash and one-dimensional about it: sugar tastes sweet, and it makes everything it comes into contact with taste sweet too. Sugar cares only about itself, salt brings out the best in others. Yes, everything salt touches becomes better as if by magic, and often in irresistible ways, like the ocean – how fresh and bracing the salty ocean is compared to the sweet freshwater of inland! I still remember how disappointed I was the first time I went swimming in the Baltic Sea, in the outer part of the Stockholm archipelago; the sea spread out before me and I dived in full of expectation, for it was summer, the sun was strong, the air was warm and the sky was high, and my body bored through the water, which was cool but not fresh, and it was as if my whole body reacted, something was missing, what on earth is this, there's hardly any salt in the water? And for the first time I had the thought that Sweden is an inland country and the Swedes an inland people. During my entire childhood and youth I believed that the archipelago outside Stockholm was a real archipelago, due mainly to the Swedish TV series *We On Saltcrow Island*, for no child growing up by the sea and watching that series could ever believe that an island that was part of an archipelago and which of all things was named Saltcrow Island, in reality lay in an inland body of water! On the way back to the city, aboard one of the many small boats that regularly ferry passengers to and from all the islands outside Stockholm, I saw it clearly: there were reeds growing in every inlet, everywhere trees grew all the way down to the edge of the water, which wasn't salt but sweet – we were sailing on a body of water in a forest. One might object that nature can't be ranked in this way; that I valued ocean higher than lakes, sea coast higher than inland shores, was obviously just because that's what I was used to, since the place where one grows up will for ever after be one's point of reference and ideal template. But this is precisely a Swedish view of the world, relativistic and evasive, nondescript and tepid, a little like the water surrounding their capital city. And after fourteen years of living near the salt-poor Baltic, in an area steeped in Swedish culture, I have a sneaking suspicion that my thinking is wrong, that the salty waves of the Atlantic smashing themselves against the Norwegian coast are in fact neutral, they don't express anything, they are just water containing roughly 3 per cent salt, brought to the ocean by rivers and brooks that have washed it out of the rock over millions of years. Salt has nothing to do with either culture or identity and almost no bearing upon human life, except for the tiny amount we need in order not to die. Salt is no agent, it is neither sophisticated nor unsophisticated. Salt is salt. And yet there are few things in the world that can measure up to diving into the ocean from a smooth rock and feeling the taste of salt on your lips as your body bores through the water, which is full of eddies and swirls and pockets seething with bubbles, and afterwards lying on the rock in the sun next to the one you love, whose suntanned skin shimmers in places under a thin, thin layer of salt, and whose lips taste of the ocean.

Earthworms

It has been raining for several days, and this morning two earthworms lay on the road beyond the hedge. They gleamed pale red against the grey-black asphalt, looking soft and swollen. They resembled small intestines or some kind of gland. When I poked one of them with a stick, it began writhing slowly, so it was alive, but clearly out of its element, like a human being in the water far out at sea. They belonged down below ground, but now for some reason they had wriggled up into the light of day, where they would die, for they couldn't withstand sunlight and they were unable to burrow down into the soil again.

I remembered seeing the same thing many times in childhood, earthworms appearing above ground in rainy weather and lying about in the garden or on the road like small slowly convulsing intestines, and yet this really quite wild sight never occasioned any surprise, that was just how things were. There also seemed to be more slugs about at these times, slimy and glistening little heaps of black in the grass and on the forest floor, as if all the water that fell and trickled and flowed everywhere had transformed the external landscape into some interior region, something soft and moist and visceral under a lid of dense cloud, and was luring out all the creatures who belonged in the world of the hidden, the sealed, the secluded. There they came, the earthworms, emerging from their dwelling in the dark earth, and there came the slugs, slithering out of their clammy, moist haunts in the shadows. As if nature was turning itself inside out, and all the creatures of the interior obeyed its call and were exposed.

As a child I had felt a pang of sorrow at the sight, for they were going to die, and now I felt the same somehow blunt sensation of sadness, watching the two earthworms lying there on the road in the grey summer light. But unless I was able to imagine their existence as they experienced it, my empathy was pointless, I thought. Perhaps for them there was no difference between life and death, perhaps to them life was like wind to a plastic bag, something which for a time moved it forward through the world, and death merely the cessation of this movement.

No, that couldn't be. Earthworms have a brain, albeit a small one, and a single nerve extending through the length of their bodies, and if their actions are mechanical, they still come about as a result of certain needs, which in one way or another must be felt as such. When the soil just beneath the surface becomes too hot during summer, earthworms burrow down to a depth of several metres, where the earth is cooler, and similarly in winter, when the topsoil becomes cold or even frozen, the earthworm moves down into the depths and lies there in a dormant state. The reason it seeks the surface when it rains heavily is that all the water makes it difficult to breathe – for the earthworm breathes through its skin – and one must imagine this ascent originating in a panicked impulse, or at least in an unpleasant sensation.

And there can be no experience of unpleasantness except based on a prior sensation of non-unpleasantness, which isn't necessarily pleasure as such but at the least some form of sober contentment, which as far as the earthworm is concerned means life underground when the soil is neither too hard packed, too dry nor too wet, neither too warm nor too cold, when it contains rotting leaves and pine needles and pieces of broken twigs. The earthworm can't see, so everything is totally black, nor can it hear, so everything is completely silent. It has five tiny hearts and a little mouth, which it also uses to make its way when the earth is hard and densely packed: it simply eats its way through. It knows neither where it is nor who it is, but none of this really matters; what matters is that it is. A string of being, that is what the earthworm is.

Ekelöf

Today is the fourth of August, and it is raining at the same time as the sun is shining. In places the grain is almost completely white, and the first of the combine harvesters, those enormous bug-like vehicles, can already be seen in some of the fields. The grain is spewed out in unbelievable quantities. I saw it this morning as I was driving to Borrby with our baby girl asleep in the back seat, I was heading to the antiquarian bookshop Hundörat ('Dog's Ear' in Swedish) to buy a wedding present. I had already bought three first editions of Gunnar Ekelöf's poems there earlier, and now I wanted to see if they had more of them. Ekelöf is the most bountiful of Scandinavian poets, his poems encompass every state of mind, every season, every epoch. And yet his tone of voice is easily recognisable, there is a sternness to it, even when he is being playful or joking. It may well be that this perceived sternness isn't really there, that I am merely reading it into his poems due to my sensitivity to authority and my fear of anything superior. But I sense the same sternness in other profound poets, such as Ezra Pound and Norway's Georg Johannessen, or Dante for that matter. These four are supreme poets, or they radiate supremacy, each in his day and within his own culture belonged among the most learned, and each in the end sought simplicity and spontaneity of expression as the greatest good. I seem to remember reading an anecdote about Ekelöf, he came late to a dinner party, he was drunk, and he walked around among the guests whispering into their ears who they really were. Surely I am not the only one whom this story fills with dread; more than anything else, I fear being found out, that someone will whisper into my ear who I really am, and I will know that what they are saying is true but I would never have been able to admit it to myself. Ekelöf stood on the outside of the party just as Count Myshkin did, an idiot or a child, one who says what he sees, but with this difference: Ekelöf knows what he is doing and where he stands, and that's what is so terrible. Something similar is going on with poets who end up seeking the simple and the free, their quest is not innocent, it merely longs for innocence. Perhaps the ring of sternness in their poems stems from this dynamic: these poets were not themselves able to experience simplicity and spontaneity, but merely wanted us to experience it, knowing full well that we would never appreciate the true value of the gift. When I arrived in Borrby, I woke the baby girl and carried her with me into Hundörat, she stood swaying with sleep in front of me, coming up to my hip, while I browsed through the bookcase containing Swedish poetry. I found four first editions by Ekelöf and bought them all. In addition I bought a volume of his posthumous poems and notes for myself. When I got home and sat down in my study with a cup of coffee, I opened the book at random and read what was on the page, it was a text called 'Apropos of Swedenborg'. It concerned the Fall. What if it wasn't a fall from good into evil, from the innocence of paradise to earthly guilt, what if man at a certain point in time separated out evil in a moral division, because man became more human, and consequently evil, in Ekelöf's words, was 'the left behind'? It follows from this that God neither has existed nor exists, but that he may arise at some point in the future. This peculiar notion is developed further in a poem in which God is immanent in life, concealed within every movement, as yet unborn, *'han har inte samlat sin ofantliga/ kropp under en vilja'* ('he has not gathered his unfathomable/ body under one will'). I have thought about that idea every single day since, that God is a possibility, always present, never realised. That God is in the combine harvesters and the spewed-out grain, in the shadows of the trees and the windings of the roads, in the roofs of the houses and the frames of the doors, in the children's movements and in their hearts, and yet is not, since totality is unfathomable and it is that which is God. And therefore God is impossible, for God is in the multitude, and if the multitude is gathered into one, it is no longer a multitude.

Bicycle

A bicycle is a mechanical means of transportation consisting of a frame with two wheels, one of which is connected to pedals via a chain. The construction is so simple and so effective that it's really rather strange that it wasn't invented until the nineteenth century. Leonardo da Vinci, who designed prototypes of aeroplanes and submarines and tanks, why didn't he think of the bicycle? Or Emanuel Swedenborg, who also drew a flying machine and was obsessed with mechanical inventions? The stroke of genius about the bicycle is the transmission of force from the pedals to the chain and on to the back wheel in a sequence in which every stage seems to augment the force, so that anyone at all, even a child, can achieve considerable speed without using more energy than is required for walking and in this way greatly expand their radius of movement. And perhaps it was due to the very simplicity of this invention, as well as its popular and democratic potential, that none of the great mechanical minds came up with it. They thought big – up into the sky, out into space, down to the bottom of the ocean – while the bicycle is small. Unlike other means of transportation its visual impact is very minor; when one sees a person riding a bicycle, it is the person one notices, not the bike. The bicycle is unimpressive and humble and doesn't protect the person riding it the way a car does, on the contrary it exposes the rider, and also his or her vulnerability. In everyday situations this vulnerability isn't so obvious, but in situations of armed conflict it becomes evident. A soldier on a bicycle is not intimidating, is not the awe-inspiring sight a soldier mounted on a horse is. It was mainly during the First World War that soldiers used bicycles, and then primarily while serving as couriers. Adolf Hitler, for example, who was a German army courier tasked with bringing messages from headquarters located behind the front, cycled the whole way to the soldiers in the trenches. As far as I know, no films or photographs exist which show him on a bicycle, but there is no reason to believe that he gave a different impression to other soldiers on bicycles, who, helmeted and uniformed and wobbling slightly as they pedal down a gravel road, seem closer to the characters portrayed by Charlie Chaplin than those depicted by Homer. Today bicycles are inconceivable in the world of military hardware, which is almost exclusively made up of large machines such as helicopters, fighter planes, submarines, rockets, tanks and aircraft carriers, and in which soldiers carry so much equipment that they themselves resemble machines. When police forces in recent years have established bicycle patrols, the aim has been to exploit the very vulnerability that the armed forces seek to avoid; by riding bicycles, the police show that they are human and minimise whatever might set them apart from the public they are supposed to serve. But in truly critical situations, such as when the police surround a house where a suspected terrorist or bank robber has taken refuge, they don't arrive by bicycle. So nowadays the bicycle really belongs only in the family sphere, but there, on the other hand, it is deeply integrated, at least in the part of the world where I live, where all children above a certain age are given their own bicycle and learning to ride one has become a ritual of initiation. I have met many grown-ups who don't know how to drive a car or who can't swim, but I have never met an adult who didn't know how to ride a bicycle. Since the bicycle doesn't protect but instead exposes its rider, mounting one may entail an apparent loss of dignity, for the aura possessed by a person driving a black BMW is radically different from that of a person riding a red Raleigh bicycle. The dignity that is lost has everything to do with the car and nothing to do with the person, for what the bicycle does is reveal the human form, or return it to itself. If you look small on a bicycle, it is because you are small. That's what I was thinking, perhaps to comfort myself, the other day when I bought myself a new bike and, wearing an equally new helmet, pushed it past the car and into the road, placed my foot on one pedal, swung the other foot over the frame and began pedalling, seated barely five feet above the road surface, wholly exposed and feeling naked. My eldest daughter, who also got a new bike that day, swung out in front of me, wobbling slightly and with her long legs pedalling rapidly up and down in too low a gear, and I was swept by a wave of affection for her, for on the bicycle her entire apparatus of protection against the world – all those forms, both physical and psychological, the make-up and the clothes and the way of speech, the arched neck and the eye-rolling – was totally eliminated by the bicycle's requirements for balance and speed, which evidently also took her back to a time when riding a bicycle was new to her, for as I came up beside her she looked up at me with eyes that sparkled with unguarded joy.

Backer

This summer I have taken maybe a hundred photographs. Most of them are of the children, but there are also many of the garden here and of the surrounding landscape – wide grain fields, the sun-filled edges of woods, great broadleaved trees, the meagre hills near the sea, the tall sky above them, often full of hanging clouds. These photos, taken with the camera in my phone, have no aura, they radiate nothing beyond a kind of facticity: this is how it was in that particular place at precisely that time, for example on this rain-drenched day in the garden in Glemmingebro on the tenth of July 2016. Every place and every moment has its own distinctiveness, but it isn't visible in these photographs, except in so far as my own memory supplies the cues. I suppose that is why other people's photos often seem so pointless; what gives them their significance is the viewer's personal relation to the viewed, whether it is people or landscapes.

A few weeks ago I was in Rio de Janeiro for the first time, and although I had seen thousands of photos of the city, it was not until I stood there, on Copacabana, with the white concrete high-rises set amid lush tropical mountains behind me and the beach before me, that the city acquired for me its own intrinsic weight. So *this* is how it is here! I had seen all of it before, but as facticity, not as reality. Reality is experienced reality. The strange thing is that paintings, as opposed to photographs, seem to convey this. There's nothing strange about that, one might object, for what paintings depict is precisely the particular place or person, conveyed through a personal presence. So is the spirit of the place, its aura, something that exists solely within ourselves? Or is it merely something within us that is fine-tuned enough to perceive it? Is the spirit of the place the same for everyone or do we each colour it in distinctive ways, according to our temperament and state of mind? What realist painting of the nineteenth century does is create a feeling of being there, not primarily through depicting the place or the person, but by depicting the *quality* of being there, in other words, presence. What happens then is that the artist's experience of the place is superseded by the viewer's experience of the painting: the painting becomes a place. All morning I have been studying a reproduction of a painting by the Norwegian artist Harriet Backer, it is one of her best-known works, the title is *Christening in Tanum Church*. I have always liked it. The scene is depicted from within the church, the perspective seems to suck the viewer from the interior of the church outwards towards the open door, where two women are on their way in, one of them carrying a small child in her arms. In one of the pews we see another woman, she is turning around to look towards the doorway, and my gaze is constantly shifting between these two, the women arriving and the woman turning to look at them.

That's all there is. One might perhaps imagine that the painting draws on a tension between the interior, the bourgeois decor, and the exterior, the wild outdoors, but it doesn't;

on the contrary, the transition between the two places or states appears gradual and harmonic. Nor is religion, the newborn child who is still a part of nature but is about to be initiated into culture, something I think about when I look at this painting, though naturally the image evokes this association too. Nor does it make me curious about who these people might be. Neither where they have been before arriving at the scene depicted, nor where they are going afterwards. For the whole point of the painting is the moment, its peculiar relation to time. It is said about Harriet Backer that she never worked on her paintings for more than twenty minutes at a time, for beyond that time the light would no longer be the same. In this particular painting the light arrives through the open door from the world outside, where no sky is visible, only dense greenery, glowing luminously the way it does on rainy days in summer. It is reflected with a faint glisten on the wooden door, becoming more matte where it strikes the floor, which gets dimmer and dimmer towards the interior of the church. These effects of the light tell us that it is late morning, probably in late June or early July. Light's fleetingness, that it is constantly changing, never motionless or fixed, connects it with time, it is almost its visualisation. In this painting's extreme sensitivity to light something occurs when the light encounters the stationary floor and the palpable walls, something that the scene depicted – the woman turning round, the women arriving – takes up into itself, in that the fleetingness of this particular moment is fixed in the immobility of the figures. Thus time becomes a place, a grotto of light dug out of the darkness, and only thus can time, which we sense but do not understand and never see, acquire its own aura.

Cynicism

Cynicism is the name given to a kind of thinking that is detached from all emotion and which therefore is often experienced as free, somewhat like the condition of teenagers whose families have left on holiday and who find themselves alone at home for the first time. Their thoughts can behave as they like, they don't need to show consideration for anything or anyone, other than for the truth, which to the cynic is hidden as if behind a veil. The veil is made up of our notions and ideas about reality, especially social reality, which is dominated by illusions we believe in and use to interpret the world, but is merely a game, something secondary which covers up the primary thing, our real motivations: self-interest, egoism, self-preservation, desire. What this means is that nothing is as it seems but is always an expression of something else. Such programmatic mistrust has only one course to follow, it cannot lead to anything other than misanthropy, which in turn has only two possible outcomes, nihilism or hedonism. Nihilism is nothingness, hedonism is pleasure devoid of empathy for others. And it is ironic that unclouded, emotionally pure, autonomous and unbounded intellect, which distinguishes human beings from all other animals, when pursued to its logical conclusion leads straight into animal behaviour, with one cruel difference: awareness of the meaninglessness of that. For the cynic, however, there is no other place to go, because it is truth that leads there. Salvation through, for instance, faith in God's grace is not an alternative, because faith is an illusion, created precisely in order to evade the truth, which is so brutal that almost no one is prepared to bear it, that almost everyone will do anything to avoid it. At the other end of the spectrum from the cynic we find the person who is naive, for whereas the cynic analyses everything and doesn't believe in anything, the naive person analyses nothing and believes everything. Nowhere is the antagonism between these two extreme positions better portrayed than in the novel *The Idiot* by Fyodor Dostoevsky. There social life is described as a game involving strategies and calculations for personal gain and the downfall of others, a game that breaks down completely when it encounters someone who refuses to play, someone who doesn't calculate but rather accepts everything at face value and believes what he sees. His goodness lies in his lack of pretence, he has no ulterior motives but lives out his emotions, like a child. The same thing occurs in the film *The Idiots* by Lars von Trier, in which a group of disillusioned Copenhageners have gathered to pretend that they are idiots, and the game breaks down when the group is confronted with a person who doesn't pretend, a woman who has lost her child. Lars von Trier is himself a cynic, and Dostoevsky must also have been, in any case he was intimately familiar with the game, with nihilism and with hedonism, and it is possible to view the work of both these artists as a battle against their cynical selves, as mighty attempts to plant meaning and life in their cynical inner wastelands. Yes, perhaps all art is really an expression of that struggle. Pure cynicism cannot create art, since its method, to regard the world as it is, without emotion and without faith, completely precludes art's method, which is to reimagine the world, filtered through emotion. Cynicism's ideal form is therefore the aphorism, the crystalline and flawless sentence, and the cynic's position of duty is that of the critic, who is really, in his or her heart of hearts, inimical to art. Pure art, on the other hand, is created by the naive, and it is greater and better the more naive the artist. The best example that I can think of is Edvard Munch, who possessed not the slightest shred of cynicism, he was an idiot, and few artists have depicted the human condition here on earth with greater truth than he has.

Plums

Just as the darkness begins to thicken at night, towards the end of July and the beginning of August, as if it is becoming a touch moister and no longer dissolves as easily in the air, the plums begin to ripen. The sweet juicy taste therefore always has a hint of melancholy about it; summer is over for now. When I began writing this book at the end of May, I asked everyone at the publishing house to write down the words they associated with summer. The list surprised me, it was so full of hope, the words were all light, airy, joyful. There were bathing beaches, bikinis, dew, cold lager served outside, white nights, smooth rocky slopes by the sea, sunburn, closed for the summer and sunglasses, there were waves, vacation, badminton, clinker-built double-enders, portable radio, sweet cherries, sandals and summer dresses. There were cabriolet, wasp stings, rosé wine, hammock, bathing under a sprinkler, reading the classics, bathing ring, skinned knees and going camping. There were summer camp, shorts, rainbow, sweat, straw hat, linen trousers and heatwave, beach bag and soft ice cream. Every word evoked expectation of one kind or another. The taste of plums, sweet in a dark and heavy, almost earthbound way, contains within it the end of this expectation. It didn't turn out the way I thought it would, says the taste of plum, and now it's too late. Today is the eighth of August, and on the old plum tree in the middle of the garden, whose horizontal branches are supported on crutches, almost all the plums facing south and west are ripe. I ate a couple earlier today, standing on the grass in the cool fresh breeze, and in the melancholy feeling which the taste evoked there was also something good, the thought of soon returning to regular life with its limitations and routines, autumn and winter, which bear no promises. The taste also made me think of my childhood, the darkness of evenings in late August, evenings when we would go scrumping in the old fruit gardens on Old Tybakken, which in my memory was connected with crab dinners, another seasonal occurrence in the final days of summer, when the wall against autumn had opened and its darkness came gliding in, along with the winds. Sometimes we went scrumping on the way to school, parked our bicycles by the fence and ran in, stuffed our sweaters with plums, holding up the hem to form a sort of sack with one hand and steering our bicycles with the other. It was my favourite time of year, I loved the hint of coolness in the morning air, when the water in the sea was still warm from summer and it felt as if two levels of reality – one belonging to autumn and school, the other belonging to summer and vacation – existed side by side. The plums were a part of this, for the plum tree blooms in late spring, the first unripe fruits appear in the middle of summer and turn ripe as summer ends, and like so much else that happens then, when the warmth and the light begin to wane, there is something ominous about them. The bees and the wasps are desperate for anything sweet, they are short-tempered and irritable, the butterflies live out their final hours, the plums get overripe and rot so quickly that it is impossible to eat them fast enough; it is as if summer flings out everything it has in one final fevered act before it dies. And if one brings plums along into autumn and winter, as we did when I was growing up and my mother made preserves of them and they stood in glass jars in the basement storeroom, then every trace of summer is gone, they lie there darkening inside jars filled with transparent sugar syrup, like little shrunken heads preserved in formalin. The skins are leathery and the taste bitter-sweet, and I don't think there is anything in the material world which more closely resembles memories.

Skin

All our notions about how something feels originate in the skin, in its encounters with the material world. It is the skin which senses that a bolt is hard and grooved while the grease covering it is soft and slightly tacky. That grass is soft and cool on a summer morning, that the plaster wall of the house is hard and cool, and that the soil in the flower bed, recently turned over with a shovel, is dry and crumbling wherever the sunlight reaches it, moister and firmer in the shade, all these experiences belong to the skin, and would do so even if the skin hadn't happened to touch any of these things on this particular morning, since all its previous experiences are stored in our consciousness, from which they are continually being brought up and collated with the information provided by our sight, so that eventually, at as early an age as two or so years, one is able to judge surfaces and to know what they feel like without having to reach out one's hand to let the skin touch them, even large complex structures such as for instance a beach, where, as even a child will know, if it has stopped at the edge of a wood and sees the beach extending for hundreds of metres up and down the shore, the sand closer to land is dry, warm and at once both silky soft and grainy if you let it trickle over your skin and run through your fingers, while where the waves coming in from the ocean peter out with a faint hissing, the sand is tightly packed, coarsely grained, hard and wet. This is also why one can have physical sensations of touching objects and their surfaces while reading in a chair, for example a text such as this as it describes a shiny steel knife with a newly honed edge sliding along the thumb, through the thin layer of skin, which opens in a narrow slit, where a second later blood wells up. The cold sharp blade, the soft skin, the sluggish trickle of blood. Everybody knows what that feels like. This reservoir of insights about how things are and what touching something will lead to is rarely brought all the way to the surface of our consciousness, but we are still ruled by them, for that is perhaps the skin's most important function, to determine the optimal conditions for the body to be in. Not too warm, not too cold, not too wet, not too dry, not too hard, not too soft. What skin most of all wants to touch, what it longs for always and what satisfies it every time, so that it calms down and becomes quiet, feeling contentment and release, is other skin. To hold a naked baby against one's own naked chest, skin touching skin, is one of the good things in life, both for the baby and for the grown-up. For grown-ups the skin of other grown-ups is the source of another form of pleasure, at times so powerful that they, as soon as they have shut the door behind them and are alone in the room together, tear each other's clothes off and press themselves against each other, for the skin's longing for other skin, soft and smooth and naked, can grow into a storm in a matter of seconds. That this is so – that skin longs for skin and that all previous touches the skin has experienced are stored in our consciousness as bodily memories, which can be reawakened by something the eye sees, even when it is out of the skin's reach – means that life is experienced in a wholly different manner when winter turns into spring and then summer, when people begin to dress in light clothing, skirts and shorts, T-shirts and tank tops, for suddenly there is naked skin everywhere, naked shoulders, naked arms, naked thighs, calves and knees, naked necks and throats, and the eye sees it, and the body knows what it feels like to stroke an arm, a thigh, a neck, to feel naked skin against its own naked skin. It feels good, yet the good feeling awakened by the sight of skin can only rarely be converted into actual touching, exchanging the eye's distance for the hand's nearness, because we organise the world in obedience to the eye, not to the hand, in a society where almost everyone is a stranger to each other. The transition from the eye's reality to the skin's corresponds to the transition from the social to the private realm, and for someone like me, who has a problem with nearness, who almost never enjoys being touched and who also almost never enjoys touching others, skin is therefore burdened with ambiguity, for my skin too wants to be near other skin, perhaps more than anything else, at the same time as it fears it and therefore seeks to avoid it, or to limit it. So that my skin's longing is like a dog and my will like a chain I rein it in with.

Butterflies

Towards the end of July and at the beginning of August there are butterflies in the garden. There are never many, and seeing one feels if not exceptional then at least special – a bit like seeing a rainbow. Our youngest girl chases the butterflies, presumably because their fluttering movements are distinct and attractive and soundless, with no hint of menace. The beauty they possess, which makes the sight of one seem to me almost like an occasion, is not something which concerns her, as far as I can make out. But what she likes about them, their air of harmlessness, does after all have a connection with beauty; it is owing to their defence-lessness against predators, which is absolute, that many butterfly species have developed patterned wings. The patterns serve either as camouflage, making the butterfly merge seamlessly with its backdrop, against which it is invisible, or as a disguise, causing the butterfly to resemble either a leaf or a twig in which its predators have no interest, or something poisonous or harmful which predators dare not approach. Last week, while I was sitting at the front of the house drinking coffee, I got the feeling that someone was looking at me, so I turned round and discovered that a butterfly was sitting on the roof gutter just behind me. Its wings had markings shaped like an eye, not a large one, but clearly outlined against a yellow and orange background. The eye was not merely an accident of nature, such as when faces and objects appear in clouds or on wood, in spots on walls or patterns in liquids, it was meant to resemble an eye, to frighten predators and deter them from attacking the butterfly whose wings bears the design. I took a photo of the butterfly with my phone and am sitting here looking at it now. It is impossible not to be astonished by this eye. Who thought it up? No one thought it up. The eye has developed without ever having been conceived of. But how then did it come about? There must have been a will at work for the evolution from a wing without an eye to a wing with an eye to have occurred. But where is that will located? Not in the butterfly, it probably doesn't know that there are eyes on its wings. Scientific theory holds that it has occurred through natural selection, in other words that butterflies with wing markings that happen to resemble an eye have proved more fit for survival than butterflies with other markings, and have therefore lived longer, allowing more of them to pass on their genes in what amounts to a slow process of refinement. There are roughly 170,000 species of butterfly, making up 10 per cent of all identified species on earth, so there is no doubt that they have found a way of existing that works well, even if it is an elaborate one: first egg, then larva, then pupa and finally, with wings that in relation to its body are enormous, the butterfly. It possesses great but also ephemeral beauty: from the moment it crawls out of the pupa and tries out its new wings, it has only a few days to reproduce before it dies. Some butterfly species are unable to eat, they have no way of taking nourishment, they just fly around looking for another butterfly to impregnate or be impregnated by while their strength lasts. So why then this whole spectacular apparatus governing their lives, from the larvae's bulgy greediness to the sarcophagus-like existence of the pupae and the magnificent display of the last few days, which this quiet metamorphosis leads up to? If the sole objective was reproduction, why couldn't butterflies simply have been small, grey, woolly and unattractive balls living on the forest floor for a few hours, just long enough to lay some very small woolly eggs? The answer is time, whose depth is so immense that any event can unfold all its possible consequences, no matter how small and insignificant they might be, in every imaginable direction. That is what the butterfly sitting on the roof gutter revealed, how infinitely ancient life is, and how vast a reservoir of possibilities time holds within it – for only a few minutes later, when I got up from the chair and went into the porch of the summer house where the tools are kept, a sudden movement almost frightened me out of my wits: it was a toad, it had found shelter beneath the leaking tap, glistening in the dim light, with its long smooth legs and its large flat head. It too was a consequence of the same thing that had brought the butterfly to our roof gutter. And I, who saw all this and am now writing it down, am yet another.

Eggs

While I was growing up we had boiled eggs for breakfast every Sunday, and even if that habit dissolved a long time ago, along with the family which maintained it, boiled eggs are still connected in my mind with the atmosphere particular to Sundays. No church bells sounded in the place where we lived, and we never went to church, there was only one family in the whole housing development that did, but the 1970s were so close to the religious past that its afterglow still remained, just as light can remain in the sky for a while after the sun has set, only fading slowly. All the shops were closed, so hardly any money was in circulation, everyone had the day off, so hardly any work was done. Instead one went for walks or so-called Sunday rides in the car, and a so-called Sunday dinner was served, which meant that it was better and more elaborately prepared than the meals on the remaining days of the week. Even though everything else was constant and both the rooms of the house and the landscape beyond the windows were unchanged, the mere sight of the egg, a chalky white vault above the brown egg cup on the kitchen table, was enough to give the day its particular stamp. Yes, it was as if it radiated from the egg itself, the mood that transformed even the light between the trees below the road into a Sunday light. Not that I was conscious of it, I just sat down at the table, struck the relatively heavy table knife against the egg some three centimetres below the top. The shell cracked and crazed and the metal sliced just a little into the softness within, so that the top, filled with stiffened egg white, could be lifted off like a lid, often with the help of the teaspoon. When that was done, I grabbed the salt shaker, held it over first the lid, then the opened egg, tapping my index finger against the top of the shaker so that grains of salt fell out. If the egg was lukewarm, they settled like tiny hard stones on what to them was a vast expanse of soft white; if the egg was hot, they melted away at once, only to be re-found seconds later by the taste buds as tiny pricks of saltiness which seemed to radiate from the mild-tasting mass which by then the egg had become inside my mouth. My mother, who was usually the one who boiled the eggs, never used a timer, so their consistency might vary from the completely soft-boiled, when the greyish and viscous egg white would float around inside the shell and the yolk too was liquid, only a little thicker, to the completely hard-boiled, when the egg white was almost rubbery and had a blueish tinge, while the yolk nestled within it like a dry yellow ball that crumbled when you stuck your spoon into it. That this egg has a connection with life is hardly an obvious thought, for there is something extremely stylised about an egg, both its perfect oval shape and its smooth surface, as well as its inner structure, where yellow rests within white, as if thoughtfully wrapped, and if there is anything not charac-teristic of life, it is stylisation, system and order. Almost everything in nature is jagged, grooved, rough-edged, gnarled and uneven, motley and boundless. That happens to

378

the egg too, when the chick hatches, and I suppose that is why the egg is central to many myths of creation, such as for instance that of Taoism, according to which the universe was first an egg which cracked into two when a god was born from it: one part became the sky, the other became the earth. Life destroys order, smashes symmetry, that is its basic condition, and if we gaze out into the universe and consider the system and orderliness that governs it, with spherical planets moving in elliptical orbits around spherical suns, which in turn are organised into spiral-shaped galaxies with vast empty spaces in between, then life down here is its antithesis, with kittens scampering at full speed until they realise too late that they are going too fast, stiffen their legs and slide straight into the wall knocking their heads against it, or boys pissing on live wires and getting electric shocks, or tipsy married couples barbecuing right under a tree that catches fire, which they stand gazing upon at a loss for what to do as we arrive home and my wife dashes inside, fetches the fire extinguisher and sprays the flames with white foam.

Fullness

Fullness is another word for richness, it means an abundance of something, more of the same thing, but the overall sum is still something more than an accumulation of individual parts. Something arises out of fullness. When we talk about fullness of meaning, for instance, we are not thinking of sharply contrasting logical opposites, not some neat bouquet of arguments, for fullness is the antithesis of logic, the enemy of limitation, the friend of endlessness. No, by fullness of meaning we mean that feeling of intensity which arises in us when we stand in front of a work of art or read a book, that very particular sense of 'more' or of 'much' which cannot be traced back to some single aspect of the work but rather radiates out from all of its parts, where it is precisely the number of parts and the parity between them that gives rise to the feeling. For example the different shades of blue in a painting, simply looking at them can elevate one's state of mind and bring the soul into contact with something that is felt to be essential. But what is this essential something? The colour blue, how and in what way does it produce meaning? And in such abundant quantities? We will never know the answer, since the question of meaning belongs to another order than meaning itself. The question of meaning is like a vessel, while the meaning is like water: if we pour the water into a vessel, it changes form, but reflecting about this form will not bring us any closer to the essential nature of water; if next we pour the water into a differently shaped vessel, it will take another shape with equal naturalness. In art meaning stands in the same relation to thought as water does to its vessel. And perhaps the distinguishing feature of art is precisely this fullness; perhaps fullness is the guiding principle from which art springs. What is certain is that our ways of evaluating art are connected with our ways of seeing our surroundings, as for example when we find that a work of art is shallow, or on the contrary deep, even though the external similarities between, say, a volume of poems and the water in a bay are few, or that the thoughts it contains are narrow or wide, or that its form belongs among the high or the low, or when we experience its language as flowering, rich and luxuriant, or on the contrary, sparse and barren and desolate. That the outside world in this way gives shape to the inner and that art is merely a feeble reflection of reality might have been a depressing thought – as grain fields are flattened by rain or hail in summer – since it makes us so earth- and place-bound, so claustrophobically shut up inside sameness, if it hadn't been for the richness of this sameness, which opens the world, even its smallest part, towards the infinite. Every summer when the grain is ripe and I drive past the fields where I live, on narrow asphalt roads winding their way through the blazing landscape, so dry and golden, for a long time perfectly still, even the wind turbines are motionless, and the trees with their dense curtain of green leaves seem to stretch themselves towards the deep blue sky, until the wind rises and everything is set in motion, and a wave seems to pass through the landscape, this is what I think about: if one could only write like that!

Ground Wasps

The ground wasp was a mysterious and feared entity when I was growing up, it was one of those creatures that the exaggerations of childhood magnified out of all proportion, a little like the greater weever fish, the blue jellyfish and the adder. But whereas those three represented a real danger – though the risk of running into one of them was small – and could actually harm people, the threat of the ground wasp was more imaginary, and our fear of it about as unfounded as our fear of the badger (who would bite until it heard bone crushing). The reason ground wasps were wrapped in legend was not just that they pursued people in huge swarms and could inflict so many stings on them that they died, it was also the fact that they dwelled in caves below ground. Wasps belonged to the air, to the sky, to everything open, so a wasp disappearing down into the underworld had an unnatural and diabolic air about it.

Personally I never saw a single ground wasp during my childhood, and as an adult I forgot all about their existence and dark power of attraction until one Sunday in late summer two years ago when we went to the beach at Sandskogen. It was overcast but warm. The sun appeared as a yellow tinge in the grey-white sky. The sea too was grey, except where the waves broke against the shore and washed whitely over the dark yellow, almost brown sand. Further inland, where the water didn't reach, the sand was beige. It rose in steep dunes with grass growing on top, tufts of pale green grass on the side facing the sea, while in the direction of the land it grew thicker and thicker up to where the woods began and the ground was covered with bushes and grass, berry-bearing shrubs and moss. We had parked the car in the small gravel parking space in the woods and walked the hundred or so metres along the path out to the beach, where we now sat looking out over the grey, calm sea while we ate biscuits and drank coffee and fruit squash. We had come there with another family, so there were eight of us. After a while the children went down to the water's edge to play, they didn't bathe but waded. There was a sandbank out beyond the beach, and the channel between the two was like a river. I went for a swim together with the father of the other family, thinking it was probably the last one of the year; it was nearly September. When I came back up, dried myself and put on a T-shirt, I realised that I hadn't seen my son for a while. I asked the others. He had walked over to the remains of the fortifications which lay some hundred metres further on. I decided to go and check how he was doing. I slid down the dune, rounded its edge and saw him lying stretched out on the beach maybe seventy or eighty metres away. He lay completely still in an unnatural position. I began to run. As I got closer, I could hear him shouting. 'Help, help, help,' he shouted. Oh hell, there was a swarm of wasps hovering around him. 'I'm coming,' I shouted. When I got there, I lifted him up out of the swarm and ran as fast as I could down the beach. When I turned round for the first time, I saw that they were following us, but only a few seconds later the swarm had dispersed. The boy cried and sobbed. I set him down on top of a dune, in the shallow pit where we often camped, and asked him where he had been stung. 'There, and there, and there,' he said between choking sobs. He had got off lightly, I thought to myself, three stings wasn't so bad considering how many wasps there had been. But he wasn't crying because of the stings, it was the fright, the panic he had felt, that he hadn't dared to move but had been trapped there, alone on the beach, with no one coming to help him. After a while he stopped crying and I didn't think any more about it, after all he had managed fine. But at the next parent–teacher conference it emerged that he had told his class about the incident, and that he had cried then too. The next summer he refused to put on shorts or T-shirts. Going bathing at Sandskogen was out of the question. And his instinct is still to cover as much skin as possible when he is going out, no matter how hot it is. That's why he walked past my window a little while ago wearing a jacket and long trousers, even though the sun is baking down and the air temperature is twenty-five degrees. Two years have passed since then and he no longer thinks he'll be stung by wasps if he dresses in light summer clothes, but he still associates long sleeves and long trousers with safety.

Circus

Last night we got home from Budapest, we had been to a wedding there, my friend Tore had got married to Hilde. The day after the ceremony and the wedding party all the guests went to a circus. My two older children were sceptical, they are approaching their teens and to them a circus was something childish, but I got them to come anyway, in the evening we took a taxi from the hotel up to the city park, where we met the other guests outside the circus building. It was hot, around thirty degrees, and the atmosphere was somewhat febrile, as it often is before performances involving tickets, seating, kiosks with long lines, people coming away with tubs of popcorn, bags of sweets, bottles of fizzy drinks. It is like that before a cinema screening, also before a football match, but not before a movie or a match shown on TV, so the expectant mood has to do with the gathering of people, that we are about to see something together with people we don't know. The buzz of voices, figures coming and going, turning round, smiling and talking. The sun was on its way down and shadows were rising in the park that extended beyond the circus at the same time as the lights there came on. We went in and found our seats. As in every circus the stage was a circle, with the audience seated in tiers around it, and not, as in a theatre, at one end. The children were sceptical because every circus show they have seen has been rather amateurish, put on by small travelling companies whose promises of excitement and magic are always bigger than the performance can deliver, and to them perhaps that was what a circus was: dramatic gestures and big words wrapped around something puny. But they got popcorn and fizzy drinks and resigned themselves to spending the next few hours watching something as uncool as people and animals performing tricks. Twenty minutes later they were sitting open-mouthed in the darkness. Sometimes they laughed, but mostly they sat staring at the circus ring with eyes at once focused and sparkling. They were spellbound. Every act was a classic. There was a tightrope walker, there were trapeze artists, there were four men standing on each others' shoulders and a woman who was catapulted through the air, landing safely in the arms of the man on top. But the high point was a man who did tricks with four top hats. He juggled them, they landed on his head and left it again one after the other in time with the music. The degree of difficulty increased at the same time as the music became more complicated, the hats now struck his forehead with their brims and were twirled around in the air before settling on his head. My youngest daughter laughed out loud. I laughed out loud too, and my two elder daughters looked at me in surprise, for in their eyes this was the least spectacular act of all. 'Why did you laugh at *that*, Dad?' they asked afterwards. I said I had laughed because their sister had laughed so hard. And because I realised that the man with the top hats must have rehearsed this act for many, many years, with as much intensity and seriousness as

Olympic champions in gymnastics practise their exercises. To accomplish that little spin of the hat as the brim struck his forehead and was twirled around in the air before landing on his head, exactly in time with the music, thereby providing the audience with a few seconds of sheer joy. In a circus everything revolves around challenging the limitations that the material world imposes on the human body, by selecting one single element and repeating it again and again, as it were freezing the moment to operate within it, until it is perfected and ready to be performed before an audience. The performance is pointless, it doesn't lead to anything other than the gasp that passes through the crowd as they watch it. The open mouth, the sparkling eyes, the inner thrill. It is easy to feel sorry for the man with the top hats, who has spent his life perfecting those minute and silly movements, there is something so small about his act, while at the same time it is also a huge triumph, for he succeeds in showing the sad beauty of life in a way that everyone immediately understands and recognises: from life there is nothing more to be hoped for than the brim of a hat striking the forehead, twirling around twice in the air before the hat lands on the head, that is the ultimate thrill we can get out of it. And it is enough, I realised as I watched him doing it, that is why I laughed.

Repetition

I like repetition. I like doing the same thing, at the same time and in the same place day in, day out. I like it because something arises out of repetition: sooner or later the whole pile-up of sameness begins to slide. That is when writing begins. The view from my window is a constant reminder of this slow and invisible process. Every day I see the same lawn, the same apple tree, the same willow. It is winter, the colours are wan, the trees are empty, then it is spring and the garden is an explosion of green. Even though I have looked out at it every day, I haven't noticed the changes in themselves, it is as if they occur on a different timescale beyond our range of vision, just as high-frequency sounds lie beyond our range of hearing. Then comes the rich expansion into flowers, fruits, warmth, birds and intense growth which we call summer here, then comes a storm, then the apples lie scattered in a circle on the ground beneath the tree. The snowflakes melt the instant they touch the ground, the leaves are brown and leathery, the branches bare, the birds have vanished; it is winter again.

When I was young I considered Cicero's claim that to be happy all one needs is a garden and a library an expression of bourgeois mentality, a truth for the boring and middle-aged, as far removed as one could possibly get from the person I wanted to be. Perhaps I thought that way because my father seemed almost obsessed with the garden, there were periods when he spent all his spare time there. Now that I myself am boring and middle-aged I have capitulated, I am resigned to it. Not only do I now see the obvious connection between literature and gardens – small areas where something in other respects undefined and boundless is nurtured – I cultivate it. I read a biography of Werner Heisenberg and it is all there, out in the garden, the atoms, the quantum leaps, the uncertainty principle. I read a book about genes and DNA, all of it is out there. I read the Bible, where is heard the voice of the Lord God, walking in the garden in the cool of the day. I like that phrase, in the cool of the day, it awakens something within me, a feeling of depth on long summer days full of sunlight, they have something of eternity within them, and then in the afternoon the winds from the sea come flowing in over the land, and then the shadows expand as the sun sinks in the sky, and then the children burst out laughing somewhere nearby. That is in the cool of the day, that is in the midst of life, and when it is over, when I am no longer here, the view from here will remain. That too is something I realise when I look out of this window, and there is something strangely comforting about it, that we notice the world while we are passing through it, but that it takes no notice of us. That is one of the tasks of literature, to remind us of our insignificance and make us understand that our own way of producing meaning is merely one of many possible in the world, along with that of the forest, the plains, the mountains, the sea and the sky.

The world is untranslatable but it is not incomprehensible, as long as you know the simple rule that nothing of what it expresses through its myriad lives and creatures is followed by a question mark, only by exclamation marks.

Crab Fishing

Crab fishing takes place in late summer and into autumn
when the crabs are at their fleshiest. You use either a crab
pot, which is a wire box containing bait which the crabs can
get into but not out of, or you stand on land shining a light at
the water in the evening and at night and rake up the crabs,
which seek out the barnacles that grow on the rocks, with a
rake or another suitable tool as they come wandering slowly
up from the bottom. I came along to fish for crabs a few times
in my childhood, and my memories of those nights are some
of my most vivid recollections, presumably because it was
like being in another reality, on a small islet out where the
ocean opened up, at night, and because everything that had
to do with crabs was foreign and felt like an adventure. For a
long time I thought it was the light they were seeking, that
from deep down below water, in their secret and inaccessible
world, they were lured up by a signal from our world, the
light that shone far above them. What could it possibly represent to them? They seemed as if hypnotised by the light, they
had to follow it, and I thought that some time in the future
spaceships the size of cities would hover in the sky above this
landscape, and that then we would be the ones to drop everything and begin walking towards them, drawn by something

irresistible which filled us to such an extent that there was no room for either fear or doubt and made us indifferent to all danger. And then there was the crabs' hardness, the shell which felt like stone and which clanked against the rock when my father raked them up out of the water. The slow movements of their claws when they lay in the tub, piled on top of each other, and their little black eyes – what did they see through them? What kind of creatures were they really, what did they think about? When we drove homeward in the boat, a clicking noise came from the tub, and if there were many of them in there, it sounded almost like the ticking of clocks. The way they clambered about, the sound of shell striking against shell. My father showed me how to hold them, you had to grip the top edge of the shell, where the claws couldn't get at you. But even though I knew the claws couldn't reach my fingers there, I didn't dare to trust in it, my fear of the sharp hairy claws was stronger than reason, the way it often is in childhood. And then there was the way they died, clambering and clicking or with slowly fumbling claws when they were dropped into the big pot of boiling water on the stove, how they at once stopped moving, capsized and turned belly up, out of the world yet still in it, with their shells and their flesh, their motionless claws and their peppercorn eyes. Next they were arranged on a large serving platter, and then they were like small statues, monuments to life under water. But where did their life go? It was as if I could feel it, what death really was: a kind of osmosis. The meal the following evening was a feast, not least because my father loved crabs and the whole ritual surrounding the eating of them, especially the claws, since that required a special technique which he had mastered fully – he cracked the claw at the joint, pushed aside the fine white sheets of cartilage which resembled insect wings, pressed the opening to his lips like a small flute, and then he sucked on it with one hard, sharp draw of breath, similar to how one blows into a blowpipe, only inwards instead of outwards, and the smooth flesh left its hard sheath and flew into his mouth. I don't think I ever saw him as happy as he was then, when the family was gathered around the table and a platter of crabs. And I felt like an apprentice, a son who would one day master all this and be happy like him.

Ladybirds

The ladybird is a beetle, but it has come to hold a very different place in our minds to other beetles, who with their hard shiny wing cases, usually black in colour, numerous legs and long antennae seem infinitely far removed from us, to the extent that we notice them at all. As with most other insects we consider beetles to be a form of living object closer to stones and sticks than to cats and dogs, and the person who shrinks from crushing a beetle under his heel or from squashing a mosquito dead between his palms is tender-hearted indeed. To kill a ladybird, however, is something few people do with a light heart. This is most likely because its appearance is pleasing to us. With its domed back and red wing cases with black spots, we find it beautiful, and when something is beautiful we want to draw it closer to ourselves. But what is special about the ladybird is that it isn't beautiful in any sublime way, unlike the eagle or the shark, whose beauty has an air of cruelty about it, creating a different kind of distance, nor is the ladybird beautiful in an exalted way, unlike butterflies, whose colours and wing markings can put one in mind of the colours and patterns formed by petrol on water, and who seem somehow aloof, which of course is one of the hallmarks of magnificence. No, the ladybird is beautiful in a childlike way. It is cute. Both its shape, that it is domed and resembles a button, and the colours of the wing cases, red with black spots, give it an air of functionality and make the ladybird look like something created to delight or to amuse, especially children, who are probably the only group capable of truly appreciating flying fire-red buttons. If one studies the ladybird's wing cases closely, the red colour actually looks like it was painted on, as if the black of the spots was the original colour and the red had come about in more or less the same way as a once black chair in the nursery was painted in cheerful colours by parents wanting to bring joy to their children. It is this cheerful air which has made the ladybird and ladybird patterns so prevalent in child culture. The little creatures look friendly and nice, happy and funny. But they are beetles, a part of the mechanistic-instinctual insect world, and when they appear in large swarms, as they sometimes do if certain conditions prevail, the chasm separating them from us becomes apparent, that deeply alien nature that insects of all kinds possess. One late summer day five years ago I saw them in that light. Together with another family we had taken the bus from the centre of Malmö out to one of the beaches just outside the city. This place was a recent discovery for us. There was a campsite nearby, and the beach therefore had every amenity, and there were trees, providing delicious shade to sit in during that overwhelmingly hot summer. Already as we were walking from the bus, with the biggest children running ahead over the grassy plain and the youngest one lying in the pram, and with cool bags and swimming gear and blankets dangling over our shoulders, we noticed that the air was full of insects, there were little black specks everywhere. They soon began to settle on our clothes and hair; I was wearing a white T-shirt, and five or six ladybirds were clearly outlined against the fabric. As we got closer to the beach, a crunching sound came from beneath our feet. In some places the ground was covered with ladybirds. I pulled at my T-shirt to shake them off, but shortly afterwards they were back, this time ten or twelve of them. I ran my fingers through my hair and shook my head to get them out of there, but new ones kept coming. There were ladybirds everywhere. We spread out the blanket on the grassy slope beneath a tree; in no time at all it was covered with ladybirds. We walked on a bit, but it was the same thing there: everywhere, on the ground and in the air, there were scores of ladybirds. They seemed to come from beyond the sound, high above the water there were enormous dark swarms moving inland. There must have been several hundred thousand of them. Even in the water ladybirds were floating. It filled me with a deep unease, for I realised, standing on the green gleaming grass and looking out over the sparkling blue strait, with the mighty span of the Öresund Bridge arching over it, that one day the world will perish, a day as beautiful and ordinary as this.

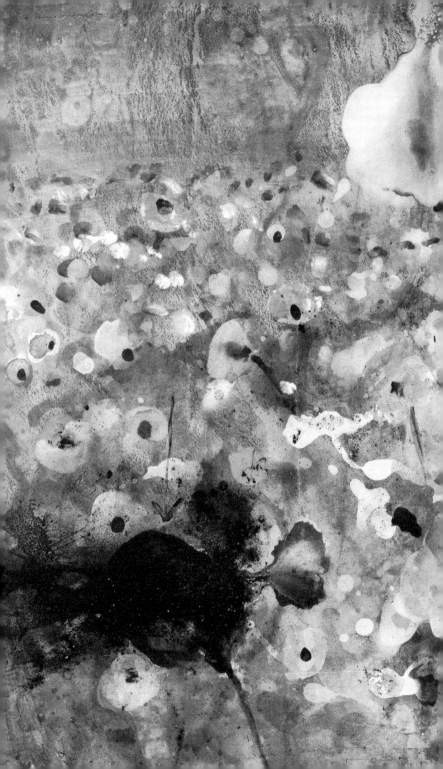

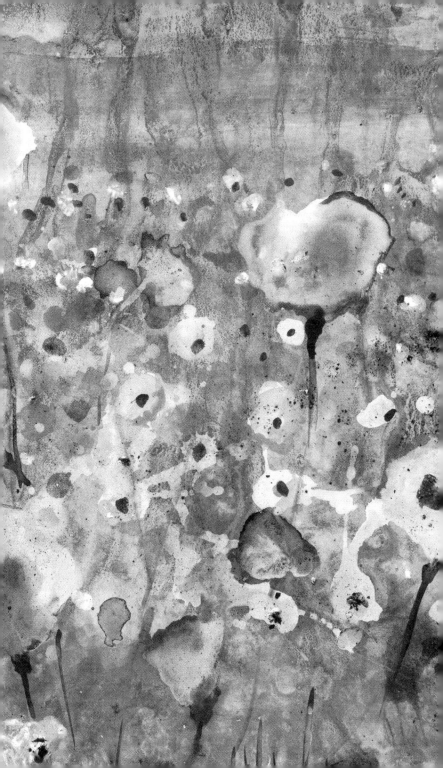

Paintings by Anselm Kiefer

Cover *Morgenthau*, 2013, Watercolour on paper, 40.3 x 50.7 cm
© Anselm Kiefer. Photograph © Georges Poncet

Pages ii, 38–39, 188–189, 290–291, 328–329 *Ich bin der ich bin*, 2015, Watercolour on plaster on cardboard, 18 pages, 57 x 48 x 6 cm © Anselm Kiefer. Photograph © Charles Duprat

Pages viii–ix *blaue Blumen*, 2015, Watercolour and pencil on plaster on cardboard, 60 x 80 cm © Anselm Kiefer.
Photograph © Charles Duprat

Page 74 *dat Rosa Miel apibus*, 2013, Watercolour on paper, 86 x 75 cm © Anselm Kiefer. Photograph © Georges Poncet

Page 112 *Extases féminines – Mechthilde de Hackeborn – Marie des Vallées . . .*, 2012, Watercolour on paper, 67 x 52 cm © Anselm Kiefer. Photograph © Charles Duprat

Page 158 *böse Blumen*, 2015, Watercolour and charcoal on plaster on cardboard, 152 x 107 cm © Anselm Kiefer.
Photograph © Charles Duprat

Page 266 *Les extases féminines*, 2013, Watercolour on paper, 116 x 51 cm © Anselm Kiefer. Photograph © Georges Poncet

Pages 402–403 *Le dormeur du val*, 2015, Watercolour and charcoal on plaster on cardboard, 50 x 70 cm © Anselm Kiefer. Photograph © Charles Duprat

Also by Karl Ove Knausgaard

A Time for Everything

My Struggle: Book 1

My Struggle: Book 2

My Struggle: Book 3

My Struggle: Book 4

My Struggle: Book 5

Home and Away: Writing the Beautiful Game
    (with Fredrik Ekelund)

Autumn (with illustrations by Vanessa Baird)

Winter (with illustrations by Lars Lerin)

Spring (with illustrations by Anna Bjerger)